VIKING ECONOMICS

VIKING ECONOMICS

How the Scandinavians Got It Right — and How We Can, Too

GEORGE LAKEY

MELVILLE HOUSE
BROOKLYN • LONDON

VIKING ECONOMICS

First Melville House Printing: July 2016

Melville House Publishing   8 Blackstock Mews
            46 John Street   and   Islington
        Brooklyn, NY 11201   London N4 2BT

mhpbooks.com   facebook.com/mhpbooks   @melvillehouse

Library of Congress Cataloging-in-Publication Data
Names: Lakey, George, author.
Title: Viking economics : how the Scandinavians got it right—and
  how we can, too / George Lakey.
Description: 1st Edition. | Brooklyn : Melville House, 2016.
Identifiers: LCCN 2016022383 (print) | LCCN 2016022598 (ebook)
  | ISBN 9781612195360 (hardback) | ISBN 9781612195377 (ebook)
Subjects: LCSH: Scandinavia—Social policy. | Social service—
  Scandinavia. | Equality—Scandinavia. | Welfare state—
  Scandinavia. | BISAC: BUSINESS & ECONOMICS /
  Government & Business. | POLITICAL SCIENCE / Public Policy
  / Economic Policy. | POLITICAL SCIENCE / Public Policy /
  Social Services & Welfare.
Classification: LCC HV318 .L35 2016 (print) | LCC HV318 (ebook) |
  DDC 330.948—dc23
LC record available at https://lccn.loc.gov/2016022383

Design by Marina Drukman

Printed in the United States of America
3   5   7   9   10   8   6   4   2

CONTENTS

Introduction: Discovering Today's Vikings Beyond
the Guidebooks   *vii*

PART I: HOW THEY GOT TO THE TOP

1. Vikings as Iconic Adventurers, Then and Now   3
2. Making Their Way in a Globalized World   11
3. Vikings Get Lost, Bankers Go Wild   27
4. Iceland Creates the Biggest Crash, then Rebounds   35
5. How Norwegians Empowered Themselves to
    Adopt the Nordic Model   53

PART II: DESIGN FOR LIVING IN THE NORDIC COUNTRIES

6. More Start-ups than the United States: Support for
    Entrepreneurs, Workers, and the Equality of Women   75
7. Family Farmers and Cooperatives: Key Players in
    the Nordic Model   95
8. Preventing Poverty: Nordics Learn How an
    Advanced Economy Can Abolish Poverty   105
9. Creating Work/Life Balance   131
10. Breaking Barriers to Education and
    Lifelong Learning   143
11. Paying for What You Get: The Viking
    Approach to Taxes   161

PART III: TODAY'S CHALLENGES, FOR THEM AND FOR US

12. Allowing Racial and Other Differences to
    Work for the Common Good   179
13. Reaching for High Goals on Climate Change   205
14. How Relevant Is the Nordic Model to
    the United States?   221

Acknowledgments   249
Notes   251

DISCOVERING TODAY'S VIKINGS BEYOND THE GUIDEBOOKS

A few years ago, I sat in a living room in the Norwegian town of Skien, surrounded by relatives. As a young man I'd married an international student from Norway, and her family had adopted me. Whenever I was back in Norway, we'd get together for pastries and coffee. I'd lived in Oslo more than half a century ago, but I'd come back many times. Gathered in the living room that day were relatives of a variety of ages and occupations: teacher, industrial worker, owner of a garden center, social worker, organic farmer, middle manager in a business.

As we talked about this and that, one of the cousins mentioned that she'd just heard about the results of an experiment for shortening the workweek. She told us with some excitement that the study measured people's productivity when their workweek was shortened from forty to thirty hours. The researchers found that the workers got more work done.

I watched the ripple of satisfaction around the room as the relatives started speculating about whether a reduction in hours could work in their jobs, too. They wondered about the implications of having more time off with the same total paycheck. On average, Norwegians work only 1,400 hours per year—the lowest in Europe—and are famous for their high productivity. I was struck by the quiet confidence everyone in the room seemed to have that as soon as the research was done, their employers would change policies easily.

"What about you, George?" a young woman asked. I had been quiet throughout the conversation. "What's the trend in hours worked in the States?"

"Actually," I said, "the trend with us is in the opposite direction. Overall, people with jobs work longer hours than before."

She was visibly surprised. "Does that mean that you take the time off in other ways, like super-long vacations? Here in Norway the national law is a month paid vacation for all, but some occupations get more because they are more stressful."

"Well . . ." I paused, trying to ensure my Norwegian vocabulary was up to the task of conveying disappointing news. "In the United States, we don't tend to have long paid vacations. Lots of people have two weeks, lots have one week, and some don't have any paid vacation."

The room became very still. I could sense my interlocutor trying to imagine living under such conditions. After a while, she chanced another question, clearly wanting to allow for cultural differences.

"Maybe people in your country don't *want* to have free time to enjoy your families, and go hiking and do recreation, and have hobbies?"

I was slow to respond. "Yes, we do want those things, just as you do. It's just that, well, we don't know that we can have them."

Hence this book. I wrote *Viking Economics* because so many of my fellow Americans experience the stark impact of our economic challenges every single day, yet feel socially powerless about solving them. One reason we've gotten stuck is that we've forgotten how successful Americans have been when we've formed social movements. Everything from child-labor laws to Social Security, after all, is a result of popular action.

But it's not just our own history we have to look toward. Too often, we're unaware of other societies that have tackled similar economic problems and taken giant strides forward; without that knowledge, it's hard to visualize the big changes we need to make.

Equality is probably the most potent example of this gap. Most Americans are deeply aware of the wealth gap—even Republican politicians are starting to talk about it.

Yet even as the wealth gap continues to grow, very few politicians seem to know what to do about it. Fortunately, bits of news are seeping into our country from the northwestern periphery of Europe. More Americans have now heard that over there, they have free higher education, robust support for families, a healthy work/life balance, active response to climate change, and an abundance of high-paying jobs for young and old alike. Almost no one connects the dots, however, to realize that these positives represent an egalitarian structure. Economists call the set of connections "the Nordic model."

The conversation in that living room in Skien reveals what's been going on: the descendants of the Vikings set themselves up to conduct experiments that support abundance for the people as a whole. Only one of the countries—Norway—struck it rich with oil, but all of them progressed in similar ways. Their economies have a sixty-year track record of delivering increased freedom and equality.

I want the United States to benefit from the living laboratory that Norwegians, Danes, Swedes, and Icelanders have created, and I'm confident that their experiments with egalitarianism can be inspiring, useful, and applicable to Americans.

The Nordics weren't always this way, of course. To get to the top of the global ratings, they paid their dues. They started out far behind: for decades Norwegians and Swedes fled poverty, emigrating to the United States and elsewhere. A century ago, their wealth gap was huge. Their economic elites, who held the power, were unwilling or unable to steer their countries toward justice and prosperity.

But eventually, the people mobilized—nonviolently—to displace their ineffective leadership and open the space for democracy. It did take open struggle, but they finally created a situation where they achieved a remarkable degree of freedom and equality key to the Nordic vision—and our own.

I believe we can catch up. We have a long tradition of citizens standing up for themselves and for their collective interests, and I have every reason to think that we can take any lessons we choose from the laboratories of the North, and run with them. I sincerely hope that *Viking Economics* can help in that effort.

PART I

HOW THEY GOT
TO THE TOP

1

VIKINGS AS ICONIC ADVENTURERS, THEN AND NOW

I'm at the Viking Ship Museum in Bygdøy, in Oslo, marveling at the open wooden ships—seventy-five feet and smaller—that braved storms and the bitter cold of the Northern seas, all without modern navigational aids.

In the 790s, Vikings swept out of Norway and across the North Sea to raid the British coast. They seized booty and killed anyone who resisted. With their light, shallow boats, which could navigate rivers as well as handle the waves of the sea, the Vikings also plundered villages upstream.

The ancient world knew the ancestors of ethnic Norwegians, Swedes, and Danes to be amazing sailors, and indeed, the very name *Viking* means, "to go on an expedition." Between the ninth and eleventh centuries, Viking men and women ventured eastward to present-day Russia, Ukraine, Turkey, and even as far as Baghdad, and sailed west to Iceland, Greenland, and Canada.

The ancient Vikings traded—depending on how willing the local people were—and they sometimes established farms and communities. They settled in such numbers in northern England and Scotland that their genes still show up in the local gene pools.

Which isn't to say that we should romanticize the Vikings and the scope of their achievements: these were people who raided and killed people near and far without provocation. They set farms afire, raped women, claimed as theirs the property of others.

Yet the positive aspects of those accomplishments have been a source of confidence to the moderns. Norwegians, Danes, Swedes and Icelanders have all looked to the ancient Vikings for inspiration. Today we still invoke a Viking spirit. It is part of the cultural DNA, still emboldening the Vikings' descendents to try new things—even when it means leaving the comforts of hearth and home.

MY ADVENTURE

I'd never been outside the United States when, at twenty-one, I boarded a transatlantic steamer bound for Oslo. I'd borrowed the money for a ticket from my grandfather, who recognized a lovesick young man when he saw one. I was determined to marry Berit Mathiesen, the Norwegian woman I met in Massachusetts, in a Quaker summer service project for students.

Five days after I got off the *S.S. Stavangerfjord* in Oslo, Berit and I were married in a red brick church with tall towers in her hometown of Skien, an old port city west of Oslo.

Berit was the first in her family to go to college, and she did it by venturing out, getting a scholarship to go to an American school. She earned her degree in Nebraska surrounded by prairie about as different from her Norwegian mountains as anything she could find.

When Berit's three brothers were young, they did what many

working-class boys did: took a turn at sea as crew members on Norwegian freighters. Einar, Kjell, and Leif Erik explored ports of call in Africa and Asia. (Tiny Norway is the sixth-largest owner of merchant ships, following Germany, Japan, China, Greece, and Russia.)

A HUMBLE BEGINNING

At the turn of the twentieth century, most Norwegians lived in economic hardship. It would have been even worse if hundreds of thousands weren't emigrating, leaving the few jobs and farms to their other family members. Small farmers supplemented their meager income by fishing and logging. Industrial workers toiled for long hours in dangerous conditions for small wages and no security. The country as a whole had little in the way of natural resources: forests, waterfalls, fish. Only 3 percent of the country was even suitable for growing food.

The tiny population, about three million, was scattered over an area larger than Great Britain, and widely distributed in small valleys separated by mountains and fjords. Trying to build roads to knit the population together was daunting given all the tunnels and bridges that were necessary, and building railroads wasn't any easier. The nation's internal market was tiny, and the dependence on global markets for the sale of commodities like timber and fish meant being at the mercy of rising and falling prices.

There were cultural limits as well. Aside from the small, indigenous Sami population in the far north, Norwegians were mostly white Lutherans. Cultural homogeneity tends to support economic stagnation.

Poverty was widespread in other Nordic countries, too. Swe-

den had significantly more natural resources and a larger population, yet it, too, hemorrhaged its white Lutheran population to
other countries where prospects were better, including the United
States.

Yet only seven decades later, Norway had achieved full employment, dramatically curbed poverty, built an efficient and
modern infrastructure, and provided good free health care, retirement benefits, and free education for all of its citizens. That
Norway achieved this before oil in the North Sea came online is
remarkable, as is the fact that Sweden, Denmark, and Iceland all
did the same—all of them without oil.

It is easy to forget the magnitude of this transformation.

When Berit and I were planning our Norwegian wedding and
how I'd spend my year in Norway with her, she said in passing
that I'd have no trouble studying at the University of Oslo. When
Matriculation Day came around, I put down my fourteen-dollar
matriculation fee and double-checked to see if I had really paid in
full. I asked a couple of university student friends how this system
could possibly make sense.

"Look," Sigurd said, "wouldn't you say that brains are an economic resource to a country?"

"Well, yes, of course," I responded.

"Then," he continued, "why wouldn't you want to develop
your resources fully instead of letting a barrier like money get in
the way?"

As I walked back to our apartment I marveled at the sheer
practicality of it.

Such policies seemed like charming eccentricities of limited
relevance in 1960, the year Berit and I returned to the United
States after a year of study. After all, in those days many Ameri-

cans did what I had been doing: working my way through a state college with a little family support and no debt to burden me when I graduated.

Today, with higher education spiraling out of reach for most Americans and public education as a whole being defunded, the Scandinavian choice to offer quality education without a financial barrier seems revolutionary.

What hadn't dawned on me in 1960 was that the free universities typical of Scandinavia already existed prior to the prosperity they became known for. The Nordics decided that it was wise to invest significantly in education at all levels, and their decision has paid off handsomely—not only in productivity, but also in the experience of personal freedom.

Norway, Sweden, Denmark, and Iceland embarked on a very specific economic adventure. It's no accident that the descendants of the Vikings designed economies with some of the same characteristics that governed their boats: a broad vision harnessed to practical action, relying on solidarity and teamwork. This combination of ambition and community promotes both freedom and equality, and those of us who share those values can learn from their story, which begins with the willingness to leave safe harbors—to venture out.

EQUALITY AND PERSONAL FREEDOM—A MATTER OF DESIGN

Like most Americans today, Norwegians a century ago didn't like the results of a wealth gap: the hunger and poverty, the crime, elderly friends warehoused or left in isolation, young people without hope of a good job. Norwegians also didn't like the attitudes that went with inequality: an inclination toward arrogance among higher-income people and the feeling among lower-income people that they were losers, defeated by the system.

Early in the twentieth century, Norway had the formal institutions of parliamentary democracy, but ordinary people were not empowered: they did not set the direction of their society. The direction was set, instead, by the economic elite, through the political parties they dominated and the businesses they ran. Career options were limited, and there was little social mobility.

The differences between then and now are striking: If you're a Norwegian teenager today and the job you're interested in pursuing doesn't require higher education, you can choose among good public vocational courses. If you learn better in a hands-on apprenticeship mode, publicly supported programs help you do that. If, instead, you prefer to develop a talent in art or music, or follow a career at sea or in engineering, you can attend a free post-secondary school.

Paid maternity and paternity leave (including for adoptive parents) is built into the system, and your job is held until you return. After the leave is over, child support is increased if you choose to be a full-time parent. If your choice is to go back to work, affordable childcare is available.

Extensive, subsidized public transport means that you probably won't need a car to get to work. High educational standards prevail in big-city schools, as well as in the suburbs. Small towns receive subsidies to make them attractive for people who might otherwise feel forced to live in a city for cultural amenities, again increasing your options. The economy subsidizes family farming both for its own sake and for food security, so farmers can earn a reasonable income, another freedom denied in many industrialized countries.

The government offers free vocational counseling, education, and job-training resources for people seeking a career change, and entrepreneurialism is encouraged through free health care and a public pension for all: In Norway, you have the freedom to fail without becoming a failure.

Money doesn't dominate the political system, so citizens are freer to participate meaningfully in political life—and they're more likely to be exposed to newspapers with a variety of points of view, because journalism is subsidized to avoid a narrowing of perspective. According to Freedom House, in 2013, Norway was tied with Sweden at number one in the world for freedom of the press. Denmark was sixth, and Iceland was tenth. (The United States was twenty-sixth.) Indeed, this approach to public life has a long lineage in the region: Sweden was the first country in the world to establish freedom of the press—in 1766.

The Nordics are among the longest-living people in the world, and older citizens continue to benefit from an economy designed for personal freedom. The Global Watch Index studied ninety-six countries and rated Norway as the best place to grow old, followed closely by Sweden.[1] The pension system enables you to live at home with health aides or in a senior living facility. You don't need to fear hunger or lack of medicines or of health care. Every small town has a music and culture center where you can enjoy the arts and pursue your hobbies.

The crime rate is very low, partly because societies with high equality tend to experience less crime. Even in their largest city, Norwegians enjoy a remarkable degree of freedom from fear about personal safety.

Designing an economy that supports freedom and equality pays off in happiness, judging from the Vikings' descendants making the top ten in the UN's International Happiness Index. In 2015, the ratings showed Denmark, Iceland, and Norway sharing first place with Switzerland, while Sweden was close to its cousins.[2]

The Organization for Economic Co-operation and Development (OECD), composed of thirty-four of the most-developed nations, compared life satisfaction experienced by the people in each country in 2013. The OECD found Norway second, Iceland third, Sweden fourth, and Denmark fifth.[3]

And yet in spite of all this security and support, the Nordic yen for adventure has not disappeared. Americans, too, have a strong yearning for both freedom and equality, so the Nordic desire for both isn't surprising. What is surprising, though, is that they went ahead and built an economy to serve those values. That's the story in this book.

Like their Viking ancestors, the moderns made mistakes in their explorations. Iceland's financial collapse of 2008 was a spectacular error, and, as I'll describe, back in the 1980s, the Norwegians and Swedes made a series of serious economic mistakes. The Nordics haven't built a utopia: Norwegians see themselves as "a nation of complainers," and this book doesn't shy away from the challenges that face them and their Nordic cousins.

Still, it's useful for us as outsiders to observe the Nordics' expeditions and to use them to reflect on our own situations. There are many important lessons to be learned.

2

MAKING THEIR WAY
IN A GLOBALIZED WORLD

What pushed the ancient Vikings to venture outside their homes?

Some believe that a growing population was using up available land. There was, meanwhile, ample room for settlement in the nearby north of England, where agricultural land abounded. Danish and Norwegian Vikings settled there in such large numbers that they established "Danelaw."

When I taught at Woodbrooke College in Northern England, Berit and I often dined with a group that included a man from Yorkshire. He seemed pleasant enough, but neither of us could understand a word he was saying—his Yorkshire dialect was too thick. Berit, the linguist in our family, suddenly solved the puzzle. "George," she said, "I figured out how to understand Peter. He pronounces his vowels in the same way as we do in Norwegian!"

Another explanation for the Vikings' mobility is that other groups that had previously dominated long-distance trade routes were in decline, which meant that there was a niche the Vikings could step into. This might explain why Vikings journeyed into Russia and as far as Baghdad.

But Greenland had almost no population to trade with, nor

did other islands like the Orkneys and Faroe Islands in the extreme north, though the Vikings went there repeatedly. Even more puzzling is the fact that the Vikings ventured westward past Greenland all the way to North America, as far as Labrador and Newfoundland.

It's tempting to conclude that the Vikings were not only driven to venture out, but also drawn by a vision of possibility.

If that's the case, that capacity for vision emerged strongly in the twentieth century. Norwegians generated abundant support for their visionaries during the previous century. It's a good thing they did, considering the economic realities they had to work with. Norway lacked the extensive land, abundant resources, and large population that enabled countries like the United States and Germany to generate robust, internally driven economies. Necessity, too, pushed Norwegians into the early experience of globalization.

MUST GLOBALIZATION HURT THE WORKING CLASS?

President Barack Obama expressed the conventional wisdom when he addressed economic suffering in the United States in his August 28, 2013, address on the fiftieth anniversary of the March 1963 on Washington. He argued that the decrease in good jobs and the proliferation of lower wages for American workers were tied to technology and global competition.

Obama's words would make little sense to Nordics, who for a century faced these challenges—technology and global competition—and nevertheless designed their economies to increase jobs and raise wages. Being at the mercy of international market forces didn't determine their destiny.

Consider Iceland, which at the beginning of the twentieth century was one of Europe's poorest economies. Two-thirds of the people were employed in agriculture, working on small fields next to glaciers and lava left from the last volcanic eruption. For much of the century there were only a quarter-million Icelanders—a minuscule internal market. Economic growth was led by the fisheries, whose prices depended on international market forces.

Even more than the other Nordic countries, Iceland should prove that globalization necessarily means a "race to the bottom," and further, that if a tiny economy is already near the bottom, globalization should keep its working people in misery.

But Icelanders rejected that narrative. They believed that an economy should serve the values of the people: equality, freedom, and solidarity. Icelanders found ways to prioritize investment in the people as part of their strategy for achieving prosperity.

While still objectively poor, the country offered free education, put its people into good housing, and gave everyone access to health care and secure old-age pensions. Icelanders learned to tap their geothermal energy for electricity and distribute it. They established a full employment policy and—as a country with the population of Buffalo, New York—built their own airline.

Although unable to reach the prosperity standard of their Viking cousins, Icelanders refused to be victims and, except for a notable recent lapse, developed an economy that served all its citizens. The idea that globalization is so powerful that it deprives people of agency is contradicted by the experience of the very countries that should be the most vulnerable.

DENMARK FINDS THAT "SMALL IS BEAUTIFUL"

In the nineteenth century, Denmark competed to be a European power: it owned both Iceland and Greenland and controlled Norway, and was rich in agriculture and trade.

Yet the Danish elite's dream of empire was dashed in 1864, when Prussian leader Otto von Bismarck seized one-third of Denmark's home base—the provinces of Schleswig and Holstein—and annexed them to Germany. Meanwhile, unemployment was rampant, and Danes were leaving their country in droves.

But thanks partly to the leadership of Lutheran bishop N.F.S. Grundtvik, the Danes recovered by developing their own society instead of preoccupying themselves with running other peoples' countries. Social movements blossomed. Farmers discovered the advantages of working together through co-ops to make Danish dairy and meat products among the best anywhere. Danes invented folk high schools to make continuing education widely available to the people, and as usual, the investment in people increased innovation and efficiency.

By the late nineteenth century, the growing numbers of shipyard and factory workers began to feel their own strength, and formed study circles to explore why Danish wealth was not more widely distributed. The workers struck for the rights to vote and unionize; they learned how to make general strikes that shifted the balance of power. They also made a strategic alliance with the farmers, as did their Viking sisters and brothers in Norway.

Danish workers created a Social Democratic Party that by 1924 had grown strong enough to form a government. Thorvald Stauning, a worker in a cigar factory who became party leader, was the longest-serving prime minister in Danish history. One of his early moves was to appoint a woman to his cabinet, a historic first.

GLOBALIZATION INTENSIFIES, AND DANES RESPOND WITH FLEXICURITY

In the 1970s, factory owners in industrial countries were moving production to the global south, in search of weak or nonexistent unions, lower wages, and fewer regulations. U.S. Steel, for example, let their American steel mills decline while opening new ones in South Korea and Brazil.

Over time, the flight of factories proved a challenge to Danes and other Europeans: relocated industries were beginning to compete successfully with factories remaining in Europe.

In the 1990s, Denmark faced the problem head-on. The Danes wanted full employment, but were reluctant to follow their neighbor Germany's policy of subsidizing inefficient firms to keep workers at their jobs.

Borrowing a 1995 Dutch concept called "flexicurity," the Danes changed the social contract between the state and the workforce. Instead of guaranteeing workers their existing jobs, the government would guarantee workers *ongoing support and retraining so they could get new jobs.*

While retraining, people laid off from their jobs received up to 90 percent of their former wages through unemployment insurance.

The Dutch had implemented a version of this policy but had given it fewer resources. The Danes brought to flexicurity a century of successful workers' struggles and its fruits: a stronger safety net, more active job creation, and better training for the unemployed, and this more-robust version of flexicurity became the "best practices" version, called the "Danish model."

Denmark's Viking cousins also adopted flexicurity, which turned out to be a win-win-win solution. Owners were relieved that they could close inefficient factories and put their capital into more-promising ventures. Workers were relieved that they would not be deprived of well-paid work that protected their standard of living. Everyone was relieved that their taxes wouldn't go ever higher to subsidize jobs that no longer paid for themselves.

Flexicurity affirmed a greatly respected Danish value: to seek the well-being of the whole. Bishop Grundtvig would have been pleased.

Flexicurity gained traction in Europe, and in 2007 the Council of the European Union recommended that its member governments consider flexicurity as they developed their economic policies. The 2008 financial crisis intervened before other countries could adopt the practice.

Four years after the 2008 crash, *Bloomberg*'s Iain Begg surveyed the European economic situation. He wrote on April 15, 2012: "In the Nordic countries, commitments to so-called active labor-market policies designed to keep people connected to the workforce have imparted resilience in employment that others envy."

When I was in New Zealand in the early 1970s, I read in a Wellington newspaper about some consultants from the International Monetary Fund who were advising the government at the time. This was my first introduction to a group of people who, as it turned out, were against the very notion of "resilience in employment." These consultants urged the government to give up its full-employment policy, and allow unemployment to rise. That, the IMF pointed out, would encourage international investors to invest money in New Zealand's economy.

I realized that this would certainly benefit some New Zealanders, but only at the expense of others. Growing unemployment would increase the number of people willing to work for less money; this, in turn, would reduce the strength of trade unions; and both these results would benefit international investors and their elite associates in New Zealand. This thinking would later come to be called the "race to the bottom."

This type of pro-unemployment strategy I first took note of in the 1970s is being implemented today in much of the Eurozone and the UK, where IMF-encouraged austerity programs throw people out of work, increase the power of capital in relation to the labor movement, and create downward pressure on wages, as well as shred the benefits that supported a decent life for the working and middle classes.

Yet the Viking countries remain on their own path. Norwegians I interviewed told me over and over that a job is a primary means for participating in society. Everyone who can work should do so. The responsibility of a country's leadership is to generate a humming and vibrant economy with jobs for all. The path to such an economy is in alignment with both freedom and equality.

BUSINESS CYCLES EXIST, SO PLAN FOR THEM!

It's a fact of economic life: business goes in cycles. Globalization increases the difficulty that this poses for the small nations that make their living through trading, but only a pessimist would assume that nothing can be done about it.

The Norwegian government, for example, long ago created *Husbanken* (the housing bank) to help people build and buy homes. When a business cycle goes into decline, *Husbanken* increases its activity, offering low-interest mortgages for first-time home buyers.

Many Norwegian renters take the new opportunity to buy homes, which also means spending on construction, furniture, and so on. This rise in consumption not only helps adjust the economy, it also produces one of the highest rates of home ownership in the world.[4]

In the wake of the Great Recession, President Barack Obama pleaded with German and other Eurozone leaders to undertake major stimulus programs to counter the plunge of the business cycle. After all, the United States has an economic stake in keeping Europe prosperous, so consumers can buy American exports. Unfortunately for the President and most of the rest of us, those leading the Eurozone and the UK had an agenda focused on austerity.

IMMIGRANTS AND GUEST WORKERS

Immigration in Norway is as old as the ancient Viking kings, and immigrants have provided important contributions to the country. Those kings found wives in foreign countries in order to strengthen their international alliances. Centuries later, the German-based Hanseatic League brought large-scale trade to Norway's west-coast cities of Bergen and Trondheim, and the civil servants working in Oslo were immigrants. Foreigners came to Kongsberg to do mining, and immigrants facilitated the industrial use of waterfalls in the nineteenth century. When we lived in Oslo in 1960, Berit and I spent a lot of time at an outdoor café on Karl Johans Gate. We would look out onto a sea of white, blue-eyed people carrying navy-blue raincoats and holding the hands of blond children. Now when I visit, I see Norwegians of many colors, wearing everything from soccer pants to head scarves. Two hundred nationalities can be found in the schools. In some classrooms, the majority of children are learning basic Norwegian.

In 1990, immigrants made up about 4 percent of Norway's population—today that number is about 14 percent: more than 700,000 people.

A few years ago, I made friends with a young man named Michael, who had come to Norway from Burundi a few years earlier. I later learned that his story was typical for immigrants who wanted to settle down in Norway.

He met with the immigration authorities and was made an offer something like this: "We pay you a living wage for a year while you spend full-time hours learning the Norwegian language and culture and taking job training to prepare you for a job for which there is a need here in Norway. We will locate you in a town or village, probably far from Oslo. You may be one of a very few Africans around, or even the only one. We will find a family that will put you up until you find your own place in the town.

"If you miss your language lessons or other responsibilities, we will dock your pay for the missing time. If your teacher believes that you need more time to master the language, you'll be eligible for an extension, while still being paid your wage. When your time is up, we will help you find a job that will use your new skills. After a certain time has elapsed you will be free to relocate anywhere in Norway.

"Norway has a great interest in your becoming a productive, tax-paying citizen. This is the contract we offer: take it or leave it (which is to say: leave the country)."

Michael was sent to a rural village among the western fjords. The only African anywhere near, he experienced the loneliest time of his life. He found the cultural differences enormous, but as his Norwegian improved he came to appreciate the life around him and began to make friends. When free to do so, he moved to Oslo, a significantly more diverse place. He feels he can now handle himself anywhere in the country and is pleased with that achievement, and he counts himself lucky to live in a country with so much freedom.

NORWEGIANS VALUE WORK

The emphasis on work as a means of participation underlies the Norwegian immigration policy. Norway followed some other European countries in restricting its open immigration policy in the 1970s, but it has continued to accept people who need asylum and many who want to join their families who previously emigrated to Norway.[5]

In 2004, Norway opened its doors again—it was required to do so to participate in the European Economic Area treaty, which gives it access to European Union (EU) markets. That year, the EU admitted several new, job-hungry member countries from Eastern and Central Europe. Gradually, workers from those countries found their way to Norway, often to take jobs in construction, retail, restaurants, and hotels. By 2012, nearly all of the 38,000 new jobs created in Norway were filled by immigrants. Three-quarters of them were taken by foreigners already settled in Norway and the rest by guest workers.

Guest workers are people who work and live in Norway for six months or less. After Norway recovered from its financial disaster in the early 1990s, its economy generated more jobs than Norwegians could fill. The government's employment office recruited tens of thousands of guest workers from other countries, especially neighbors like Poland and the Baltic States.

When the 2008 global financial breakdown resulted in increased unemployment elsewhere, it was even easier to attract workers from other countries. Over 100,000 guest workers worked in Norway in 2010, from Poland, Estonia, Latvia, Lithuania, Germany, and the UK, among others. The skill levels of guest workers range from engineers and consultants to unskilled agricultural and forestry workers.

The guest-worker system requires that workers pay the standard payroll taxes even though they will not be around to collect pensions at the end of their working lives. On the other hand, the payroll taxes entitle them to unemployment compensation when their jobs in Norway run out, and depending on opportunities in their home countries, many stick around and collect unemployment while seeking fresh Norwegian jobs. But that's not always easy, as Martins Selickis, a twenty-seven-year-old carpenter from Latvia, told then-newspaper *Aftenposten*: "[Employers] demand that we speak Norwegian and they only take on those who have worked for them before."

Still, Norway is ranked number one among the twenty-seven richest countries for its policies on migration: acceptance of asylum-seekers and refugees, open borders to immigrants and students from developing countries, and friendly integration practices.[6]

FOREIGN AID

Denmark, Sweden, and Norway ranked first, second, and third in the Commitment to Development index in 2015. A lot of their aid goes into multilateral programs. They do not require recipient countries to buy goods and services from the donor. They set the standard for the amount of their economy that is given to poor countries at about 1 percent.[7]

Norway's aid budget has doubled in nine years, to the level of 30 billion kroner, and a lot of that goes into multilateral programs. Along with Sweden, Norway is also one of the largest contributors to the United Nations.

Norwegians like to target their unilateral aid to reflect their values: assisting the poor, empowering women, and reducing climate change. Three of the countries that get consistent attention are Sri Lanka, Chile, and Cambodia. Norway tries to improve those countries' access to trade so they can in turn earn more capital for development. Recognizing that some governments hinder development due to their own corruption and incompetency, Norwegians target some aid to try to solve those problems, such as unsound taxation systems and illicit money flows.

In many cases, Norwegian aid is directed to women, as with access to contraception. This is based on the notion that promoting the agency of women gives a head start to any country trying to climb out of poverty.

Norwegian aid is also heavily invested in environmental issues, such as green energy initiatives. The country also prioritizes programs to combat deforestation, especially in Brazil, Indonesia, Guyana, and Tanzania.

But to some internationalists, the Norwegian aid program is best known for its emphasis on conflict resolution. Through training and hands-on mediation, Norwegians have for many years worked in areas of bloody conflict to increase the chance for peace with justice.

NORWAY AND THE EUROPEAN UNION—A SURPRISE

When a new European vision came along in the 1950s, proposing a degree of economic integration, Norway looked at it with interest. Norway prided itself on its internationalist tradition and the contribution of Norwegian Trygve Lie, the labor leader who in 1946 became the UN's first-ever Secretary-General.

Norway applied for membership in the European Economic Community (EEC) in 1962, along with the United Kingdom and others, but the UK was rebuffed and instead set up a parallel group, the European Free Trade Area. Norway joined its "big brother" in EFTA.

Norway did not expect EFTA to be a permanent arrangement; its main trading partners, after all, were members of the EEC. For the next ten years, Norway negotiated with the EEC and prepared itself for membership. All of the major political parties agreed with this. Only the tiny Communist Party dissented.

In January 1972, the Storting—Norway's parliament—voted to join the EEC. Members of parliament were then stunned by an enormous protest at the grassroots level. The Labor government was forced to agree to a referendum. That fall, 53.5 percent of the popular votes were against membership.

The Labor Party was shocked. Because the nature of the issue went to the heart of Norway's future direction, the party regarded the referendum as a vote of no-confidence and resigned. The resignation, however, led to chaos because no major party could step into its place. All had supported membership in the EEC.

Finally a governing coalition was patched together and an interim agreement was signed with the EEC, in lieu of membership, that supported a strong trading relationship for Norway. That relationship continued when the EEC transformed into the European Union (EU).

The Labor Party hoped that, with further education, the grassroots opposition would wither. It set up another referendum for 1994, but again the proposal for membership failed. 2013 polls showed about 70 percent of Norwegians still oppose joining the EU, and the Socialist Left Party (a junior partner that joined the Labor Party in the governing coalition in 2005) went beyond that opposition, urging departure from the European Economic Agreement that interfaces with the EU.

Denmark and Sweden have differed from Norway and Iceland when it comes to this issue: the two Nordics whose boundaries meet the rest of Europe have joined the European Union. Denmark and Sweden carefully avoided joining the Eurozone, however. They retained their own currencies, giving them flexibility that other EU countries have lacked when facing the top-down controlling austerity measures that followed 2008.

While interviewing Norwegians about the EU, I found that, in addition to voting based on their material interests, they also reflected the visionary dimension of the Viking heritage.

Those who most opposed membership in what is now the EU saw the member countries faltering in whatever loyalty they formerly had to social democratic ideals. Almost everywhere these Norwegians looked, the economic elite seemed to be in charge. Joining the EU, the dissenters feared, would mean that their small country would surrender to the domination of giant banks and corporations.

Norwegians had corrected their errant banks in the early 1990s, but most countries had not done so. When the EU members' economies took a dive, would governments expect the resulting mess to be paid for by the workers rather than those who caused the disaster? The answer turned out to be yes.

Giant corporations continue to make threats that add evidence to the case made by Norwegians concerned about being out-maneuvered. Writer Asbjørn Wahl tells us that the multi-national Kraft Corporation, which bought the iconic Norwegian chocolate firm Freia, pressed workers in Oslo to accept night shifts. If they refused, Kraft said, it would take the jobs to another European country.[8]

Those suspicious of the EU expected that high Norwegian standards, such as worker protection and compensation, democratic participation, support for the weakest, and access to economic necessities such as public education, would be pressed downward. Norwegians know how to maintain the stability of their kroner—what might happen with the euro?

My brother-in-law Leif Erik, who lives outside Skien next to farmers, told me that one reason Norwegian agricultural products get such high prices in the EU is because they are reliably of high quality, which cannot be said any longer of most EU farmers' products. Since Denmark joined the EU, he said, farmers have become so specialized that the country has lost its food security. In contrast, Norway still meets its own needs for meat and dairy products despite its limited arable land base. What will happen to food security, and the beauty of Norway's landscape, if the country joins the EU, loses its ability to subsidize its agricultural sector, and sees its farms returned to trees and logging?

Labor Party consultant Dag Seierstad told me during our meeting in the Storting that the growing trend toward a joint foreign policy in the EU also collides with the Norwegian vision of peace. "We must retain our independence," he said, "in order to follow our own responsibilities as peacemakers."

And so we have the irony that the people who give the highest per-capita contribution to foreign-aid efforts like the UN Development Program, and who consider their internationalism second to none, stubbornly resist joining the integration process closest to them. The Norwegian Vikings, it seems, remain visionaries.

3

VIKINGS GET LOST, BANKERS GO WILD

It's hard to understand how the descendants of Vikings could have steered into an economic glacier.

Sweden, Norway, and Iceland had made enormous economic gains for half a century by emphasizing the development of human capital and guiding the economy for the common good. They were small ships in shark-infested international waters, and the crews thrived because they had developed resilient structures and chose reliable stars to navigate by.

In the 1980s, Norway and Sweden turned away from what had been working for them and deregulated, giving the financial sectors the chance to act in their own, short-range interests. The private banks speculated, creating housing bubbles. The bubbles burst. Both nations headed into crisis.

To understand what might seem incomprehensible, we need to understand the larger context. It is not easy for small nations to stay focused on their own vision and the wisdom of their own experience when giant nations are telling them they are wrong. Ronald Reagan was elected U.S. president in 1980. Margaret Thatcher became British prime minister in 1979. Both countries were widely respected in Scandinavia.

Reagan and Thatcher shared an alternative vision: instead of freeing all individuals through increasing their opportunities, it was time to free owners to make more money, and that, they claimed, would trickle down and benefit everyone.

It's not a new idea, but it found some fertile soil in Norway. A severe international oil shock had come in 1973–74, resulting from the Organization of the Petroleum Exporting Countries (OPEC) hiking the price of oil. The shock triggered the deepest world economic recession since the 1930s. World trade and production grew at a much weaker pace, hurting the Nordics, and Norway in particular. Norwegian economist Lars Mjøset argues that the Labor government's policy responses included mistakes that contributed to a worrying period of stagflation: economic growth was slowing but inflation was moving upward and unemployment was straining to do so as well.

The neoliberal gospel also had some resonance because Viking economics includes many rules and regulations. I remember Berit's dad Johannes complaining about the red tape involved with his gardening business; land-use regulations meant getting permission to make some changes that he wanted to make. That's a common experience in Norway, and over time it can chafe.

Perhaps, some Norwegian economists were saying, the market does have its own wisdom that will yield the best result when rules are dropped and each owner seizes the moment without worrying about consequences. If great and respected nations like the United States and the UK take this chance, why not little Norway?

In 1981, the Norwegian Conservative Party formed a minority government, which it expanded in 1983 into a center-right majority coalition. The coalition deregulated the credit market in 1984. For the first time in decades, the bankers could pursue their own short-term interests.

SWEDEN FOLLOWS NORWAY

The Social Democrats remained the governing party in Sweden, but in 1985 they followed the Norwegian Conservatives' deregulation move. Now Swedish bankers could expand like their Norwegian colleagues. By 1990, all of Sweden's largest banks were speculating on commercial property and the bubble grew. Despite the bankers' gamble that what goes up can stay up, the bubble burst. In the next few years, 90 percent of the banking sector experienced massive losses.

The government nationalized two of the banks, sheltered some that looked like they could survive, and took the attitude that the rest could go bankrupt. Stockholders were left empty-handed.

As it turned out, three of the large banks were able to raise necessary capital privately. Regulation was reimposed and Sweden began to recover, taking care to retain its famous safety net to undergird the economy and to protect individual Swedes.

The mid-1990s were nevertheless a challenging time for many Swedes because of the fallout from the bank crisis. The government poured money into professional training and university courses, which of course stimulated the economy. In that period, according to Sweden's present prime minister, Stefan Løfven, "Almost a million people got a chance to raise their education, which was very good, because when things started to go well, people were on a higher level."[9] Løfven is a welder by occupation and was the leader of the national metal workers' union before becoming a politician.

The Swedish version of financial-sector "tough love" put the economy in such a strong position that when the 2008 financial crisis hit most of Europe, Sweden could use a series of flexible measures that minimized disruption. The banks had already been cleaned up. The Swedes used counter-cyclical measures to stimulate demand. Even though it was a member of the European Union, Sweden retained the *krona*, which gave it the advantage of flexibility not retained by nations in the Eurozone. In addition, their famous social safety net worked to keep Swedes accessing health care, education, and job training programs, and maintained the jobs that provided those services.

From this experience, some Swedish economists conclude that a high level of ongoing, thoughtful governmental intervention in the economy works better than occasional large spurts of stimulus.

The result: by 2011, *The Washington Post* was calling Sweden the "rock star of the recovery," with a growth rate twice that of the United States, much less unemployment, and a strong currency.

"THE NATIONAL MOTHER" TAKES LEADERSHIP IN NORWAY

In the 1985 elections, the Norwegians voted out the center-right coalition. Labor came back in as a minority government, led by Gro Harlem Brundtland. Norway would not have a majority-based government again until 2005. Brundtland had several terms as prime minister; she strongly influenced Norwegian politics and society and was nicknamed "the national mother."

Brundtland was a medical doctor by trade, and one of her achievements was to put climate change on the global agenda. She did not, however, reimpose strong regulations on the banks.

Though Norwegian banks began to wobble in the next few years, few imagined major trouble was coming. But, as in Sweden, the Norwegian bankers' bubble burst. In 1991, the commercial banking sector collapsed.

In decisive action, Brundtland's government seized the three biggest banks of Norway (which were the biggest culprits and together represented half the banking sector), fired the senior management, and made sure the shareholders didn't get a *krone*.

The now publicly owned banks were given new, accountable management and time to clean up. The government told the rest of the private banking sector that they were on their own: if they in fact had money in their mattresses with which they could recapitalize, fine; if not, they could go bankrupt. No way would Norwegian citizens bail them out.

Regulations were put back into place. The lesson to the entire financial sector was unmistakable: risk your own money, not other people's.

The government gradually sold shares in the banks it had seized and made a net profit. It kept a majority stake in the largest bank, DNB NOR, reportedly as a safeguard to prevent the bank from being sold to foreign banks.

A couple of decades later, in 2011, Norwegian State Secretary Morten Søberg reflected on what Norway learned from its harrowing experience. One lesson was to make the first step the elimination of shareholder equity in the banks chosen for government intervention:

In this way, those responsible for the banks' business and risk management—the owners—suffered losses before everyone else, while the transfer of risk from private actors to the public purse was accompanied by control and ownership of future profits. This recipe for crisis management contrasts with many other approaches during various crises. Too often, governments have implemented support measures without charging those responsible for the problems properly. This gives rise to the proverbial "privatization of profits and socialization of costs," and very bad incentives for good banking. The Norwegian approach to crisis management, on the other hand, provides healthy incentives for good banking, as banks and their owners can expect that any new losses due to high risk-taking must be borne by themselves.

DENMARK AVOIDS A CRASH

In order to implement neoliberal policies in her own country, British prime minister Margaret Thatcher needed to weaken the labor movement. In 1984, she confronted the coal miners, whose strike deepened into a general strike. Through archival research reporters recently discovered that at the time, Thatcher considered imposing a state of emergency and mobilizing troops.[10]

Denmark's center-right government was in that same period seeking to impose austerity measures and also encountered strenuous opposition from labor, including a strike that fared better than that against Thatcher.[11] Labor went on the offensive, and campaigned for a 4 percent pay hike, a thirty-five-hour work week, and increased taxes on corporations.

When the government tried to impose a settlement and ban the strike, some 100,000 workers gathered outside the Parliament building in Copenhagen. They barred lawmakers from going into the building and delayed debate on the government's legislation. Municipal workers refused to clear Copenhagen streets of the overnight snowfall, while other Danes slogged through the snow to join the protest. Wildcat strikes erupted in many sectors, and the illegal, nonviolent strike spread until about 320,000 workers joined (in a country of only 5 million).[12]

The government decided to urge compromise and settled the strike, with the employers' association making concessions.[13]

The government largely gave up the Thatcherite agenda. Danish banks struggled in the 1980s but escaped the Norwegian and Swedish crashes. The Danes retained a stronger regulatory regime on finance, and their banks maintained higher cash reserves as well.

NORWAY AND SWEDEN RECOVER QUICKLY

Norway and Sweden bounced back quickly from their collapses through tough and effective governmental intervention, avoiding the "lost decade" syndrome that dogged Japan after its early-1990s crash, and that seems to be the continuing reality of the United States and much of Europe post-2008.[14]

When the 2008 banking crisis hit countries like Britain, France, and Germany, the Norwegian and Swedish banks were unscathed. Of course, the fact that giants around them were toppling had a negative impact on their economies as a whole, but Denmark, Sweden, and Norway all found it easier to regain their footing because their stronger democracies made sure their banks were clean, transparent, and accountable. Rejecting free-market ideology, they had largely returned to what works.

St. Louis Federal Reserve Bank vice president Richard G. Anderson studied the responses of Sweden and Norway to their financial crises. He wrote, "The Nordic bank resolution is widely regarded as among the most successful in history."

Two financial crack-ups by Viking descendants would seem to be enough, but a decade later the Icelanders set up an even greater disaster. How the Icelanders did it and then played the rebel in charting their recovery is told in the next chapter.

4

ICELAND CREATES THE BIGGEST CRASH, THEN REBOUNDS

I was impatient to meet the man who led Iceland's "Pots and Pans Revolution"—the mass movement that mobilized Iceland after its economy spun out of control in 2008.

Hørdur Torfason asked me to meet him at an outdoor table of his favorite café in downtown Reykjavik. A small park lay between us and the plaza in front of Iceland's House of Parliament. Hørdur (pronounced roughly like "Harder") suggested I take a seat where I could easily see the epicenter of the Icelandic awakening. I remembered, taking in this grinning and powerful elfin man, that he was a performer and would want to set the stage before he recounted his story.

It turned out that Hørdur carried in his personal history an ancient Viking theme.

In the earliest centuries of settlement in Iceland, when free-spirited Vikings got in trouble with their community, they were banished. That's what happened when Hørdur, in the 1970s a popular Icelandic actor and singer, came out as gay.

"Jobs dried up," he said with a shrug, but I saw the pain in his eyes.

"The thing was, I couldn't any longer bear my profile as a matinee idol, making love to women on the stage, when my real life was in the closet. Still, I didn't expect I'd lose my ability to make a living." He paused and took another sip of coffee. "I went into exile, to Copenhagen."

Hørdur made a living in Denmark, but his longing to return to his own country led him to set up annual concert tours in Icelandic towns, performing one-man shows night after night to empty theaters.

"If the janitor would stay and listen to me, I'd perform for him," Hørdur told me. "I would tell him, 'Next year I'll be back, and if you liked my songs, I hope you'll bring your family and friends.'"

Hørdur returned Iceland each year, gradually rebuilding his audience until finally it became possible once again to make a living as a performer in his native land. Those who knew him saw him as a man of enormous determination and strength. It was that reputation that led grassroots Icelanders to turn to him as someone who could lead them in a crisis.

THE ICELANDERS' ROOTS IN DEMOCRACY

After World War II, Iceland developed important features in common with their Viking cousins. To learn more about Iceland's political economy, I met with Professor Thorvaldur Gylfason. The internationally known University of Iceland economist welcomed me into his large flat, high in a building by the sea in downtown Reykjevik. The walls were covered with art he'd collected in his travels to numerous overseas consultancies and conferences. As we relaxed in his living room, Thorvaldur told me that in some respects Iceland didn't fully fit "the Nordic model."

I objected. After all, Iceland had free university education, universal health care, universal pensions, and full employment. Thorvaldur agreed, but said Iceland's historic poverty meant that it did not achieve the level of expenditures on education and health care that the Swedes and the others did, nor was its labor force as highly skilled. He also said that Iceland's democracy is not as robust as that of the others. Compared with the citizens of Sweden, Denmark, and Norway, a much higher percentage of Icelanders regard their own government as corrupt.

For Thorvaldur, the cooperative movement's decline in the second half of the last century was a sign of this corruption. Co-ops had once been a major force for Iceland's economic development as it had been the others. Iceland's co-op leaders, however, began to leverage political connections to gain subsidies while maintaining the movement's inefficiencies, instead of innovating to solve problems. He saw cooperatives operating like "crony capitalists." Sweden, Denmark, and Norway, Thorvaldur said, would not tolerate crony capitalism.

Despite Thorvaldur's points, I still include Iceland in most of this book's references to "the Nordics." Except for Finland, whose ancestry is quite different, the Nordics descended historically from the ancient Vikings, and Iceland retains the closest cultural connection to the early Vikings of any of the four. Icelanders still read eddas and sagas in the spoken language of the ancient Vikings.

Iceland's everyday egalitarianism is reflected in everyone's being on a first-name basis with everyone else. The Norway I first encountered in the late 1950s placed such importance on honorific titles so important that I even gained a title when I became a university student. Whereas even the listings in the Icelandic telephone book are alphabetized by first name.

All four nations founded by the Vikings have similar parliamentary systems, but Iceland was the first among them—indeed, first in the world—to invent a national representative assembly where decisions are made through deliberation and voting. In 930 AD, and still, Icelanders call it the *Allting*, the assembly of all.

The actual site of the original *Allting* lies in a starkly magical valley where the European and American tectonic plates meet. The giant plates forming the earth's crust have been separating from each other, at the rate of a centimeter per year, at that very spot. It was a perfect place to launch a governance structure so attractive that a millennium later representative democracy could still inspire movements to shake up kings, dictators, and oligarchs alike.

Thorvaldur believes that despite their historic head start, modern Icelanders have not evolved the highest degree of democracy in the world. Iceland became top-heavy, its political class overlapping with owners of fishing fleets.[15] In the early 1900s, unlike in Sweden and Norway, Iceland's trade union–linked party, the Social Democratic Alliance, had been unable to form a government.

I acknowledge that the minority position of the political left is one more reason to question Iceland's inclusion among "the Nordics." However, Icelanders resemble Swedes and Norwegians one crucial way. In their march toward a modern economy, Icelanders also gained ownership of major banks, via the state and cooperatives.

The people's agency in the economy, however, was undermined as the twentieth century came to a close.

SIGNS OF THE CRISIS TO COME

Iceland's 1995 election planted the seeds of its 2008 crisis. The victors, a center-right coalition, began to deregulate the financial sector. Unlike their Viking cousins' earlier behavior, Icelanders took it to an extreme. Iceland joined the international trend initiated by the United States' repeal of the Glass-Steagall Act (an act that separates investment banking from ordinary banking). By 2003, the government fully privatized most banking. Now Icelandic bankers were free to take ownership stakes in their customers' companies.

Iceland's economy was especially strong in the early years of the twenty-first century: pharmaceuticals, fish processing, retailing, real estate, transportation. Building on that economic credibility, Iceland's largest banks opened branches abroad and even bought foreign financial institutions.

Internally, the bankers created a reckless culture for their executives by offering stock-options and other compensation policies that incentivized risk-taking. They made the Norwegian and Swedish banks' mistake of creating a real estate bubble, but they also doubled down on those bad bets by making high-risk loans to holding companies.

As the economy heated up, Iceland's government lowered the traditionally high taxation rates. The popular perception of what was happening was a boom, so ordinary Icelanders joined in by buying consumer goods on credit and failing to save, increasing the underlying vulnerability of the economy.

The now-private banks leveraged their capital base to buy up banking assets worth several times Iceland's gross national product. Landsbanki handled its difficult cash-flow situation by opening an online subsidiary, Icesave, offering high interest rates and taking deposits from 400,000 people in the UK and the Netherlands. (Iceland's entire population is 330,000.) Other banks followed suit. In effect, the banks themselves were operating a Ponzi scheme.

By 2007, Iceland had become the fifth-richest country in the world. Its per capita income was 60 percent higher than that of the United States. The *Wall Street Journal* told its readers about "the greatest success story in the world" and called it "Miracle on Iceland."[16] President Ronald Reagan's economic advisor Arthur Laffer's endorsement of Icelandic financial strategy was titled, "Overheating Is Not Dangerous."[17]

But it was dangerous. Even allowing for the fact that the U.S. Wall Street crowd was egging them on, Icelanders had—in their own "neighborhood"—the recent disasters in Norway and Sweden to learn from. Thorvaldur's father was a former finance minister; he was born into the political class. He told me that during the go-go years prior to the 2008 collapse, not once did he hear anyone refer to Norway's and Sweden's disastrous 1980s flirtations with neoliberalism.

THE RACE TO THE CLIFF ACCELERATES

When Icelanders went shopping for assets internationally they especially favored buying in the UK. In 1976, Iceland won its third Cod War with Britain over who had the rights to fish within what Iceland claimed to be its territorial waters. The Cod War left some bitterness. How sweet it must have been for Icelanders now to buy British assets.

Iceland also had a historic grievance against Denmark, their colonial master for 600 years. A few Icelanders told me mean jokes about Norway, their senior partner in an economic alliance called the European Economic Area (EEA), where equality-hungry Icelanders believed that Norway pulled rank and failed to adequately consult its junior partner.[18] It must have been exhilarating to be loaded with cash and buy assets in Denmark and in Norway.

Snapping up assets internationally gave rise to the phrase "Viking capitalists," referring (positively in some Icelanders' minds) to the ancient practice of raiding other countries and seizing booty.

I turned to political scientist Eirikur Bergmann, author of a leading book on the Icelandic boom and bust,[19] to get more perspective. Eirikur is Director of the Centre for European Studies at Bifrøst University, and he greeted me in a high-rise office building largely tenanted by other academics, a stone's throw away from the wharves and surf of the North Atlantic. Still a young man, he was in blue jeans and an Icelandic sweater.

Eirikur reminded me that Iceland is an old nation but a new republic, only gaining its independence from Denmark in 1944. Iceland can also be seen as a micro-state, with only 330,000 people to uphold a unique language and culture. Many regard Iceland's sovereignty as fragile.

Icelanders' insecurity, Eirikur said, helps to account for their nationalistic politics, their resistance to joining the European Union, and their excitement about suddenly appearing, a decade ago, to be on the top of the economic heap—*Viking capitalists!*

In 2006, both Fitch Ratings and the Danish Bank publically criticized Icelandic banking behavior. Iceland's chamber of commerce went to Columbia University Business School professor Frederic Mishkin and paid him $124,000 to coauthor a report on Iceland's economy and banking systems. In the report "Financial

Stability in Iceland," Mishkin offered an optimistic picture of Iceland's future. He failed to mention who was paying him to write the report, as shown in the Oscar-winning documentary film about the global financial crisis of 2008, *Inside Job*.[20]

THE PLUNGE TO DISASTER

In October 2008, just two years after the Danske Bank issued its warning, Iceland suffered one of the worst banking implosions in history. The stock market tanked. Hundreds of thousands of people in Britain and elsewhere demanded their money back.

Iceland's was the first modern economy in which virtually the entire banking sector went belly up, and making it worse, the currency collapsed.

Unemployment and inflation shot up. Many Icelanders, encouraged by their government and banks, had spent their savings and had nothing to live on. Because the government had lowered taxes, another mistake frequently made by neoliberals, Iceland had no "rainy-day fund" for contingencies. Some in the Western mass media described Iceland as a failed state.

A few activists organized small demonstrations at the Parliament building, across the lawn from where six years later Hørdur Torfason and I sat in the sun drinking coffee. Hørdur told me that key activists came to him, acknowledging that they didn't really know how to orchestrate a movement. They asked him to accept the leadership. He warned them that he was a performer, not a community organizer committed to democratic process, so his leadership style would be highly personal. They accepted his terms, and a team formed around him.

THE PEOPLE TAKE CHARGE

In mid-October, Hørdur stood across the street from the parliament building with an open microphone, inviting passersby to speak. People gathered in the park, next to an old memorial rock that, fittingly enough, has an inscription celebrating civil disobedience.

Icelanders responded strongly to Hørdur's leadership, each week increasing in numbers while tactics evolved and creativity reigned. Three collective demands emerged: the government must resign and hold an election, the heads of the Central Bank and financial supervisory authority must be fired, and Iceland's political economy must be reformed, for example by writing a new constitution.

In his book, Eirikur describes what happened next:

> Initially the government tried to dismiss the protesters as frustrated wannabe politicians and disillusioned youngsters who did not understand the complexity of the situation. But when our grandmothers put down their knitting needles, strapped their boots on and took to the streets shouting for an election we saw that the disgust was almost universal.

When Parliament recessed for the Christmas holiday, the people also took a much-needed break. It was a cold winter for demonstrating. When Parliament went back into session on January 20, 2009, a mass of people returned.

As Eirikur describes it:

The protesters put forward a clear demand for an early election. Ignoring them, the ministers and parliamentarians tried to sit out the protest, hiding inside the old building in central Reykjavik. This time it didn't work. The protests grew and the people kept warm by burning torches in front of the building. They were going nowhere. The Parliament remained under siege well into this dark night in Iceland's history, and the vigil resumed the following morning.[21]

The crowds grew to thousands, then to more than ten thousand. In a population of 330,000, that is over 3 percent. (In the United States, that would be like over 10 million people hitting the streets.)

Hørdur told me that the tactic that gave the movement its name in history came from a security guard inside Parliament. One of Hørdur's strategies was always to talk with everyone, and he made a point of seeking conversations with the whole political spectrum from ardent allies to strident opponents. He paid extra attention to people whose role it was to maintain safety, like police and security, and who might be commanded to repress the increasing thousands who were taking to the streets.

A security guard who worked inside the deliberation chamber of the Parliament building told him that sometimes, when the crowd outside was singing or chanting, it was difficult for the members of Parliament to hear one another. Hørdur therefore put out the word that at the next demonstration the people were to bring cooking pots, frying pans, and utensils. At a signal the din began. Sure enough, it brought Parliamentary work to a halt.

Prime Minister Geir H. Haarde announced that he and his cabinet would resign and new elections would be held. On February 1, 2009, the government was replaced by a caretaker government composed of the Social Democratic Alliance (SDA) in coalition with the Left Green Movement, a party to the left of the SDA.

The new parliamentary leader was Johanna Sigurdardottir, a well-known social activist and a leader of the SDA. She became Iceland's first female prime minister, and the first openly gay prime minister in the world.[22]

Three major officials of the Central Bank were immediately replaced, and the director and board of the financial regulatory agency were fired.

As had earlier happened in Norway and Sweden, the Social Democrats allowed the three largest banks to fail rather than bailing them out. It made sure that domestic depositors got their money back and gave debt relief to struggling homeowners. For businesses facing bankruptcy but having a positive cash flow, debts were forgiven. Instead of trying to pacify international investors, Iceland created controls on the movement of capital.

Because Iceland controlled its own currency, it could devalue it in order to support its important export market. The government began the process of developing tough regulations for the restarted financial sector.

In spring the election was held as demanded by the movement. The Social Democratic Alliance won and formed a government with the Left Green Movement—the first left wing government ever to lead Iceland.

FIGHTING WITH THE IMF

The obvious recourse for help in getting Iceland's financial sector back on its feet was the International Monetary Fund, but Icelandic socialists and the IMF understandably had difficulty seeing eye to eye.

The IMF famously believes in austerity, bailing out the owning class at the expense of the majority of the people, while the new government insisted on its own strategy: increase taxes on the rich, reduce taxes on the working class, force banks to write off mortgages for householders under water. Alarmingly, from the IMF's point of view, the government even wanted to strengthen the social safety net!

Health economist David Stuckler was called in by the Icelandic government for consultation. Officials knew that Stuckler's statistical studies showed that economic depression triggers psychological depression, predictably increasing numbers of heart attacks, suicides, and other symptoms.[23]

The IMF argued that, in order to receive its rescue package, the Icelandic government should cut its health-care funding by 30 percent, defining health care as a "luxury good."[24] Thirty percent would be twice IMF's proposed cut for the military.

Iceland's health minister resigned, refusing to make the cuts.

Consultant Stuckler knew that the IMF wanted to shrink Icelandic government services because the IMF believed that governmental spending hurts the economy. Checking the IMF's numbers, he learned that the IMF didn't use hard data in determining the multiplier effect of government spending, relying instead on incorrect theoretical modeling. By using actual data, Stuckler's team showed that government spending on health care and education had a high multiplier effect, and would therefore help the economy recover from the crash as well as save lives.

Iceland's leftists held firm in their negotiations with the IMF and at the same time sought unilateral aid from other potential lenders, like the United States, Norway, and Sweden. The governments of those countries urged Iceland to work it out with the IMF instead.

The situation intensified. Norwegians at the grassroots became aware of the plight of their Viking cousins and pressured their government to break ranks with the IMF and help the people.

The IMF finally accepted Iceland's refusal to adopt austerity. A deal was made that included major funding from Norway, Sweden, and Poland, along with the IMF.

I asked Thorvaldur what broke the stalemate between the IMF and the Icelandic government. I understood that the Icelandic government represented a massive people's movement ready to go into the streets at any moment—the people had their government's back. The growth of Norwegian solidarity at the grassroots also mattered. Because Norway is a democracy, its government would likely follow the will of the people, and the IMF might worry about the loss of its hegemony on these matters.

Thorvaldur added another piece of the puzzle. The IMF has been so roundly criticized on five continents for its austerity programs and the misery it has caused that it decided it needed a public-relations win. "Being cuddly with Iceland," he said, "could provide a welcome change in image."

The Icelandic government did lose on one major point in the negotiations. In the Icesave program, UK and Dutch citizens had deposited billions of dollars through online subsidiaries of Icelandic banks. The Dutch and British governments naturally expected Iceland to repay their citizens, many of them seniors who had sunk their life savings into Icelandic banks. The Icelandic government argued that it was the banks' idea to offer outlandish interest rates that couldn't be made good on, and the banks' decision to gamble on (among other things) U.S.–created mortgage default swaps. The banks were privately owned. The Icelandic public had no responsibility in the matter.

The IMF said if the government didn't accept responsibility, there would be no deal.

The pressure aroused fierce indignation within Iceland against foreign meddling with Iceland's sovereignty, exacerbated when Britain invoked antiterror legislation against Iceland. Nevertheless, because the Icelandic government saw no other option in its desperate situation, it acceded to the IMF demand. Ironically, that one governmental concession, deemed a betrayal by many Icelanders, later played a major role in sinking the fortunes of the Social Democrats and Green Socialists in the election of 2013. A majority of voters did not forgive the left's acceptance of the IMF's demand for Icesave repayments, even though no viable alternative existed.

Not entirely acquiescing to the IMF, the government did bring the matter to an international tribunal even while knowing that the tribunal would take years to rule on it. The tribunal did eventually rule in Iceland's favor, asserting that the people as a whole do not have responsibility for the debts incurred by private bank owners.

In the meantime, the government agreed, reluctantly, to repay the Icesave depositors. Escalating, the people launched another initiative. Before the government could actually implement the Icesave deal, the people demanded, and got, a referendum on the question—its first referendum since the vote on independence in 1944.

In March 2010, 93 percent of the participants voted "Nei"—a refusal to repay the lenders. Stock markets reacted negatively to the vote.

Iceland's 1 percent pushed for a second referendum on the question, arguing fiercely that a "Ja" was essential for Iceland's credibility in the world. Once again the citizens repudiated the debt.

The move sent shudders through the international financial world. Ordinary Icelanders were refusing to accept responsibility for the frenzied behavior of their bankers.

HOW DID ICELAND'S RECOVERY PLAN WORK OUT?

Despite a banking collapse that makes the United States' and most of Europe's 2008 troubles look modest, Iceland moved briskly toward recovery. People continued to live in their homes. The unemployment rate marched steadily downward.[25]

Observing the upbeat Icelandic atmosphere during my May 2014 visit, I thought of the trend in schools back home in the United States, where hundreds of thousands of teachers have been laid off and teachers still employed in hard-hit districts buy school supplies personally, accept cuts in pay or benefits, and manage without school librarians, nurses, counselors, and extracurricular activities that motivate and stimulate their students.

Nobel Prize–winning economist Paul Krugman contrasted Iceland's approach with that of the United States, the UK, and most European countries after 2008. "Where everyone else bailed out the bankers and made the public pay the price, Iceland let the banks go bust and actually expanded its social safety net."

By June 2015, the Icelandic unemployment rate declined to 3.2 percent.[26] Prime Minister Sigmundur D. Gunnlaugsson had announced an unemployment goal of 2 percent, which *Bloomberg* believed realistic.[27] The OECD predicted economic growth.[28] The government repaid many of its international loans early.

Health economists David Stuckler and Sanjay Basu continued to track the data to see whether Icelanders took a public-health hit similar to those felt in the countries choosing austerity, such as the staggering health impacts in Greece and Spain. The team checked their typical measures of heart attacks, suicides, mental health problems, and others, and they learned that Icelanders' health did not suffer.

To the contrary, many Icelanders reported an uptick in their sense of well-being, and in the first UN World Happiness Report in 2012, Iceland came in at number one in the world.

When I read that statistic, I remembered a study of several U.S. cities during the 1960s civil rights movement. The researchers found that in communities where African Americans waged campaigns there were decreased symptoms of pathology, as compared with communities where they did not wage campaigns. I wondered: perhaps ordinary Icelanders taking charge of their country gained the health rewards that go with empowerment.

Journalist Ben Chu, writing in *The Independent*, points out how extraordinarily self-respecting the Icelanders were. Ever since the 2008 international crisis, both European politicians and ratings agencies "have demanded that national governments honor the debts of their banking sectors, protect their exchange rates, eschew capital movement restrictions, and impose massive austerity to earn back the confidence of bond markets."

Had they taken that road, up to one-third of Icelanders might have fallen into poverty. Instead, the people of Iceland refused to be victims, and ignored the neoliberal demands.

Interestingly, the international financial world did not shun them as a result. In fact, when Iceland's government issued $1 billion in sovereign debt at 6 percent interest in June 2011, investors oversubscribed the offering!

Nobel Prize–winning economist Joseph Stiglitz said, "What Iceland did was right. It would have been wrong to burden future generations with the mistakes of the financial system."

5

HOW NORWEGIANS EMPOWERED THEMSELVES TO ADOPT THE NORDIC MODEL

When I give lectures in the United States on Viking economics, people often ask, "*How* did Norwegians move from a majority-poor, underdeveloped country to the top of the heap on international ratings?"[29]

Sometimes they are asking about the specific policies or major features of the Nordic model. But sometimes they mean something quite different: *How did they gain the political consensus to make such drastic changes?*

The short answer is, they didn't. Decades went by when Norway, to take one example, became more polarized instead of moving toward consensus. The long answer is, and now I'm talking about half a century, they *did* gain consensus. First, polarized Norwegians, put in power the group that had a vision of economic democracy. Only later did most Norwegians who resisted change realize that the change actually was a big improvement on the bad old days.

In other words, Norwegians created a small, visionary social movement that grew, engaged in struggle, attracted allies, and won. By winning nonviolently, the movement minimized push-back after the victory and consolidated its gains. Today, even though Norwegians will tell you they are "a nation of complainers," when you frame the conversation in global terms, almost everyone across the political spectrum would rather keep their Nordic model than operate like any other country in the world.

I'm happy to tell the story of those who made it happen: the little movement that could.

THE EARLY DAYS: HOPE AGAINST HOPE

Imagine a poor family dependent on Lars, the sole breadwinner, who tells his wife and children, "We decided to go on strike, so I won't be bringing in any pay for a while." And the response of his wife, who says, "But last time you went out we got hungry *and* you lost the strike. What makes you think that this time you'll win?"

The husband replies, "Nobody can be sure we'll win, but we have to try!"

By the 1880s, families were having this conversation across Norway. The first small factories were built in those years and the workers began to form unions. The owners refused to accept them, so workers struck and went hungry in towns like Drammen, not far from Berit's hometown of Skien. During Drammen's 1885 strike, the owners turned to the government for help. The army intervened and opened fire at a demonstration, killing one and injuring others.

In 1887, the infant union movement took its next step, creating *Det Norske Arbeiderparti* (DNA, the Norwegian Labor Party). The party admitted only union members, expecting to represent them in the *Storting*.

Norwegian labor leaders wanted a national labor federation, but struggled to organize on a national level. One challenge was the linguistic division of Norway, understandable in a geographically decentralized population. The country has hundreds of valleys separated by ice-capped mountains. Each valley contained clusters of farms, a village, and usually a trading town at the end of the fjord that snaked its way into the countryside through mountain passes. Most Norwegians rarely had a chance to talk to anyone besides their neighbors.

The Norwegian language has so many dialects that linguists can't agree on the number. Dialects can be very different from one another. A hundred years ago, someone from one valley might not understand a worker from another. Even today, most ethnic Norwegians use their local dialect for everyday speech, and linguistic diversity (not even counting the indigenous Sami language) is abundant. When Norway was trying to build a nation that could become independent, they made heroic efforts to identify a common language that all Norwegians would acknowledge. The best they could do was to come up with *two* official versions of Norwegian. Both are still used today.

Despite these difficulties, in 1899 unions across the country reached agreement to create the Workers National Trade Union. Their action stimulated an equivalent on the employers' side: the Norwegian Employers Confederation. That same year twenty-year-old Martin Tranmael joined with others in the northern city of Trondheim to found a newspaper, called *Ny Tid* (New Time, or New Era). A year later the newspaper became the official organ of the Labor Party, and young Tranmael made a name for himself.

Martin Olsen Tranmael had left the family farm to become

a painter and construction worker. When he was seventeen he joined his first union. Like most workers he had little schooling, but he was a natural organizer and used his fascination with history to develop a big picture that empowered him for leadership.

He joined the movement at a time when a significant number of labor leaders were turning to Marxism, which meant that they organized workers for immediate gains and also for the overthrow of capitalism. Deviating from Marxist orthodoxy, however, the Norwegian leaders decided that when they achieved power they would not collectivize agriculture. Instead, they would protect and extend family farms and clear more land for development. This choice created a potential bond between industrial workers and small farmers.

Hungry for broader experience, Martin Tranmael went to the United States and found work in Minnesota as a painter. He stayed for three years while learning from the much more advanced U.S. labor movement.

Tranmael returned to Norway in 1902 with more to offer the *Ny Tid* newspaper and his fellow organizers. His reputation as an effective agitator grew. Workers elected him chair of a local branch of the Labor Party. One of his favorite tactics was to soapbox churchgoers as they left their Sunday-morning services.

BREAKING WITH SWEDEN: NORWEGIANS YEARN FOR FREEDOM

The growth of the labor movement coincided with the increase of Norwegian nationalism. For ninety years Norway had been yoked to Sweden as a result of the 1814 settlement of the Napoleonic

War. Denmark, on the losing side of that war, had lost its Norwegian colony to Sweden.

Norwegian leaders tried to declare independence by gathering northeast of Oslo, at the town of Eidsvoll, to write a national constitution. They proclaimed their constitution on May 17, 1814, a date still celebrated as Norway's Independence Day.

Sweden's government, however, was unimpressed by the Eidsvoll declaration, and installed its king as the monarch of Norway, determining that country's foreign policy rather than letting the Norwegian Storting decide vital issues affecting foreign trade.

Sweden had industrialized earlier than Norway, and by the beginning of the twentieth century, Sweden's labor movement was more advanced. That proved lucky for Norway. When in 1905 the mounting tension between the two countries came to a boiling point, the Swedish workers were strong enough to make a difference.

The impatient Norwegians wanted to make their move unilaterally and walk out of the union. Sweden countered by demanding that there be a plebiscite. Then 99.95 percent of Norwegians voted to leave! Both Swedes and Norwegians deployed military forces at the border. Sweden was richer and more powerful, and it had a far larger army than Norway's. Right-wing Swedish politicians pushed for a hard-line response.

Norway needed allies, and found one in an unusual Swedish journalist named Hjalmar Branting. Branting had been a young scientist who in 1884 switched to journalism to advocate for his vision of a just society. As editor of socialist newspapers he was imprisoned for three months in 1888, the same year that Swedes formed their national trade union confederation. A year later, Branting joined others to found the Swedish Social Democratic

Party, and in 1896 he became the first one of his party to be elected to parliament.

The Social Democratic Party grew rapidly, but many of its supporters weren't allowed to vote because of limited suffrage. For that reason there were few socialists in parliament. When the possibility of war heated up, the parliament was of little use for resistance.

Fortunately, Branting and the Swedish working class knew that there is power outside parliament, in direct action. Later this knowledge would turn out to be crucial for making the Nordic model possible.

Branting created a slogan that was trumpeted around the country: "Hands off Norway, King!" The movement anticipated that if the Swedish-led government declared war on Norway, it would need to call up the reserves. To preempt that possibility, the movement organized reservists, getting them to pledge that they would not respond to the government's call-up. Labor's next step was to plan for, and publicize their plan for, a general strike.

Faced with all this, Swedish diplomats negotiated an agreement that Norway could make its own decisions and leave the union with Sweden.

CLASS STRUGGLE HEATS UP

Now that Norway was on its own, the question still remained: would it be governed by those who considered themselves "born to rule," or might the workers force some kind of economic democracy?

In 1907, the ironworkers signed the nation's first collective agreement with an employer. Encouraged, union activity increased and more workers studied the writing of socialist visionaries. The cooperative movement grew in this period as well; twenty-eight consumer co-ops banded together to form the Norwegian Cooperative Association to act as their wholesaler. (That association is now Coop Norge SA, with 1.3 million members—one in four Norwegians.)

The class struggle became even more visible. By 1913, the Labor Party had twenty-four newspapers around the country, and six more were added that year. It also had its own publishing house.

Threatened by the trend, the government imprisoned Martin Tranmael in 1915 and repeatedly thereafter. The still-young leader gained even more prominence within the movement. He and his colleagues closely followed the developments in neighboring Russia, where the czar had led his country into a bloodbath that came to be called World War I. In 1917, Russians overthrew the czar. Inspired by the Bolsheviks' role in the revolution, Tranmael and others led the Norwegian Labor Party to respond positively in 1918 when V. I. Lenin invited the Norwegians to join the Communist International (Comintern).

Postwar times were tough, even though Norway had remained neutral in the war. During 1919 and 1920, the Norwegian cost of living rose by 16 percent. 60,000 workers in different parts of Norway responded by organizing strikes that gained higher wages. At the same time, increasing turbulence in the global economy hit export businesses hard. In 1921, employers therefore demanded a 33 percent wage reduction.

Across the Atlantic in the U.S. ports, the U.S. Seafarers' Union faced a similar situation. The Americans stopped work to resist the wage cut. Inspired, Norwegian marine workers did the same, and truckers struck in solidarity. The Norwegian Federation of Labor then announced that it would launch a general strike, and two weeks later—on May 26—some 120,000 workers stopped going to work.

Revolution was in the air. Workers in Norway's northernmost town, Hammerfest, formed a commune to be led by workers councils. The army intervened to crush the initiative.

At this point history becomes a family story. A young man living at the southern end of Norway, Johannes Mathiesen, heard about the army's intervention and concluded that he should become a conscientious objector and refuse army service. This was the man who later married, and fathered a baby named Berit, who became my wife. Deeply religious, my father-in-law had no inclination for war anyway, but he told me that, as a young man, the thought of being conscripted to kill other workers made him a pacifist.

The general strike continued, but the employers were able to hold on longer than the workers. The national unions temporarily surrendered. The U.S. marine workers lost their strike as well. Localized strikes continued through the 1920s including a bitter ironworkers' strike in 1923–24 and a fresh wave of strikes in 1928.

ENTER MIDDLE-CLASS INTELLECTUALS

Erling Falk came from a politically active middle-class family in the north of Norway. In 1907, he moved to Duluth, Minnesota. He was twenty. In the eleven years that he lived in the United States, he threw himself into activism and found various jobs, including a stint as accountant for the Industrial Workers of the World (the "Wobblies").

Falk returned to Norway in 1918 to take up university studies. Oslo had Norway's only university at the time and therefore graduated much of Norway's future leadership. Its student association—the Norwegian Students Society—was a political hotbed, and Falk became active immediately.

Falk quickly asserted his leadership and gathered a group of students to publish a new periodical, *Mot Dag*, with him as editor. The magazine's full title was, "Toward the Day: For Workers and Academics." Its first edition, September 1921, set the tone: "*Mot Dag* seeks an intellectual leadership. Every academic does not belong here, only the ones who think."

In a few years the magazine had 6,500 subscribers and was the biggest and perhaps the most influential political periodical in the Nordic countries.

A year after the magazine's start-up, Falk founded a membership organization, also called *Mot Dag*, that lasted from 1922 until 1936. The group was influenced by syndicalism and radical humanism as well as Marxism. Falk wanted a group of young workers and students who would make the revolution their first priority and work together, in a disciplined way, to influence the labor movement.

Members of the group joined the Labor Party and became a visible caucus within it, joining the revolutionary wing led by Martin Tranmael. While some of the group's inspiration came from the United States, it was also an extension of the radical student tradition of celebrated thinkers like the Norwegian writer Henrik Wergeland.

In 1923, Falk joined Tranmael to write a proposal that the Norwegian Labor Party should act independently of the Communist International, of which it was a member. In Moscow the

Comintern was displeased and put the question on the agenda for an enlarged meeting of its executive committee. Falk went to Moscow along with Tranmael and other Labor Party leaders to face the music, and reportedly distinguished himself with his antiauthoritarian sarcasm. Top Soviet leader Bakunin demanded that the Norwegians choose between the Comintern and the young upstart Erling Falk.

A majority of Norwegian labor leaders had grown disenchanted with high-handed instructions from Soviets who were out of touch with Norwegian realities. One of the Soviet instructions was to prepare for armed struggle. Tranmael and Falk were certainly not alone in their strong anti-militarist inclination, and the Russians' bloody and destructive civil war following 1917 must have set a miserable example.

Not everyone in the Labor Party wanted to leave the Comintern, however. When the party had its annual convention later that year, a minority of workers and labor leaders demanded that the party remain in the Comintern. That meant a split in the party—a very emotional moment for a movement that so highly valued solidarity. It was hard enough that two years before, in 1921, a split had led to the creation of the moderate Social Democratic Labor Party. Now, in 1923, a new minority formed the Communist Party of Norway to remain a member of the Soviet-dominated Communist International.

The main body, having now lost members on both its left and right wings, opened its membership to anyone whether or not in a unionized workplace. Many rural farmworkers and small farmers joined. The members of the Social Democratic Labor Party then came back. More middle-class students, influenced by *Mot Dag*, joined as well.

One of these was twenty-four-year-old Karl Evang, a medical student who later became a celebrated doctor who co-founded and chaired the World Health Organization. As a student, Evang threw himself into *Mot Dag*'s new evening school for workers. He also helped build a parallel association for middle-class young people, *Clarté*.

Like *Mot Dag*, *Clarté* (French for "clarity") was socialist and pacifist, but unlike *Mot Dag* members, *Clarté* young adults didn't accept a group discipline that centered one's life on the revolution. It had started as a French-based organization and had Swedish, Danish, and Finnish branches. *Mot Dag* members edited *Clarté*'s periodical and offered other leadership.

Young Karl Evang experienced the growing intensity of *Mot Dag*'s community life. The group welcomed psychoanalysis—in the 1920s a revolutionary idea—and sought to replace middle-class individualism with a collective spirit. Evang's medical studies led to fresh considerations of sexuality. His flair for writing made his articles popular in *Mot Dag*'s outreach, including among the proliferating workers' study groups. He also helped *Mot Dag* lead the Norwegian Students Society; he was elected chair of that association in 1931 even while the government held him in prison for conscientious objection.

As *Mot Dag*'s influence grew, however, detractors called it a sect and a "black magic order of monks." Others saw it as "the most together political organization that ever existed in the Nordic countries."

Mot Dag became a breeding ground for national leadership; many members became valued civil servants and advisors to Labor members of Parliament. Evang himself became the government's health minister and led campaigns that eradicated poliomyelitis and reduced tuberculosis. A popular radio speaker, lecturer, and author, he later spoke against Norwegian participation in the Korean War and in NATO. In 1972, he helped lead the movement that kept Norway out of the European Union.

THE OWNING CLASS STRIKES BACK

By the middle of the 1920s, some members of the Norwegian owning class began to doubt the effectiveness of the army for repression of the labor movement. My future father-in-law Johannes Mathiesen was far from alone in his passionate rejection of the military. The Labor Party tried calling for a military strike; the government retaliated and threw party functionaries in jail. Nobody knew how reliable the army would remain in defending the status quo.

The Patriotic League was their answer. Launched in 1926, the League's mission was to wade into labor strikes and violently defend replacement workers from the efforts that union members made to keep "scabs" from taking their jobs. By the 1930s, the League had recruited tens of thousands of members.

This resort to street violence to try to keep the Norwegian labor movement from winning had of course been preceded by the rise of Hitler's Nazis in Germany and Mussolini's Fascist "blackshirts" in Italy. Sir Oswald Mosley was a frustrated politician in the United Kingdom whose meeting with Mussolini in 1932 inspired the English version, called the British Union of Fascists. Its paramilitary wing also called itself the "blackshirts." Mosley was supported by an array of wealthy funders and members of the British nobility.

The Great Depression hit Norway hard, resulting in a higher rate of unemployment than in any other Nordic country. In a shrewd move, the union movement decided to continue the membership of unemployed workers, even those who couldn't afford their union dues. It was another way to generate solidarity, and to reduce the chance of former union members turning, in their desperation to feed their families, into scabs.

The year 1931 was one of widespread hunger and suffering. The unions organized boycotts and eighty-two strikes. The Norwegian Employers Confederation tried to force the unions to accept a reduction of wages for workers who still had jobs, and used the technique of the lockout—locking the doors of their factories and shipyards to prevent workers from working. Workers fought back nonviolently, with massive demonstrations. The four-month struggle had no clear victor.

In 1932, the total number of union campaigns increased again, to ninety-one unions fighting for a living wage, union recognition, and the right to strike. A middle-aged Norwegian politician named Vidkun Quisling believed that the time had come for a coup d'état to establish military rule and crush the left.

Quisling had begun his career in the military, where he joined the General Staff on the eve of World War I. He was said to detest the strong Norwegian pacifist movement that achieved its goal of keeping Norway out of that war. After the war, Quisling did diplomatic work, using his administrative skills to help Fridjof Nansen with international humanitarian projects. He then drifted rightward in his politics. He explored the value of militias, published an openly racist book, and advocated war against Bolshevism.

In 1931, he became defense minister in a government led by the Agrarian Party, although Quisling was not himself a member of the party. One of his first tasks as defense minister was to deal with a conflict at Norsk Hydro's plant near Berit's hometown of Skien. Coincidentally, Quisling had also lived in Skien as a boy.

Norsk Hydro had joined the national employers' strategy of locking out their workers, but then the local management hired some replacement workers for limited production. One hundred police guarded the replacement workers while 2,000 striking workers marched to the port and warehouse at Menstad. The police were overwhelmed by the demonstrators, some of whom supplemented the power of their numbers by throwing stones and pieces of iron pipe.

Quisling's solution was to send in the army, evoking a storm of popular protest.

Quisling grew more contemptuous of what he regarded as weakness in the Agrarian-led government. In 1932, he secretly laid plans to overthrow the elected prime minister so he could seize power with the help of the military. He couldn't secure the support of top military officers.

In 1933, since his personal popularity was soaring among right-wing Norwegians, Quisling decided to strike out on his own and organize a new political party: the Nasjonal Samling (National Unity). The party mixed romantic nationalism and Norse paganism with admiration for the Nazi movement. In parallel with the early days of similar movements in Britain, Italy, and Germany, Quisling's uniformed paramilitary wing was called the *Hird*, an ancient Norwegian word for warriors. The *Hird* held marches to provoke violent clashes with working-class activists.

In national elections, Quisling's new party never got more than 2.5 percent of the votes. Still, its drama reflected the polarization of the country. Because Norwegians knew about the Nazis' attacks on German unions and the left, and knew about the support Hitler received from the German owning class, Quisling's activity heightened their sense of urgency about resolving Norway's own question: which class will direct the future of Norwegian society?

SWEDEN MAKES A CHOICE

Sweden, too, wrestled with that very question. As in the Norwegian labor battle in Skien, the boiling point in Sweden's Ådalen Valley was the use of strikebreakers. By 1931, three lumber mills were involved. Four thousand striking workers picketed and rallied against the owners and the political authorities who backed them. National soldiers were mobilized, killing five and injuring five more.

Thousands attended funerals of the slain workers.

The parties representing the owning class had been losing ground in elections, while the labor-based Social Democrats made steady gains. The Liberal-led coalition government's choice to defend capitalism by killing workers lost the coalition most of its remaining credibility with middle-of-the-road Swedes. The government fell, an election was called, and Swedes elected the Social Democrats in 1932 to give them a fresh start.

The policymakers faced an economy in deep trouble. One of the creative Swedish economists they turned to was Gunnar Myrdal, a name familiar to many Americans for the landmark study of black-white relations in the United States entitled *An American Dilemma*.[30]

Myrdal had broken with the classical economists and offered breakthrough thinking that later won him the Nobel Prize in Economics. He argued that the reason the classical economists were unable to imagine an economy that included well-being for workers was because they were not holistic enough. He believed that it was possible to design an egalitarian economy that would prevent poverty and be productive at the same time. His theory encouraged an investment in the individual person as a resource for economic growth—a pillar of what came to be called the Nordic model.

Myrdal urged the new policymakers in the Swedish government to let go of the old, negative understanding of incentives for work held by classical economists—that it was a struggle for existence—and design a positive framework of incentives for economic participation.

Swedish voters reelected the Social Democrats to lead their society almost without a break until 1976, by which time the Nordic model was firmly established.

In 1932 in Norway, however, the battle continued.

NORWAY AT THE BRINK

In 1933, the government continued to flounder in the face of depression. More Norwegians went hungry. Farm families could find something to eat, but they were unable to keep up payment on their debts. Banks tried to foreclose on farmers, and crowds gathered at farms nonviolently to prevent seizure. Workers launched ninety-three strikes in Norway in 1933.

The 1933 general election did not resolve the deepening conflict. Labor got more votes than ever and added twenty-two more members of parliament than it got in the 1930 election. Nevertheless, the Labor Party missed by seven seats the number required for a majority in the Storting.

The Conservatives had made a blunder in Norway's second-largest city, Bergen. For the local election it formed an alliance with Quisling's new party, the National Union. Because Quisling was widely regarded as Norway's Hitler, the generally democratic Norwegians were shocked to see their party of the economic elite make that alliance. In the general election, the Conservatives lost a quarter of their popular vote and thirteen parliamentary seats.

The parliamentary majority was held by what Norwegians call the four "bourgeois" parties, but that coalition had no real mandate. Politically, Norway was split fairly evenly. A former prime minister from a right-of-center party put together a caretaker government.

Significantly, the minority Labor Party did not try to move to the right and make a deal that would enable it to form a government. The Norwegian workers' theory of change, after years of study groups and educational debates, accepted the need for polarization in order to bring about a new society.

The Agrarian Party, however, formerly in coalition with the Conservative Party, began to reposition itself. Labor had been wooing family farmers for decades, and it was obvious that the Conservatives had no idea how to get out of the depression. The Agrarian Party's experience with Quisling in its government's cabinet was bruising, and it needed to look elsewhere for answers.

The workers' nonviolent direct action intensified. In 1935, the strike total hit 103. The bourgeois parties saw that they could not, in fact, govern. The Agrarian Party switched sides in the Storting and supported the Labor Party to form a government. But the power struggle between labor and capital was not yet resolved, and the Labor government could initiate only limited Keynesian measures to expand the economy and start an old-age pension scheme for hungry workers.

The poorest members of the labor movement pushed their leadership to alleviate the pain immediately, rather than to continue to struggle for the complete overthrow of capitalism as stated in the party's manifesto. Labor's leadership began to consider compromise.

On the other side, the employers' federation had waged decades of open struggle against the growing workers' movement and had its back to the wall. It knew that the Labor Party's manifesto envisioned a socialist society. Norway has a common border in the north with Russia. The owners were well aware that the Russian revolution left no room for capitalist survival. The owners had to wonder: if they were not willing to compromise, would the Norwegian workers and farmers and middle-class allies surge ahead and leave them with nothing?

In 1935, the owners met with the labor leaders. Together they hammered out what came to be called the "Basic Agreement."

The owners' federation agreed to accept the right of unionization throughout Norway, including collective bargaining, and accepted the workers' right to strike (except during the life of a contract). Owners agreed to political strikes and sympathy strikes.

Labor leaders agreed that the owners could continue to own and guide their firms. Labor expected that their political instrument, the Labor Party, would restrict owners through government regulation and control the overall direction of the economy. The intensifying nonviolent struggle by workers and farmers, plus middle-class allies, created a fundamental power shift.

In 1937, the Labor Party won the largest share of the vote (although still a minority, in a multi-party election), stepped up its Keynesian stimulus of the economy to counter the depression, and distributed more relief to the poor.

More middle-class people swung to support the Labor Party, both because the Party was recruiting them more actively (through family ties to workers, for example), and because some middle-class people began to see that Labor could deliver concrete benefits for the people.

The Labor Party's vision of nonviolent revolution resulting in a completely socialist society remained in its manifesto until 1949, reminding the owning class that another round of militant capitalist resistance to change might lead to a more radical outcome than what they already were living with.

THE CONSENSUS EMERGES

Not until 1965—three decades after the Basic Agreement—did the Conservative Party get a chance to govern, leading a coalition of bourgeois parties. By then the Nordic model was securely in place and the Conservatives accepted the basic changes in the rules of the game.

This came fully home to me only when I sat in the Mathiesen living room in Skien in 1973 and watched a televised election debate among national party leaders. I commented to Berit that it hardly seemed a debate; it was almost boring. I spoke in English so her father Johannes, also watching, wouldn't think I was trivializing his country's politics. But Berit agreed that the major parties no longer fought over the design of the economy.

In the debate, I heard little attraction to the command economy of the Soviet Union next door, nor to the free-market economy of the United States across the sea. Norwegians didn't completely scorn the market. After all, a market can provide flexibility and the constant feedback and corrections that support the well-being of the whole. They thought a small stock market could be useful but needed regulation so its own excesses didn't destroy it. The financial sector remained small, and a good deal of it was owned publicly and the rest highly regulated.

After the bitter strikes and loss of productivity that resulted from the class struggle back in the day, the election debate I watched in the Mathiesen living room reflected industrial peace. By 1973, Norwegians seemed to have consensus on a carefully guided market, full employment, free and universal health care, free higher education, and efficient and affordable public transportation. The party spokespeople agreed on the goal of good housing for all but argued that their own party would get it faster than the other parties would. Taxes weren't really an issue; the people knew they needed to pay high taxes to get abundant services.

In my experience, Norwegians don't like to talk about "the bad old days" of harsh polarization and open struggle. Most enjoy their reputation in the wider world as consensus-seekers and experts in conflict resolution. Their backstory, however, is different: they needed to fight to achieve the amount of freedom and equality they now enjoy. As Martin Luther King, Jr., observed, "Freedom is not free."

PART II

DESIGN FOR LIVING IN THE NORDIC COUNTRIES

6

MORE START-UPS THAN THE UNITED STATES: SUPPORT FOR ENTREPRENEURS, WORKERS, AND THE EQUALITY OF WOMEN

When Berit was a teenager, she often babysat for Finn Gjaerum, an entrepreneur in her hometown of Skien. When I moved to Norway she was eager for me to meet Finn's young family, with whom she'd gone on trips. I had a delightful time, drank a lot of coffee, and asked Finn what it was like to run his chemical import firm in Norway.

"It's absorbing, and satisfying," he said. "I like to make decisions and I'm okay with the responsibility of meeting payroll. I like being my own boss. And Norwegian workers are very reliable and conscientious, so I don't have to worry about setting and meeting deadlines."

Over time I realized that, even under a government usually run by the workers' party, Norwegians recognize their entrepreneurs. Take Kjell Inge Røkke. He started out as a fisherman, reportedly too dyslexic to finish secondary school. He worked on fishing trawlers in Alaska and returned to Norway to become an industrialist with assets reportedly worth $3 billion. My own town has reason to be grateful to him: his shipbuilding firm Aker saved the Philadelphia Navy Yard from giving up its centuries-old mission of building ships.

Rates of start-up creation in Norway are among the highest in the developed world, and Norway has more entrepreneurs per capita than the United States, according to a report by a Boston-based research consortium.[31]

The flurry of new Norwegian enterprise was news to me. I assumed that my own country would consistently lead the start-up economy. But the U.S. Small Business Administration released a study in 2010 reporting that U.S. start-up activity fell behind not only Norway but also Canada, Denmark, and Switzerland.

HOW THE ECONOMIC DESIGN SUPPORTS ENTREPRENEURS

In 2010, Max Chafkin did a survey of Norwegian entrepreneurs for *Inc. Magazine*, where he was a senior writer. While in Norway he noted the liveliness of the start-up scene. When he returned home he consulted Zoltan J. Acs, the chief economist for the U.S. Small Business Administration's Office of Advocacy. Chafkin asked why more Norwegians than Americans would be taking the risk of starting their own businesses. Acs said, "The three things we as Americans worry about—education, retirement, and medical expenses—are things that Norwegians don't worry about."[32]

Mark Zandi, chief economist for Moody's Analytics, in 2014 added another reason for start-ups lagging in the United States. Thirty-somethings, a demographic usually productive of risk-taking and start-ups, are often held back by student loan debt.[33]

The Nordic model's free higher education opens doors. The Norwegian Entrepreneurship Program is a collaboration of all seven of the Norwegian universities, nine university colleges, and some business and architecture schools. The program cooperates with international partners, including the University of California at Berkeley. Budding entrepreneurs take academic and practical courses and spend three months working in a start-up company with a technological focus.

Because the Norwegian Entrepreneurship Program is for Norwegians wanting to make a major commitment, the government has set up other programs that are more introductory, designed to clarify people's intention. Oslo offers free introductory courses on how to start a company. The course instructors teach in English in order to catch new immigrants whose Norwegian skills may not be very secure yet.

Many immigrants live in the city of Drammen, where workers went on one of Norway's earliest strikes. Drammen now hosts a national pilot program for immigrants to support entrepreneurial spirit and professionalization, and the project emphasizes the contribution of immigrants.[34]

INNOVATION AND EQUALITY: THE TRACK RECORD

Conventional wisdom links innovation to wide *in*equality. The belief is that inequality motivates, by increasing both the risk and potential reward, attracting talented people who love adventure. The bold ones make the breakthroughs that propel invention and innovation. It sounds reasonable.

Three researchers at the London School of Economics put this assumption to the test by examining, among other things, patent filings in different countries. They found that Sweden, which gets sneers from some red-in-tooth-and-claw capitalists as a "nanny state," had more patent filings per resident than the United States for most of the last half-century. The LSE researchers then turned to the Global Innovation Index and compared innovation with inequality. They found that innovation in the United States lags behind a number of OECD countries that have lower inequality.[35]

The advocates of inequality invoke the concept of meritocracy. They point to the olden days in the United States when high rates of upward mobility showed that the poor with talent and grit found our country a land of opportunity, and that this was an important measure of freedom.

In 2012, *The New York Times* reported on economist Markus Jantti's studies of mobility.[36] Professor Jantti asked how different countries compare in giving young people the chance of upward mobility.

To measure this, Jantti looked at the rates of sons and daughters moving in just one generation from their father's spot in the income ladder to a higher spot for themselves. The most dramatic change, he reasoned, would be for children whose fathers were in the bottom fifth of earners to leap to the top fifth.

Jantti found that in Norway, Denmark, and Sweden, the daughters and sons from the bottom fifth had a much better chance of making that leap than they do in the UK and the United States.[37] His finding lines up with equality studies comparing the OECD countries that found that the more equal a society is, the more mobility it has.

It turns out that freedom (shown by mobility and innovation) and equality are not necessarily opposed. In fact, by these measures, *equality supports freedom.* The track record suggests that the Nordic economic design has features that are synergistic: the more equality, the more freedom.[38]

One reason why Norway picked up quickly on the Danish model of flexicurity is because it increases an entrepreneur's freedom. If the business you own can no longer compete in the world market, it's fine with the Norwegian government for you to close it and lay off your workers. Flexicurity means the government has a social contract with those laid-off workers to do everything possible to help them land a new job that's just as good or better for them. Your unproductive capital becomes available for a new start-up.

Still another way that the government helps is to minimize the red tape for start-ups. According to a World Bank report published in 2012, the time it takes in Norway to establish a new company is seven days.

WOMEN AS LEADERS AND PRODUCERS

Norwegian-American Susanne Kromberg told me that the gender dynamic is an important part of the Viking economic story. She asked me to consider what was happening in Norwegian villages a thousand years ago while men were "going Viking." "The women," she said, "had to have legal authority, to be able to defend themselves, and manage every aspect of life in the village without the men present."

Viking women could hold property and easily obtain a divorce in response to her husband beating her or for some other reason.[39]

That was then. By the nineteenth century, Norwegian women had fallen into a Victorian oppression that stirred Norwegian dramatist Henrik Ibsen to rage against sexism in his plays.

Sexism was still very much alive in the 1950s. When Berit graduated from the junior college in Skien that specializes in business administration, she placed first in her class. In that school, placing first marked the grad as CEO material. The college principal, however, told Berit's mother in congratulating her that Berit would some day make a CEO a fine executive secretary!

Since those days, Nordic women have gained more freedom and equality, tracking closely with the growing sophistication of the economic design. In 1986, newly elected Labor prime minister Gro Harlem Brundtland made history by announcing a cabinet that was dubbed "the women's government." Eight of the eighteen ministers were women.

The Nordic countries now have high women's participation in their parliaments, an average of 40 percent, and most have had a woman prime minister. Norway became the first to adopt affirmative action for corporate boards of directors, requiring by law at least 40 percent women on the board.[40]

The descendants of the Vikings have the world's highest employment rates for women. Over three-quarters of Norwegian women work outside the home, compared with 68 percent in the United States and 65 percent in the European Union.

The heritage of sexism, however, still shows up in several ways. One is that women comprise the majority of employees in the public sector while men make up the vast majority of workers in the private sector. Another is that women are less likely to be in top managerial positions. I'm told that this is changing, but the most recent figures I've found were from 2005, when women's percentages in top management were in the low twenties. Even in middle-level management spots, women in private companies made up only 27 percent.

A factor that will likely make a difference over time is that three of five students at universities and colleges are now women. Women form the majority of students in the traditionally high-status schools of law and medicine. The fact that the universities are free increases the freedom of women to develop fully their careers.

DESIGNING FOR THE FREEDOM AND PARTICIPATION OF WOMEN—A WIN-WIN

Two male cabinet members in the recent Norwegian Labor government, justice minister Knut Storberget and minister of equality Audun Lysbakken, took three and four months off while in office to look after the new children in each of their families. A major preoccupation in Norway is increasing innovation and productivity by breaking out of rigid gender roles.

Former Norwegian prime minister Jens Stoltenberg is an economist by trade. In 2011, *The New York Times* interviewed him during his second term as prime minister. The reporter asked for the secret of Norway's economic success. He said, "One Norwegian lesson is that if you can raise female participation, it helps the economy, birth rates, and the budget."

I traced this trend back to Jens's mother, Karin Stoltenberg, who in the 1980s was one of those pioneer cabinet ministers in Gro Brundtland's government. She earned wide respect by working hard to support an expanded role for women in the workforce.

She pushed for lengthy maternity leave at full pay, subsidized after-school programs for children, and the right to paid leave when a child was ill.

Karin Stoltenberg believed that freeing women to combine career with family and encouraging couples to share responsibility at home would be a win-win for freedom and also for productivity. When her son Jens became prime minister and formed his cabinet in 2005, he made it the first in Norwegian history to have a majority of women.

The Stoltenbergs, mother and son both, love families and at the same time want parents to be in jobs and paying taxes. Norway ranks first in Europe not only in participation of women in the workforce but also in birth rates.

Save the Children ranks all countries in the world to find "the best place to be a mother." Year after year, the Nordic countries trade places among the top few ranking spots. In 2015, the top five were Norway, Finland, Iceland, Denmark, and Sweden. The UK was twenty-fourth, and United States thirty-third.[41]

Norway offers new parents two options for its national, government-funded parental leave. The first option is to take fifty-six weeks of leave at 80 percent of your pay.[42] The second is to take forty-six weeks at 100 percent of your pay. This is true if you're adopting a child (up to age fifteen), or if you're giving birth.

The law guarantees that the parents can come back to their old jobs when their leave is completed. If a parent wants to continue as a stay-at-home caretaker, he or she will be paid by the state for that job. Some women aren't in the workforce and don't have a job from which they can take a leave if they become mothers. In that case, they can claim a grant, which in 2009 was about $5,000 USD.

The Nordic countries realize that if all the parental leave is taken by the mother, she will be less likely to keep up over time with advancement opportunities at work, and therefore she will fall behind in lifetime earnings and career achievement. That's a built-in dynamic of inequality between the genders: once again, the more inequality, the less freedom. Further, a mom taking the parental leave means she'll probably become the primary caregiver for the youngster, instead of caregiving being shared equally.

That means the dad needs to step up and take responsibility for childcare. When I'm on the streets of Norway during the working day, I'm struck by the large number of young dads who now push baby carriages and play with young children in the parks. The basic design of Viking economics promotes not only justice but also productivity. Economics writer James Surowiecki reports in *The New Yorker* that a recent worldwide study of four thousand research-and-development teams found gender-diverse teams much better at driving "radical innovation."[43]

HOW UNIONS SUPPORT EQUALITY AND THE COMMON GOOD

These days, the Nordic middle class of professionals and managers is becoming larger than the working class. In the shifting coalitions of electoral politics, the labor-social democratic parties are not always leading their governments.

Nevertheless, trade unions play a crucial role in Nordic economies. Strong labor movements bring an organizational cohesion and persistent advocacy that prevent an unraveling of the economic design for equality and freedom. John Weeks studied inequality in Australia, Canada, Germany, Japan, Sweden, the United Kingdom, and the United States for the decades of the 1980s and '90s, finding that declines in trade union membership were closely associated with widening income differences.[44]

Then came the 2008 lurch of the financial sector outside of Norway and Sweden. The United States was one of the countries where inequality accelerated; according to the *Fiscal Times*, "for most Americans, wages aren't just stagnating—they're falling. Low-income workers have taken the biggest hit, especially restaurant workers . . . The declines get worse the father you move down the income scale."[45] The Nordic labor movements do not tolerate this kind of trend, on principle and because of the suffering and because it leads to the kind of political alienation we see in the United States, when many white male workers follow demagogues like Donald Trump.

A convenient way to look at social classes is to see them performing different functions for the economy as a whole. In Nordic as in other modern industrial economies, people in middle-class jobs mostly perform the functions of managing, teaching, designing the work of, and supporting the health of the working class. Working-class jobs produce most of the goods and services that keep the economy humming.

Economic functions generate particular values carried by each class within the larger system. Each economic class carries a kind of culture that supports its function. Working-class people generate the value of social solidarity; one reflection of that is giving a higher percentage of their income to charity than do people in other classes.

I'm not suggesting that individuals can't support values that are mostly promoted by cultures other than their own. The solidarity championed by workers and their allies has been adopted more broadly in the Nordic countries. We see, for example, Norwegians across a wide class spectrum taking pride in their small country being among the top contributors to the United Nations.

In the early 1900s, a coalition of Nordic workers and small farmers pushed for an economics of solidarity, attracting middle-class allies and leading to the invention of Viking economics. In the 1980s, when the coalition's confidence in their invention was shaken and they flirted with the neoliberalism promoted by the upper classes, their economies plunged toward disaster. When they returned to the root value expressed in the old slogan "All for one and one for all," they once again prospered.

One of the arguments used by neoliberals is that a "flexible labor market" contributes to economic strength, i.e., the common good. Nobel Prize–winning economist Joseph E. Stiglitz challenges that idea. "That the American labor market performed so poorly in the Great Recession and that American workers have done so badly for three decades should cast doubt on the mythical virtues of a flexible labor market."[46] He notes that unions fight for strong worker protections, which "correct what would otherwise be an imbalance of economic power." In other words, powerful trade unions are an essential ingredient of why the Nordic countries outperform the American economy.

I told the dramatic story earlier of how the Nordics made the transition from majority-poor to top-of-the-charts economies, emphasizing the role of union-led nonviolent direct action campaigns. For day-to-day influence in the direction of the overall economy, however, the unions depend on a political party that is accountable to them, the Social Democrats or Labor. In the United States, we see what happens without that mechanism: the Democratic Party pays almost no attention to labor except at election time, and it fails decade after decade to enact labor's legislative priorities even when in control of both Congress and the White House.[47]

I've been struck in researching this book by the consistency with which the many international rating systems for the human development and well-being of a country correlate with percentage of workers in unions. The high-union-density Nordics nearly always appear in the top group, and the United Kingdom, with its lower union density, shows up farther down the list. We find the very-low-union-density United States yet another jump down the list. It appears that the habit in the United States of labeling unions as "special-interest groups" has little relation to reality; according to the evidence the unions should be called "common-interest groups."[48]

However, Norwegian writer Asbjørn Wahl shows that the solidarity base for Viking economics cannot be taken for granted. When neoliberal-influenced governments in Denmark and Sweden acted openly to weaken unions, both union power and membership dropped.[49] In 1992, Sweden's national employer confederation declared openly that it had broken with the social partnership model that had worked for decades to create unprecedented prosperity and productivity, and then refused central negotiations with the labor federation.[50] This coincided in time with the worst Swedish economic performance in half a century.

Even though the Nordic economic elite cannot rule the roost as it did before the 1930s, the class struggle continues in Nordic countries.

HIGH UNION MEMBERSHIP AND PRODUCTIVITY

Neil Brooks and Thaddeus Hwong at the Canadian Centre for Policy Alternatives did a comparative study of the six Anglo-American countries in the OECD with a group of Nordics: Norway, Sweden, Denmark, and Finland. They used data from 1990 to 2002. The group average for labor density in the Anglo-American countries was 24 percent; for the Nordics, 71 percent. Among the many interesting social indicators they compared were institutional legitimacy and labor productivity.

The Anglo-American countries had little confidence in their legislatures, 32.1 percent, compared with the Nordics' 52.7 percent. The average in the first group for confidence in the justice system was 45.8 percent compared with 68.9 percent. The Anglo-Americans also believe that there is more governmental corruption in their countries than do the Nordics: on a scale of perception of governmental corruption, where "0" equals "most corruption" and "10" equals "least corruption," the Anglo-American countries average 8.4 and the Nordics 9.3.

Perhaps most surprising to Americans will be the study's comparison of labor productivity. The group of countries where the majority of workers are in unions were also those that experienced higher productivity. "On average, Nordic country workers produce goods and services valued at $44.10 an hour, while Anglo-American workers only produce goods and services valued at $38.20 an hour."

Comparing two countries at the extremes of the OECD spectrum on union density, Brooks and Huang note that "American workers tend to be very productive, on average producing goods and services worth $46.3 per hour. However, it might be noted that they are not nearly as productive as workers in Norway, who produce goods and services worth $56.6 per hour."[51]

The United States operates a different economic model, which values *insecurity*. The model keeps unemployment high and sustains poverty and hunger. A family depends on a job that might disappear tomorrow; it lands in a feeble safety net; it has few prospects for finding another job as good or better. Small wonder that U.S. unions sometimes defend inefficient labor practices and outmoded organization of work, even though undermining productivity—whatever it takes to keep workers in jobs. In other words, compared with the high-productivity Nordic model, the U.S. insecurity approach creates *an incentive to resist efficiency.*

U.S. economist James Galbraith helps us see how productivity-reducing the U.S. model is in comparison with the experience of Nordic corporate managers. Over there, labor costs are high and there are few barriers to trade. "If you are a business in Sweden or Norway, you are free to import, export, and outsource as you like," Galbraith writes. "There is, however, one thing you are not free to do: you are not free to cut your wages. You are not free to compete by going after cut-rate workers, either native or immigrant. You are not free to undercut the union rate."[52]

Galbraith explains that these strong rules incentivize productivity. They guard against lazy or incompetent managers who try to maintain profit by underpaying employees rather than doing their job of increasing efficiency. Strong unions fight for the Nordic model, which incentivizes productivity.

HOW MANAGERS INCREASE PRODUCTIVITY BY KEEPING QUALITY WORKERS

Finn Gjaerum, the CEO for whom Berit babysat when she was young, cited the reliability and competence of his workers as one reason for his satisfaction as an entrepreneur. Max Chaflin, the senior writer that *Inc. Magazine* sent to Norway to dig into such matters, interviewed entrepreneurs about finding and keeping good workers.

Chaflin interviewed Wiggo Dalmo, owner of a $44 million company that mostly employs mechanics and machinists. In his industry, the employee turnover rate is 7 percent, but Dalmo keeps his turnover below 2 percent. He does that by treating them like Google engineers. He employs a chef who prepares lunch for the staff each day. He throws a blowout annual party—last year the cost was more than $100,000. He also adds private health insurance on top of the insurance that all Norwegians get free, enabling treatment in private hospitals for conditions that might not be treated as quickly in the public ones.

Chaflin notes that "it takes more than perks to keep a worker motivated in Norway. In a country with low unemployment and generous unemployment benefits, a worker's threat to quit is more credible than it is in the United States, giving workers more leverage over employers. And though Norway makes it easy to lay off workers in cases of [the firm's] economic hardship, firing an employee for cause typically takes months, and employers generally end up paying at least three months' severance."

Bjørn Holte is the founder and CEO of bMenu, a start-up that makes mobile versions of websites. Chaflin reports that Holte pays himself $125,000 a year while his lowest-paid employee makes more than $60,000. He quotes Holte: "You can't just treat them like machines. If you do, they'll be gone."[53]

Readers who are mystified by the respectful attitudes often shown by Nordic entrepreneurs will be helped by a study of their U.S. counterparts done by economics writers Brian Miller and Mike Lapham. The book contains interviews with fifteen U.S. entrepreneurs, including Warren Buffett, who have in common an ability to see through "the self-made myth" that haunts U.S. business culture. Because the fifteen understand, as Nordic entrepreneurs do, the social and governmental context that made their success possible, they pay attention to the larger picture of co-creation of economic value.[54]

INCOME POLICIES THAT ADVANCE FREEDOM AND EQUALITY

One measure of inequality is wealth. On the international charts, Denmark, Sweden, and Norway do not do as well on wealth equality as they do on income, although even on the wealth measure they do better than the United States. New Credit Suisse became curious about why the Nordics are not superstars in the wealth-equality ratings and conducted a study. The researchers concluded that the very fact that individuals' future is so secure in the Nordic countries reduces the incentive for working- and middle-class people to save. Owning-class people do invest because they cannot spend all their income, and their investments pile up in the form of wealth and assets.[55] The difference in typical saving behavior between the different classes means that the Nordic spectrum of wealth is much wider than the Nordic spectrum of income. As we'll see in the chapter on taxes, the Norwegians acknowledge wealth inequality by having a wealth tax.

What matters most for people's everyday life is income. Among thirty-two OECD countries, the ten most equal countries include Denmark, Norway, Iceland, and Sweden. The United States and the UK are among the five most unequal, along with Turkey and Mexico.[56]

Henry Ford famously announced that he paid his workers high wages (compared to those at other automobile firms) because he wanted them to be able to afford to buy his cars. The genius industrialist anticipated the modern economic reality in which a nation's productivity is partly driven by consumer demand.

The social-democratic Nordics are surprisingly in agreement with arch-capitalist Ford. Together they've been the outliers, because they challenged the prevailing assumption made by Soviet and capitalist leaders alike: underpay your workers and farmers to force capital accumulation to finance economic development.

Norway was on a front line of the U.S.-Soviet struggle. It was a member of NATO, but also had an active Communist Party and a common border with the Soviets. Norwegians could hear clearly the economic arguments of both sides.

Both the Soviets and the capitalists needed a maxim to justify maintaining their high levels of poverty, reassuring their 99 percent that the sacrifice would someday be rewarded by shared abundance. The Soviet version was, "Communist rule will one day shower you with goods and services." According to the U.S. version, "A rising tide lifts all boats."

Both promises turned out to be profoundly untrue. In economic development terms, the Nordic model has proven far more practical than either the Soviet's command economy or the free market. The workers' parties that led the Nordics had a belief in equality that correctly distrusted a huge income gap. They also shared the economic shrewdness that Ford expressed. They distributed income to those who would use it for needed goods and services rather than allowing it to be skimmed off the top by owners who would do God only knows what with it.

The way that Norwegians designed their globalized economy was to create a national mechanism for setting wages. Both labor and employers have national federations that look after the interests of their constituents. They meet periodically to negotiate wages. Their first step is to pay attention to Norway's export industries and ask what the global wage situation is for those workers. Then they negotiate Norwegian wages that make sense in light of the global market.

Wages for other workers are then decided in that context, assuming—as do most Norwegians—that high wages, high taxes, and abundant services create a productive and prosperous economy. The typical starting wage for a Norwegian graduate of the country's upper high school, which is roughly the equivalent of a U.S. two-year community college, is $45,000.

In that way, Norway's economic "boat" is balanced for successful use in the turbulent global seas and the more peaceful domestic lakes, an economic feature that reminds me of those early Viking ships that were designed to serve well in both shallow rivers and deep water.

Highly productive, unionized workers create more wealth. Workers are more likely to be productive if they are in jobs that are right for them. Family-support policies and quality vocational education matter, as does support for retraining and career change. Universal, single-payer health care prevents workers from being locked into jobs that bore them in order to keep employer-paid benefits. Productivity and equality-promoting services join to produce individual freedom in the labor market.

7

FAMILY FARMERS AND COOPERATIVES: KEY PLAYERS IN THE NORDIC MODEL

In the United States, the business news on television and the daily newspaper focuses on the excitement of corporate deal-making, the volatility of the stock market, and, occasionally, a union's threat to strike. Rarely attracting media attention is the international network of cooperatives, which, in total, do business equal to the seventh-largest economy in the world.[57]

Cooperatives have played a significant role in building the Viking economic model. Cooperatives have been growing internationally in recent years. For example, *The Economist* reports that since the 2008 financial crisis, European cooperative banks have been increasing their market share. Germany's *Bundesbank* (Central Bank) investigated the trend and found out why: co-op banks are financially more stable and less likely to fail than shareholder-owned institutions.[58]

Exceptions do exist. Even though a co-op's board of directors—who are customer-members—is elected by the other customer-members, a board can fail to do due diligence and can allow management to go off the rails. In Germany, the cooperative bank DZ lost one billion euros in 2008 because it had made high-risk investments.

Nevertheless, a recent scholarly study of the 2008 crash showed that overall, co-ops were more resilient than shareholder-owned banks, since they aren't driven by a need to make profits for investors and huge bonuses for managers.[59]

In Iceland, co-ops played a pivotal role in economic development for the first half of the twentieth century and then went into decline. Now they are growing again. In Denmark, Norway, and Sweden, cooperatives remained a dynamic part of economic life. A Danish financial services and insurance co-op, *Beierholm*, made the 2013 list of twenty-five "best large workplaces in Europe."[60] The Oslo-based KLP Insurance is eighty-first in the top 300 co-ops in the world, with revenues of $3.9 billion.[61]

The Swedish co-op *Folksam* represents the overall growth trend. The 106-year-old insurance co-op grew by aggressively marketing to immigrants to Sweden, who make up one-fifth of the population. Folksam set up a multilingual call center over a decade ago that now handles calls in seventeen languages, including Somali, Farsi, Arabic, and Kurdish. Folksam claims the lion's share of the insurance market in immigrant communities.

The high productivity and efficiency of businesses organized on the co-op model also shows up in the United States. A study found that worker co-ops had only one-third the chance of failing compared with public companies. This might be related to their extraordinary ability to retain the people in their workforce. A 2013 study found annual turnover averaging 15 percent, compared with industry norms of 40 to 60 percent![62]

A LONG TRACK RECORD IN SWEDEN

Starting early in the nineteenth century, Swedes organized co-ops for a variety of purposes. Now we find industrial production, banking and insurance, retail sales, and agriculture. People often band together to build an apartment complex and then share the ownership of it. The co-ops helped move Sweden from mid-nineteenth-century poverty, which pushed people to flee to America, to its present prosperity.

In their early days, co-ops were often organized by activists from the temperance movement, the farmers' movement, the trade unions, and a dissenting wing of the state Lutheran church. Activist workers who were members of the Social Democratic Party were prominent, although co-ops formally abstained from party politics.

In the 1870s, workers increasingly came together to build homes, investing their savings in their new housing co-ops. The cooperative movement expanded rapidly in the 1930s, when the Social Democrats replaced the Conservatives and began their long tenure in leading the economy.

The housing co-op movement not only provided homes but also created jobs for construction workers. Today, some 860,000 Swedes are members of housing co-ops, holding 18 percent of the country's housing stock with about 750,000 apartments.[63]

The co-op ownership model supports a variety of dwelling sizes, from one-family homes to large apartment buildings. The large units usually incorporate co-op-owned space for shopping centers, schools, and day-care centers.

Parent co-ops provide between 10 and 15 percent of childcare in Sweden. First developed in the 1970s as an alternative to the childcare offered by municipalities, they grew significantly in 1985 when they began to get public funding.[64]

Swedes in industrial co-ops today produce a variety of goods: automobile tires, paper, earthenware, even plastics. A kind of hybrid is the recent trend toward co-op wind power. For technical reasons these are defined in Swedish law as consumer co-ops, but the cooperative companies in fact produce electricity. From 2009 to 2012, the number of members in wind-power co-ops increased from 19,300 to 25,000.[65]

The members of all the co-ops, as co-owners, have the right of participation in decisions through a representative, democratic process. The *Folksam* insurance firm's governance structure is interesting because it was founded by both the co-ops and the trade unions. Its highest decision-making body of 108 delegates are elected half by the co-op movement and half by labor.

Today, groups wanting to start up a new co-op are called "nontraditional entrepreneurs" by the state-supported consulting agency, *Coompanion*. Many of these start-ups are from immigrant groups who see unmet needs among their people. Coompanion's 100 advisers can often steer them toward start-up funds from the government's assistance program.

In the meantime, Swedish consumer co-ops have grown to include 1.9 million members.

NORWAY'S SLOW START

The Norwegian Co-operative Association was founded in 1906 but remained weak until 1914. The combined membership of local consumer cooperative societies was a smaller proportion of the population than it was in other countries that got started at about the same time. The 1844 Rochdale principles—which were the international hallmark of viable co-ops—had little impact; Norwegians attracted to the consumer movement had little ideological coherence and failed to agree on an organizational practice.

Not until the Association borrowed from Sweden the idea of setting up a wholesale operation serving their local stores did the movement take hold. Norwegians increased their unity, and in the single decade before 1920 the number of local societies increased tenfold.[66]

Now a thousand co-op stores together have 1.2 million members, which is about half the number of households in Norway. More than 22,000 people work in the extensive Norwegian network of consumer co-ops. Co-op grocery stores have 24 percent market share of food sales. The network not only provides useful goods and services at competitive prices, but also acts as an interest group advocating on consumer issues nationally.

Norwegians were inspired by the success of the early Swedish housing co-op model, so construction workers in Oslo started a housing co-op of their own with the close collaboration of the city government. It wasn't until after the Nazi occupation during World War II, however, that large-scale cooperative housing was seriously undertaken.[67]

Now in Oslo, 40 percent of the housing is owned cooperatively; the portion for the country as a whole is 15 percent. The average housing co-op has apartments for fifty families or individuals. Nationally, the housing co-ops have about 800,000 members—a large number in a population of only five million.

The need for fire insurance spurred in Norway a local fire

insurance cooperative in 1689. There was little building on that, however, until some local start-ups in the nineteenth century finally joined together to create *Gjensidige*, now one of the biggest Norwegian insurance companies with about 966,000 members.

There's nothing more hardcore in Norway than fishing. Co-ops are significant for getting the fish and shrimp to market. Each of the six co-ops is owned by the fishermen in that particular geographical area.

All told, more than 2 million Norwegians are co-op members, and many individuals are actually members of several co-ops. The government has been backing this continued growth. In 2008, the Storting passed new legislation to encourage more co-ops of all kinds in Norway.

Cooperatives have an impact beyond the economy because they provide visible evidence that *cooperation works*. Culturally, co-ops serve the need in small countries for a defense against the unrelenting message from corporate globalization that only ruthless competition produces results.

HOW NORWAY SUPPORTS FARMERS

Norwegians and Danes were already keeping cattle in the days when Vikings were discovering North America. At that time, the most valuable product was butter, which was used as a kind of currency and means of payment.[68]

When Norwegian national feeling grew in the eighteenth and nineteenth centuries, urban intellectuals realized that the closest connection the country had to the ancient Vikings was through the farmers, since the Vikings were mostly farmers and the family farms in remote valleys still had some continuity with old Norse practices.

When in 1959 I first went to Norway, there were still nearly 200,000 farms, but the number now is about a third of that. The national government anticipated this trend and began to build cultural and educational programs to strengthen rural life. Berit and I saw an early sign of the program on my first ski vacation in a remote valley. We skied over to the local grange hall, where we joined local farmers watching a movie brought by a travelling culture worker.

The governmental program worked: nearly a quarter of Norwegians still live outside towns and cities. Most of the agricultural land itself is still worked, absorbed by the remaining farms. The law requires that agricultural land must continue to be used for farming, and the owner of the farm has to live there; this protects farming from developers. The result is that the agricultural story of Norway is still one of family farms.

Mechanization and fertilizer have meant increasing output, and Norwegian farms keep their country self-sufficient in animal products, although not in cereals. Switching to organic farming is a growing trend.[69]

Farmers hire help from wherever they can get it—Poland, Turkey, even as far as Vietnam. Farming "internships" offer American students and others the chance to experience Norway, with free room and board, in exchange for bringing in the harvest.

Globalization and agribusiness have decimated the family farm in some countries, so Norwegian farmers feel themselves under threat and count on pro-farm government policies. They deeply distrust the European Union. Norwegian farmers get a larger proportion of their income from government subsidies than any other country in the OECD, which reflects the national importance given to food security and tradition despite the challenges of a short growing season and international competition.

Still, there's lively debate about how much subsidy is the right amount. Agricultural subsidies amounted to nearly 7 percent of the national budget in 1980 but declined to 1.3 percent by 2010, according to the newspaper *Nationen*.[70] A majority of farmers do something else to supplement their income, like fishing or logging. From farming alone, the average income is only $22,000. That average, however, includes what Norwegians call "hobbying" farmers with little production.[71]

Farmers also have unions—two of them. Together they negotiate with the government about the annual agricultural marketing agreement. The larger of the two, with 61,000 members, is *Norges Bondelag*, the Norwegian Agrarian Association. Founded in 1896, it created its own political party in 1920, then called the Agrarian Party and now called the Centre Party. Today called the Centre Party, it is now independent of the union, although largely composed of farmers still, and it joined the Socialist Left and Labor Party to form the government in 2005.

The Norwegian Farmers and Smallholders Union (Norsk Bonde-og Småbrukarlag) was started in 1913 and has about 7,000 members. It's not affiliated with a political party and states that its primary values are solidarity and equality. It practices solidarity through programs with farmers in the global south.

This younger, more aggressive farmers union is willing to resort to nonviolent direct action when the government acts against farmers' needs. In 2005, the NFU protested the breakdown of negotiations with the government by emptying milk into streets, blocking entrances to flour mills to stop bread production, dumping manure, placing cows in front of government buildings, blockading motorways with tractors, and temporarily kidnapping county mayors.

In Sweden, too, the government has a role in supporting the viability of agriculture. It ensures that farmers have a chance to maintain equal income with other population groups. The government bargains with a farmers' trade union of some 150,000 members.

Farmers are fiercely loyal to the cooperative way of doing business. Back in 1915, Norwegian farmers formed a credit union to get a new source of loans; it has grown to about 12,000 members.

Most Norwegian farmers—about 50,000 of them—own cooperatives that process and market their products. Co-ops produce nearly all the milk, half the cheese, and 70 percent of the eggs in Norway. Timber is still one of Norway's major industries, and timber co-ops produce 80 percent of the timber. The co-ops have 17,000 employees to handle the processing and marketing of the farmers' production.[72]

Swedish farmers also built co-ops to process and market their products. 75 percent of Swedish agricultural output goes through their co-ops.[73] Most Swedish farms are medium-sized family farms; the average is 66 acres that can be cultivated.

Many countries buy dairy products from Denmark, but consumers may not realize they are buying from cooperative dairies that acquire 97 percent of Danish farmers' milk.[74] Agricultural cooperatives in Denmark have roots in the fourteenth century, and they were given fresh impetus by Bishop Grundtvik and the folk high school movement. While the Danish consumer co-op sector may have lost its dynamism, the hugely important agricultural sector of the economy remains a triumph of cooperativism.

When I reflect on the Nordic model's role for cooperatives and farming, I see a careful balancing act in which the needs of the whole are weighed along with the needs of the parts. That shows up in the local cooperative societies, and also in the debates of the national parliament. It's very pluralistic—farmers are members of a union, one or more co-ops, and a political party, all of which weigh in on the hot-button issue of the moment. Urban dwellers are likewise members of one or more co-ops and benefit from an unpolluted natural environment and delicious local food that wouldn't be there if greed were their bottom line.

8

PREVENTING POVERTY: NORDICS LEARN HOW AN ADVANCED ECONOMY CAN ABOLISH POVERTY

The Vikings' descendants can be stubborn. That's what the German Nazis learned when they occupied Norway and Denmark during World War II. It will help us understand the determination postwar Vikings brought to the task of abolishing poverty if we first look at examples of how Danes and Norwegians resisted enemy occupation.

When Norwegians wore small potatoes in their lapels to symbolize their resistance, Nazi authorities outlawed the practice. Then Norwegians substituted a pair of paperclips. The Germans faced a dilemma: how do you arrest tens of thousands of people for wearing paperclips in their lapels without looking utterly foolish?

In Denmark, across the open water of the *Skaggerak*, workers began to hold protest strikes. The occupiers outlawed strikes. Danish workers then left the factories early, insisting they weren't on strike—they just needed to go home while there was still daylight, to water their gardens. Do you arrest tens of thousands of workers

for watering their gardens when what you most want is high productivity to harness for Hitler's faltering war effort?

The Danes became masters of the art of low productivity.
They generated an epidemic of low-key industrial accidents that
hurt no one. They insisted on working according by the rule book
even though it created bottlenecks. Germany, previously counting
on the skilled Danish ship workers to produce ships for its war
effort, ended up towing half-finished ships back to German yards
for completion.

The Danes also frustrated the Nazi plan to wipe out the Jew-
ish population. The Danish resistance to occupation was largely
nonviolent, which may have encouraged the leak that revealed
when the round-up of the Jews was to take place. Forewarned,
nearly all the Danish Jews joined the "underground railroad"
that took them under cover of night to points along the Danish
coast where fishermen's boats lay in wait. More than 7,000 Jews
crowded into the boats and were taken across the Øresund strait
to safety in neutral Sweden.

In Norway, the schoolteachers could see what was coming
when the Nazis began by using "salami tactics": changes imposed
one slice at a time. One move put Quisling's portrait on the wall
of each classroom. Another increased the role of the German language in the curriculum.

Among themselves, the teachers drew a line in the sand: when
their own union was shut down in favor of a Nazi association, they
would resist. When that day came, nearly all the eleven thousand
teachers wrote to the ministry of education, refusing to join the
new association.

A colleague in the Oslo school where I taught was a teacher
during the occupation. He told me what happened after the teach-

ers wrote their defiant letters. Police were instructed to arrest a couple of teachers at each public school as an example, and send them to a new prison camp in southern Norway. My colleague said that the faculty had a hurried meeting and talked candidly about who would be most suited to be arrested: young, physically fit, without children. Such teachers volunteered. Police were quietly told the way to meet their quota should be by arresting the volunteers.

The arrests didn't achieve compliance from the mass of teachers who remained free, so Norwegian Nazi leader Vidkun Quisling closed the schools. Teachers then met their classes in the homes of the parents, while communities banded together to meet the basic needs of the teachers.

Quisling increased the pressure by sending the imprisoned teachers to a concentration camp north of the Arctic Circle to do hard work in desperately cold conditions with little food. Some died. Each day the suffering teachers were offered the chance to go home if they simply pledged to join the Nazi teachers association. Almost none of them signed the pledge.

Quisling's goal of converting the school system into a building block for the new Nazi society became the reverse: a cause that increased the level of Norwegian resistance. He realized his mistake, reopened the schools, and brought the teachers back to teach.

Even though the German army had one soldier per ten Norwegians in the country, Quisling got nowhere in his four-year effort to Nazify the country.

Even while confronting overwhelming force, Norwegians and Danes acted as if they had agency. Rather than bow to inevitability, they rolled up their sleeves and tackled the threat. After the war, they took that same attitude toward the "inevitability" of poverty.

In common with their Swedish and Icelandic cousins, they had a new vision: the abolition of poverty.

The postwar Nordic attack on the causes of poverty required the determination and sense of agency they'd shown during the war. In addition to challenging mainstream notions like the free market, they found that they needed to innovate on many levels. They found no panacea, no one economic policy that did the trick. In effect, they created a laboratory for testing multiple interventions for poverty prevention, and in the process came up with a set of "best practices" that set today's global standard.

WHAT DO WE MEAN BY "POVERTY?"

Two very different definitions of "poverty" live side by side in social statistics: "relative" and "absolute."

Journalist Nina Berglund reported an example of relative poverty when she described a Norwegian family of three. The mom can't work and relies on social assistance. For her and her two children, the income covers the costs of rent, utilities, clothes and food, but it does not leave much for recreation.

Many international statistical comparisons use the relative definition of poverty. Researchers identify the median income, calculate what 50 percent (sometimes 60 percent) of that would be, and consider that result the poverty line.

Using this relative definition, UNICEF's 2012 table of child poverty among rich countries shows the following percentages:

Iceland, 4.7 percent (the lowest child poverty in the OECD)

Norway, 6.1 percent (tied for third-lowest)

Denmark, 6.5 percent (seventh-lowest)

Sweden, 7.3 percent (eighth-lowest)

UK, 12.1 percent (the twenty-second-lowest).

USA, 23.1 percent (thirty-fourth-lowest; only Romania
    exceeds the United States in this ranking of nations'
    child poverty.[75]

UNICEF offers this relative definition of poor: "those whose resources (material, cultural and social) are so limited as to exclude them from the minimum acceptable way of life in the Member States in which they live."[76]

When people are excluded from the acceptable way of life, their children are marginalized. They are less likely to graduate from school, get a good job; they are more likely to fall into drugs and crime. Yes, "relative poverty" is partly a matter of perception, but it has real consequences. The measure has the advantage that it can compare different countries at different periods.

The problem with the procedure for arriving at the statistic, however, is that a lot depends on the amount and distribution of incomes that are in that population. The measure can be misleading. In Sweden, for example, *relative* poverty grew dramatically between 2003 and 2012 because of changes in the distribution of incomes, but *absolute* poverty remained the same or dropped a bit![77]

The usual definition of absolute poverty is the one used in the United States, which focuses on the actual degree of material need, regardless of what a society's range and distribution of incomes is. The official poverty line in the United States is based on the amount it cost in 1964 to feed a family of three or more with economical food, multiplied by three. The purpose of the multiplier was for rent, heat, clothing, and other needs. The total is adjusted annually by the price of food inflation. People whose income is below this total are considered poor.[78]

In this book, I lean toward the absolute definition, because I think of someone who can't reliably afford the necessities of life as poor. In the metropolitan area where I live, Philadelphia, a growing number of people go to bed hungry at night, and a steady percentage don't even have a bed of their own. I know personally a dad who for a period had to swap with his teenage son the one pair of good shoes they had between them. Because I see that reality, the absolute definition speaks to me, especially as reflected in hunger and homelessness.

The Norwegian family that Nina Berglund described has little income beyond that needed for food, rent, and utilities. By that relative definition the family is poor, even though they do have enough food and a home. They also have free health care, childcare, education through grad school, old-age pension, highly subsidized transit, and many other services that many poor American families don't have.[79]

When I look at Norway, Sweden, Iceland, and Denmark through my American eyes, I see countries that have virtually wiped out poverty. How did they do this?

THEY USED A COMPLEX UNDERSTANDING OF WHAT GENERATES POVERTY

The largely Christian Nordics set aside the Biblical saying, "The poor ye shall always have with you." Even though their experience

included widespread poverty, the labor movements and their allies chose a different vision. If the Norwegians, for example, could
tackle their economic elite and then resist the Nazi German invaders, why not see what could be done with poverty?

Successive Labor governments found that tackling poverty is
not rocket science, although they found it much more complex
than simply bulldozing Oslo's slums and building new housing,
something they did early on. Labor found that economists *can* design a system that virtually eliminates poverty, when hired to do
so. When the working class takes power in a society, it can apply
the economists' policies and hire social scientists to evaluate the
effects and stimulate course corrections.

Fortunately, the Nordics resisted the temptation to believe
that poverty comes from one major cause. Take, for example, the
view I've heard in my country that single-parent households are a
major cause of poverty.

In UNICEF's large 2000 study of child poverty in rich countries, researchers examined factors that show up in the wide dis-
parity in poverty rates among the OECD nations. They explored
what they called the "lone-parent theory" and found that it didn't
hold up. "Canada and Finland have almost the same proportion of
children in lone-parent families, but the child poverty rate is over
15 per cent in Canada and less than 5 per cent in Finland."[80]

In Sweden, one of every five children lives with only one parent, which is slightly higher than the proportion in the United
States and the UK. Sweden's child poverty rate, however, is under
3 percent as compared with about 20 percent in the United States
and the UK.[81]

Getting everyone married clearly does not take care of the
problem! Poverty is complex. What the Norwegians did in their

first four decades after the power shift in the 1930s, *before* the oil began to flow, was to use multiple tools. One of them was to maximize participation in the labor market.

THE CENTRAL ROLE OF WORK IN ANTI-POVERTY STRATEGY

In interviewing for this book, I learned that Norwegians see work as a key expectation of a citizen. If they are able to work, Norwegians *should* work as a way to participate in society. Tone Fløtten, a young policy analyst at the Norwegian research institute Fafø, described to me a typical conflict between the government's labor department and the social work department:

A labor department caseworker says, "Ole Johansen should have a job."

The social worker says, "You know that's impossible. Ole has been a drunk for twenty years."

"Then encourage him to take a rehab program and learn to control his alcoholism. He needs to be working."

"We've tried that," the social worker replies, "and Ole always relapses. On Friday he goes on a binge. He's out of it until Tuesday when he finally sobers up."

"Well, then," says the employment worker, "find him a part-time job, for Wednesdays and Thursdays. He needs to be a productive citizen; he needs at least that much self-respect."

For the Norwegians' economic design, paid work is fundamental. Many countries operate differently; they build in *unemployment*, as the IMF advised the government of New Zealand to do when I was there on a training mission.

When the government raises the unemployment rate, some blame the unemployed themselves for lacking jobs. The psychological dynamic follows accordingly. Picture a teenager who's had a rough start in life, with family pathology and a history of family poverty. Teenagers, with few jobs to apply for, can be overwhelmed by discouragement, especially when they are told that it must be *their* fault that they are "losers."

In Norway, however, society says something very different. It tells such a teen that *the economic system was built for everyone*, and therefore jobs are available, and free training and support are available, and working is important for self-respect and the economic productivity of the country. In short, the government's policy is full employment.[82]

When I learned that the unemployment rate is actually a choice made by those who lead their economies, I looked more closely at the Norwegian unemployment rates. I'd read that Norway's long-term average unemployment is considered by economists to be "full employment" because it allows for the people who are in the labor market but in transition from one job to another. The average for the period between 1997 and 2013 was 3.44 percent, according to worldfinance.com.[83]

I then looked for a bigger picture that included the period before the oil started flowing in the mid-seventies.

The Economic Journal published a study showing four decades of unemployment rates in the OECD from 1960 to 2002. In that period, Norway's five-year averages varied from 1.7 percent to 5.2 percent. To my surprise, Norwegian unemployment averaged lower before the oil started flowing than afterward. Clearly, the Norwegian success in handling poverty is not related to their "black gold."

The statistic also shows that having a goal of full employment doesn't guarantee its achievement. There is, after all, such a thing as the business cycle. In those years when the unemployment rate went up, the government made both fiscal and budgetary tweaks to increase the number of jobs.

Still, the same UNICEF researchers who disparaged the lone-parent theory caution against believing that employment rates *alone* determine the amount of poverty. The team found that Spain and Japan had widely different employment rates but about the same amount of child poverty. In the period examined, the United States and Mexico had fairly low unemployment but high levels of poverty, while in the same period Finland had high unemployment and *low* child poverty.

UNICEF researchers found that what mattered more than *whether* people were employed was *what their wages were*. If they are low-paid, they may be unable to keep their families out of poverty, especially if there is a minimum of other social and economic support for children. The Nordics famously pay workers well; their highly unionized labor force makes sure of that.

Another advantage of the Nordic income policy is that in social assistance the cash payments can be set low enough to motivate people to get paid jobs rather than "live off the system," and on the other hand can be set high enough so people aren't actually suffering in poverty.

By breaking down the statistics, UNICEF found another key dimension of employment—*distribution* of the jobs. If a high-unemployment area has available jobs well distributed through the population, child poverty will be lower than in an area where overall employment is higher but concentrated among fewer families—for example, in two- and three-income households—therefore leaving more households with no one holding a job.[84]

By understanding the importance of how jobs are distributed among households, we can see another way that the Nordic economic design reduces poverty. The design encourages single parents to hold jobs by having free or affordable childcare available at the work site or near the home. Few children, therefore, live in a household where no one has a job.

DOESN'T IMMIGRATION PROMOTE POVERTY?

Another notion I sometimes hear is that a major cause of poverty is immigration. In the mid-1990s in Sweden, that view seemed supported by the fact that poverty rates climbed at the same time that Sweden opened its doors to a wave of poor immigrants.

When we look more closely, we see that immigration increased in the 1990s, at precisely the time that Sweden was recovering from its bankers having gone wild, taking their country to the brink. Thanks to the Swedes' flirtation with neoliberalism, the country had higher-than-usual unemployment. Sweden needed time to generate jobs for its own people, not to mention jobs for newcomers without Swedish language skills and often without job skills appropriate to Sweden's economy.

Fortunately, the design of Viking economics came through in Sweden. It enabled basic resolution of the poverty problem for immigrants, even though racist reactions did erupt within the population and lingering problems remain. Poverty rates went down as the year 2000 approached, thanks not only to increased and well-paid jobs, but also to the educational and social infrastructure.

That being said, it remains true in all four countries that immigrants are over-represented in the poverty statistics. Linguistic and cultural obstacles and lack of job skills for the economy of the host country matter, and they take time to be handled in a way that creates the win-win promise of diversity.

The Swedes' social safety net helped them rise to the 1990s poverty challenge. UNICEF's poverty researchers, however, warn against counting on the net as a fix-all approach. Yes, choosing the share of national income devoted to unemployment benefits, family allowances and services, disability and sickness benefits, housing benefits, and other forms of social assistance does matter. But so do other factors, the researchers say, like well-paid jobs and how they are distributed, and the training and education programs that support them.

Even though UNICEF warns against putting all the anti-poverty eggs into the social safety net, the researchers comment that "no country with a high rate of gross social expenditure has a high rate of child poverty."[85]

THE FUNDAMENTAL DESIGN CHOICE: PROGRAMS FOR THE POOR, OR UNIVERSAL PROGRAMS?

In the nineteenth century, the Danes, Swedes, Norwegians, and Icelanders tried to help the poor, motivated by a religious impulse toward charity. What they found was that programs for the poor are poor programs.

In the big picture, the track record of programs for the poor is miserable. No country has come close to abolishing poverty through programs for the poor, no matter *how* wealthy the country itself was. Why?

First, programs designed for the poor are inherently inefficient. Consider the bureaucracy involved in means-testing—all
that paper-shuffling needs to be paid for! The programs create an
incentive to "game the system," again cutting into productivity.
One way to generate waste is to have a lot of people sitting around
trying to game the system, while others sit around trying to stop
them from gaming the system.

Of course human beings will be human, and some will try to
cheat. What a smart economy does not do is design programs offering *incentives* to cheat, which is what programs for the poor do.

Another characteristic of programs for the poor is that they
are under-funded and skimp on quality, partly because the poor
have don't have the political power to insist that their programs
be top-flight. In reality, the poor are likely to need even *higher-
quality* support than people brought up with more social capital
and other advantages. Programs for the poor give less service to
precisely those who need more.

The social workers and teachers of the poor are often expected
to be heroes—who else would choose to work with people who are
believed to be more challenging? If these professionals turn out to
be more like other human beings (non-heroes simply trying to do
a satisfying day's work), and if the conditions of their workplace
are bad (typical in programs for the poor), then many will burn
out. In the big picture, burnout is another source of waste.

Observers in the United States have noted since at least the
1930s that individuals thrown out of work even in a depression
or recession often blame themselves for their situation. I remember my dad, one of the hardest workers I've ever known, bringing home government-surplus cheese and milk with defeat on his
face. (Our family needed the supplements.) Programs for the poor

are the front-line echo chamber for a largely false message: "Your trouble is your own fault rather than the result of a societal phenomenon; if you are here, you reveal your inherent unworthiness as a 'loser.'"

I have collected unemployment checks myself. But no social worker revealed to me the truth: the unemployment rate comes from choices made by those who lead the economy.

Conservatives worry that out-of-work people may blame the system, regard themselves as victims, and refuse to take responsibility for themselves. Lapsing into dependency, they may reject the principle that humans co-create their own reality.

The principle of co-creation is fundamental for me as well; this book is full of examples of people asserting their power, their agency. Programs for the poor, however, undermine agency when they reinforce individuals' sense of themselves as losers. This insight was initially present at the heart of the 1965 launch of the U.S. "war on poverty."[86]

The original conceptualizers of President Lyndon Baines Johnson's "war on poverty" understood how much the initiative of the poor is related to empowerment. They therefore planned for representative councils of the poor to guide the new initiative. Their phrase was "maximum feasible participation of the poor." This design element was, however, dropped.

Informal groups empower individuals for economic advancement by supporting their agency. American observers have long noted that immigrant groups arriving with their families intact usually advance themselves through combinations of relatives: the family-run Chinese restaurant is the classic example. A unique feature of African American history is that the slavery system systematically attacked family ties and other cultural supports.

Despite the fact that informal groups and family networks can be a resource, programs for the poor are usually atomistic, responding to the poor one individual at a time. They systematically ignore other, broader means for empowerment.

The twentieth-century descendants of the Vikings figured out that the individualistic charity model of the nineteenth century simply could not alleviate poverty. In each country, the designers turned against programs for the poor and created universal systems instead.

UNIVERSAL SYSTEMS ARE POLITICALLY SUSTAINABLE

I grew up among hardworking people who were compassionate but began to worry if someone appeared to be shirking their share of the labor. That reflexive worry is triggered by talk about people "on welfare"—why are they benefiting while I'm working and paying taxes? In Nordic countries the worry is also present. I suspect that if the Nordics had the American system, most of their political support for quality assistance to the poor would evaporate.

Arguably, what motivates Nordics to pay high taxes for services is that the services are universal rather than targeted to a subgroup of "the needy." *Everyone* benefits from quality health care, schools, transportation and pensions, but those who benefit most of all are the political majority composed of the working and middle classes. When someone proposes chipping away at the quality of universal systems, a political defense is mounted by the majority almost regardless of the party they belong to. The Norwegian Progress Party and the Danish People's Party, for example, are branded as "right-wing" because of their anti-immigration stance, but both parties pledge to safeguard the continued high quality of universal services, which in the United States would put both of these "right-wing parties" well to the left of the Democratic Party. The Progress Party has even urged that some of Norway's oil income should be diverted from the pension fund to be used to enhance universal services![87]

WHAT DO UNIVERSAL SERVICES LOOK LIKE?

In Norway, all babies can be born in birth centers and hospitals without regard to income, and all moms and dads can take time off from work with pay to take care of the young ones. All parents have access to day care. All parents, whatever their means, automatically get a family allowance for children below the age of 18. This applies to all adopted children, and to same-sex parents.

Education is free to all, as is retraining for a new job and support while looking for one. Public transportation is subsidized for all, and so are tickets to the new opera house in Oslo.

When they need assisted living, Norwegian elders have a choice of whether to move to a retirement center or stay at home. Most stay in their homes, while between one-third and one-fourth choose to move. Those who stay home can receive between a few hours a month to a few hours a day of extra assistance. The cost of the service is subsidized for all, but there is a charge. Unusually for Norway, means-testing enters into the pricing of this service: if an elder's income falls below a certain threshold, he or she is charged only a nominal amount.

The Norwegian love for freedom and flexibility shows up in

the eldercare system. Most implementation is left to local authorities, in order to encourage innovation and allow for local differences. An OECD study found that Norway and Sweden were among the top three countries in providing eldercare. Since elders are particularly vulnerable to poverty, and in the Nordic countries elders live practically forever, the attention to elders through universal programs goes a long way toward eliminating overall poverty.[88]

Rent control, cooperatives, and public responsibility for the supply of shelter creates affordable housing for all. Rural areas are subsidized, so farmers and people brought up in the countryside aren't put at a disadvantage. Disability benefits are available whether or not one has a background of wealth. Single-payer health insurance for all with small co-payments make very expensive treatments available to working-class as well as rich people.

A "NANNY STATE?"

Some critics deride the Nordic design as a "nanny state," picturing passive inhabitants dependent on swollen welfare programs that meet their every need from womb to tomb.

Part of this misunderstanding comes from carelessly labeling the Nordics as "welfare states" in the sense of the U.S. word "welfare." Believing that the word means the same thing in both systems leads critics completely astray.

The Viking descendants turned *against* the "welfare" system that they formerly had—and that we mostly still have in the United States—and replaced it with universal services. The Nordics are not actually welfare states. They are "universal services states."

If the Vikings had simply pumped up their programs for the poor, today they *would* have nanny states with monstrous bureaucracies, little freedom or equality, and disempowered populations.

I am one of those Americans who would not want a "nanny state." The Nordics don't want one, either, and so they have built something very different. The new design was built in the 1930s by empowered citizens who took charge of their own country. Together they created a cooperative system for meeting needs that most people have at various points in their lives.

That being said, the Viking-economics model is a work in progress. The Nordics' biggest achievement may be in refusing to think of themselves simply as objects of mysterious "market forces." Freedom means accepting agency. Citizens freely debate economic design proposals; changes become the intentional acts of a democracy.

I attended a lecture in which then–Health Minister Karl Evang gave a concrete example of what a difference the universal-services paradigm makes. He said that when the Norwegian Labor government initiated universal health care, it realized that many people had poor teeth. If the service started out by covering dentistry, the new system would go bankrupt.

In that postwar time, Norway had nothing like the wealth of the United States, where dentistry could perhaps have been included when President Harry Truman proposed launching a universal single-payer health system.

The creators of the Norwegian system researched the problem of dental health. They found that in postwar Norway, poor and working-class people were drinking little milk because it was expensive. They found a universal solution: subsidize milk for all children and then, when Norway could afford it, create universal free dental care for all children to the age of eighteen—who by then didn't have as many cavities.

The sheer efficiency of a comprehensive and universal health-care system shows up in study after study. The United States spent over 16 percent of its gross domestic product for health care in 2013, according to the OECD. That's almost twice as much as Norway and Iceland spend. Nevertheless, the Nordic countries keep their citizens healthier than the United States does. Ellen Nolte and Martin McKee looked at sixteen high-income countries in the OECD, analyzing deaths that occurred before age seventy-five from causes like treatable cancer and diabetes, childhood infections, and complications from surgeries. They found that tens of thousands of Americans died annually during the period they studied because the U.S. system was less effective than the universal systems.[89]

Another way to look at this comparison is through per-capita spending on health care. In 2013, Denmark spent $4,553 per person on average, and Sweden $4,904. The United States spent nearly double: $8,713, and even so left millions uninsured. All four of the countries studied for this book have higher life expectancies and lower suicide rates than the United States.[90]

Economist Dean Baker proposes another intervention that could dramatically reduce the United States' swollen health-care costs. Baker, head of the Center for Economic and Policy Research, has a history of being ahead of the curve; as early as 2002 he published his warning that the United States had a housing bubble that would lead to disaster. Baker also sees systemic waste in the health-care system that creates crises for some families and hardship for many others. He proposes that the government simply buy up patents that, left in the hands of pharmaceutical companies, enable them to overcharge for drugs. The hundreds of billions of dollars Americans now spend on prescription drugs could fall to one-tenth that amount. Even the government would realize savings on this universal plan, because most drugs would then cost $5 to $10 per prescription, much closer to the prices paid in other countries. People who are presently forced to choose between buying their medicine and buying adequate food would experience immediate relief.[91]

"FUEL POVERTY"

International researchers investigating the causes of the spike in winter deaths among older people have brought attention to what they call fuel poverty—people's inability to buy enough fuel, at to-day's higher energy prices, to keep their homes warm. According to a 2013 report, an estimated 5,000,000 UK households—19.2 percent of the total—are now in fuel poverty, nearly the worst of the sixteen European countries studied.[92] "A household is considered to be in fuel poverty if more than 20 percent of its total income is spent on adequate heating," according to the story in *The Independent*.

It seems that the British should have a much easier time keep-ing their homes warm in the winter than people in much colder countries, like the Swedes. Surprisingly, the UK has a 23 percent higher rate of excess deaths in the winter than Sweden.

Do Swedes pay less for their electricity and find it therefore easier to heat their houses against wintry storms? No, electricity prices are higher in Sweden, and the Swedish per-capita average income is about the same as that of the British, so the Swedes have no advantage there.

Researchers finally found the culprit. British homes lose three times more heat than Swedish ones—because of poor insulation.[93]

Norway, Iceland, and Denmark join Sweden in having little fuel poverty, despite their much colder winters. The universal principle works again: Nordic housing, much of it built by cooperatives and the state, is well insulated. The Nordics chose another universal economic design feature that reduces poverty and saves lives.

Comparing track records shows universal programs winning, hands down.

REDUCING POVERTY THROUGH CRIMINAL REHABILITATION

For a very long time, criminologists have noticed a connection between poverty and crime. For that reason, it's not surprising that Norway has a very low crime rate, as do the other Viking descendants. Sweden has one of the lowest incarceration rates in the world—70 per 100,000. Norway and Denmark are nearly as low, at 73 and 74 per 100,000.[94] United Nations statistics show more generally that more unequal countries have higher rates of imprisonment than more equal countries. The U.S. rate is over four times higher than that of the UK, which in turn is far higher than the Nordics.[95]

The Nordic rarity of actual crime doesn't, however, prevent Icelander Arnaldur Indridason, Swede Henning Mankell, and Norwegian Jo Nesbø from making a lot of money writing imaginative crime novels!

Iceland's scarcity of crime even attracted the attention of the

BBC, which did a story, "Why violent crime is so rare in Iceland."[96] Iceland made international headlines in 2013 when police shot a man to death for the first time since the founding of the republic in 1944. The shooting was precipitated by a mentally ill man firing at the police with his gun. Nevertheless, the nation went into grieving and the police department, without saying that the shooting was wrong, expressed its own deep sadness. Icelandic police are unarmed and must request a gun for a specific occasion.[97]

Although Iceland is the nation that identifies most strongly with the ancient Vikings culturally, it joins the other three descendant nations in opposing violence. The criminal justice systems of the four reflect this thinking. When Norwegians, for example, send someone to jail, they do not look for additional ways to punish the prisoner. Because freedom matters so much to them, they see the deprivation of freedom by itself as a significant loss. They therefore set up correctional institutions for rehabilitation. Norway has no capital punishment or life sentencing. Prison terms are short and families are encouraged to stay close to their incarcerated member.

Repeat offenses are among the lowest in the world. Their prisons are not training schools for a life of crime; instead they are part of an economic system that wants offenders to rejoin the community—and become taxpayers as soon as possible.

Even with this track record Norwegians try to bring criminality lower still by working closely with offenders on job training and job placement. The process begins in the prison itself, where programs focus on rehabilitation rather than punishment.

British reporter Ryan Duffy visited the island prison of Bastøy in 2010 and was shocked to see drug dealers and murderers running ferries, operating farming equipment, and playing soccer. There were no walls or chains, and the guards carried no weapons.

Time magazine reported that "within two years of their release, 20 percent of Norway's prisoners end up back in jail. In the UK and the United States, the figure hovers between 50 percent and 60 percent."

Norwegians recently showed the stubbornness I talked about in the beginning of this chapter, and they decided on another experiment. They built an expensive new prison, Halden, with an even more radically "soft" rehabilitation program. They expect to see, over time, the Halden graduates setting new records for going straight.

Because Norway has an extensive social-science research industry, studying and restudying all the anti-poverty measures mentioned in this chapter, you can believe that they are studying their effort to reduce criminality to a minimum. One of the most recent criminological studies looked at every prisoner released between 2003 and 2006 and tracked his or her employment record, along with possible arrests.

The study found that there was a high association between employment and staying out of trouble. Once again, the investment in job rehabilitation and training and job placement created a win-win-win: the former inmates and their families won, crime was reduced, and more people took a step out of poverty.

The persistence in creating systems for the marginalized to return to society works for chronic addicts as well. The Nordics have a lower percentage of drug addiction than many countries; drug addiction, as well as obesity, follows the usual pattern of pathology in which higher addiction rates correlate with greater economic inequality.

New York Times business writer Landon Thomas, Jr., reported from Norway on May 14, 2009, when most Western countries were reeling with recession. In his article, he mentioned that Norwegian banks represent only 2 percent of the economy and that they were so tightly regulated by that time that Norway didn't join the crash of the neoliberals. Instead, Thomas said, the country was riding out the storm.

Thomas reported, however, that around the corner from the Norwegian central bank in Oslo he found a man injecting himself with a drug. For many years an addict, the man told Thomas that he'd never had a job and was in no shape to have one. The man said that the social assistance he gets monthly, $1,500 in high-priced Oslo, keeps him fed and alive.[98]

The opportunity Thomas didn't report is that if the addicted man becomes inspired to make a fresh start, the system is there to help him. Not only can he get free in-patient drug rehabilitation treatment but when he gets out he can be paid a living wage to take active job retraining and reenter the work force. Norwegians call it "occupational rehabilitation."

THE CHALLENGE FOR THE DESCENDANTS OF THE VIKINGS

Most of us in the United States, used to defining poverty as the inability to meet basic needs on a reliable basis, would want to consider how to adopt or adapt the best practices of the Nordics in our own country. Denmark, Sweden, Norway, and Iceland, however, might want to go further and tackle "relative poverty"—the economic marginalization that is measured internationally. That challenge is difficult because relative poverty is more nuanced than food and fuel insecurity and homelessness.

In looking for relative poverty, people need to observe closely where the marginalizing happens: the expected well-packed lunch from home that has *not* accompanied a youngster on the school trip, the expected new dress for the school dance that is *not* worn on the big occasion. These are "discretionary items," but in the real-life world of peers, such items aren't discretionary at all. Even though signs of relative poverty may be more nuanced, a teacher's sharp eye might implement a universal provision of things like packed lunches for school trips that, to more privileged and perhaps clueless well-off people, appear to represent no barrier at all.

Fortunately, the political discourse in the Nordic countries suggests that ending relative poverty has become a widely shared goal. In Norway's 2001 national election, the Conservatives ran on a platform that attacked the incumbent Labor government for not doing enough to fully abolish relative poverty.

9

CREATING WORK/LIFE BALANCE

In the introduction to this book, I told the story about a party at Berit's brother's house in Skien, where I had my eyes opened to how different the Nordic model is from that of most countries. Our host Leif Erik was retired by then, but most of the adults presently worked at a variety of occupations: teacher, corporate middle manager, industrial worker and more. They all seemed to have found good niches for themselves, and at the same time perked up their ears when they learned that Norwegians—already at 1,400 hours working the fewest hours per year of any nation in Europe— were researching how to increase productivity while working still fewer hours.

The party came to a shocked stop when I told the relatives how long, on average, people in my country work. Their shock motivated me to look into the difference between their perspective and mine. It turns out that the Nordic model assumes a rested worker is a productive worker.

By the 1960s, a five-day week became the Norwegian norm. But when you factor in the paid vacations and holidays, the comparison is startling: according to the OECD's 2012 data, the average number of hours a person works in a year in Norway is 1,418.

In Denmark, the number is 1,430; in Sweden, 1,621; in Iceland, 1,706; and in the United States, 1,790.[99]

Another OECD study showed Norwegian workers producing, compared with the United States, 27.8 percent more per hour for the hours worked.[100]

Sweden is not satisfied with its work/life balance and set up an experiment with the six-hour day in the city of Gothenburg. City workers will be divided randomly, with half continuing the eight-hour day and the other half engaging in the experiment. The goal is to gain higher productivity per hour and have fewer sick days. The researchers are encouraged by positive results from Toyota's similar experiment in its Gothenburg factory.[101]

Washington Post reporter Brigid Schulte told Terry Gross on National Public Radio's *Fresh Air* that Danish women felt social pressure to leave the office punctually at the end of the day rather than spend extra time "finishing up" at their desks. They did not want to give their colleagues and supervisors the impression that they could not do their job fully within the framework of regular hours.[102]

By law, Norwegians are entitled to twenty-five vacation days every year, as are the Danes. Working hours may not exceed nine hours per day or forty hours per week.[103] Flextime is increasing; employees can choose their own work hours as long as they are at the worksite in the middle of the day for meetings and common tasks.

Economist Sam Bowles at the University of Massachusetts studied working hours in all the OECD countries and found that more unequal countries tend to have longer working hours. He checked the trends over time and discovered that, in those countries where inequality changes over time, the working hours

change in tandem. People in more unequal countries do the equivalent of two or three months' extra work per year.[104]

Does all this emphasis on work/life balance mean that the
Nordic peoples shirk work? On the contrary, more people there
work than in comparable countries. The numbers reported by the
Better Life Index show that the following percentages of people
aged fifteen to sixty-four have paid jobs: Denmark, seventy-three;
Sweden, seventy-four; Norway, seventy-five; and Iceland, seventy-
nine. The OECD average is 66 percent. In the UK, it is 70 percent,
and in the United States, 67.[105]

Just as there is no necessary contradiction between equality
and freedom, there may be no contradiction between work and
life. The design-crazy Scandinavians, when encountering apparent
tensions, prefer rolling up their sleeves to shrugging their shoulders. Their advanced democracies make design solutions possible.

TACKLING GENDER ROLES

Seen in that light, an obvious design flaw in the patriarchal system inherited by most economies is the gendered division of labor
within the family.

Norway was the first country in the world to establish a
scheme that incentivizes dads to take more responsibility for their
children. A paid leave of absence from the job is set aside for the
father; if he doesn't take it, the couple can't transfer that time to
the mom. The policy is working: by 2008, 90 percent of fathers
were using their quota, and 16.5 percent were extending their leave
beyond the reserved amount.[106]

In Denmark, the current system is this: families receive a total of 52 weeks of parental leave, with full pay. Mothers take eighteen weeks and fathers get a dedicated two weeks. If they don't use it, the couple loses it. The rest of the paid time off is up to the family to use as they wish, again building in the freedom for couples to decide what works best for them.[107]

Dads can't breast-feed, and most Norwegians do recognize the health and other benefits of breast-feeding their children. In Norway, a new mother at her job has the right to two hours of break time each day to permit breast-feeding.[108]

If the dad takes care of the baby at home when the mom resumes her job, he can bring the baby to the workplace for feedings. For moms who combine job with baby, many workplaces have day care for their employees' children on-site. If a child is primarily being taking care of by a job-holding dad, he has an equal right to access the day care on-site.

Affordable, publicly financed day-care institutions are available if a parent's worksite doesn't have one. Either parent has the right to stay at home with sick children at least twenty days per year.

Many heterosexual couples aren't choosing marriage these days, but that's not stopping them from having children; Norwegian fertility is high. In 2005, unmarried moms living with their partners accounted for 42 percent of all births. Single mothers accounted for 10 percent.[109]

When I heard Schulte's interview on NPR describing the office pressure to leave work after eight hours, I remembered the Wall Street firms who are reportedly pressuring young analysts to work fifteen hours a day. A Penn professor published a study finding that people at two investment banks spent up to 120 hours per week on the job. Goldman Sachs, New York economics writer

James Surowiecki wrote, recently broke ranks by announcing that analysts shouldn't work more than 70 to 75 hours per week![110]

In the United States, neither women nor men are able to advance in competitive workplaces like large law firms and academia and still strike a sane work/life balance. I understand the passion that can drive some individuals to clock incredible hours to finish that painting or bring in the harvest or heal the refugee children. What I respect is the choosing, rather than a workplace pressure that takes away employees' freedom to create meaningful lives on their own, individual terms. This is one of the starkest contrasts I have found in exploring the Nordic model: the extraordinary lack of freedom available to individuals in the United States to place work in the perspective that makes sense to them.

KEEPING LIFE BALANCED: THE EASY-TO-ACCESS HEALTH-CARE SYSTEM

When we moved to Oslo, Berit found a primary-care physician for us both—the doctor-patient relationship is important to Norwegians. I usually catch the flu once each winter, and the Norwegian snow didn't give me an exception. I felt too feverish and miserable to go to the doctor, so the doctor came to our little apartment and treated me. He gave me an invoice and I paid him with cash. He told me that when I was better I should take the invoice to the health office and get my cash back minus a very small service charge.

That was it. Procedures change over time, but the basic model remains the same: a doctor-patient relationship, and whatever care is needed paid by the publicly funded insurance system. If I were living at the other end of the country, north of the Arctic Circle, and got a brain tumor that required the kind of surgery that's only done in a hospital in Oslo, the system would fly me to Oslo and handle the surgery. I learned that everyone is covered equally— even an American who fell in love with a Norwegian.

As in my first encounter with the university, I asked as a stranger in a strange land, "How does it make sense for the whole society to pay for medical care? Isn't that a burden on the economy?" I learned two things.

The total cost per capita is a little more than half what the United States pays for health care. That's partly because of an emphasis on prevention of illness instead of waiting until it's a matter for the emergency room. Another reason is that the Norwegian system is so much easier to administer—another shock, since I believed that a "welfare state" would be so full of bureaucracy and paperwork that everything would cost more to get done, not less. The Danes also pay less than the United States, even though Danes on average visit their primary-care physician seven times a year.[111]

It turns out that there's far more bureaucracy and paper-work in the U.S. market-based health-care system, with multiple insurance companies and their multiple plans covering different things, with multiple employees acting as gatekeepers. In the United States, the plans keep changing their policies on which prescriptions they will and won't cover. Medical practices are so burdened with paperwork that some doctors simply leave their vocation. In health care, so-called "market efficiency" is actually "market wastefulness." So wasteful, in fact, that despite the Affordable Care Act (so-called "ObamaCare") tens of millions of Americans don't get covered at all, and countless others who are insured still don't get the treatment they need.

The second thing I learned was that Norwegians believe there is a relationship between health and productivity. I heard a talk by Dr. Karl Evang, the legendary Norwegian health minister who went on to lead the World Health Organization. He said that long ago the Norwegian Medical Society was among those pushing for a socialized system because doctors admitted there was no other way that Norwegian health could be protected at a high standard. As I listened to him, I realized the other economic payoff: a healthy population is a productive population. Health may be a human right, as Norwegians believe, but it is also a necessity for optimum work performance and work/life balance.

All this was still hard to wrap my mind around, but by putting "free health care" together with "free higher education," the paradox was getting clearer: Norwegians believe they get what they pay for, and that they need to pay for what they get. They notice when it's more practical for that payment to be made by the community rather than by individuals. They also acknowledge that collective care for the health of the nation is an expression of solidarity and equality.

Nordic health-care systems are also less expensive because health problems are more common in unequal countries. Epidemiologists Wilkinson and Pickett did the math on this question. At one end of their graph describing rich countries are the Nordics and Japan, which are both more equal and have better health, and at the other end are the UK, Portugal, and the United States. The authors double-checked by creating a different graph that related health problems to national average income, and found a weak relationship. Per-capita average income is a poor predictor of rate of health problems, whereas the degree of inequality predicts very accurately, far beyond what chance alone could produce. This pattern also holds true among our states in the United States: high inequality correlates with worse health.[112]

EFFICIENT COMMUTES AND NATURE

When I began to teach in an Oslo high school, I worried about getting to work on time, since I lived at the opposite end of the city from the school. Berit tried to reassure me, but I found myself starting my morning journey long before I needed to, sure that my first trolley would be late, that I would miss the connection to the subway, and then miss the connection to my next trolley. For one thing, I kept thinking about the winter snow and ice that certainly would wreak havoc with trolley schedules.

I finally accepted that the 7:30 morning trolley would be there at 7:30, if not 7:29, and not even snow would make me late for school.

This isn't only a result of substantial public investment to create a quick, efficient and affordable public transportation system. Nor is it all about taxing cars and gas so hugely that many Norwegians find it expedient to use public transportation for routine travel. My experience also reflects a pro-work and pro-freedom orientation to how Norwegians use space.

In 1999, Norway passed a law banning large shopping malls outside city centers. It was done "to revitalize city centers, reduce sprawl, and encourage use of public transportation." Within the framework of that national law, most land-use decisions are made on the level of the municipal government, as large as Oslo or as small as a village. The decision-making is democratic rather than largely influenced by corporate interests.

As a result, everyone—even in the largest cities—lives close to nature, an easy ride by trolley or bus to a stress-reducing walk in the woods.[113] I asked Berit about the large bins that were attached to the backs of Oslo trolleys when winter came. She laughed. "You'll see," she said. On weekends I saw people load their skis in the bins, ride to the end of the trolley line, and go cross-country skiing all day.

The equality theme, expressed through policies that are universal rather than tied to income and consumer prices, has a particular meaning when we think about land use. It turns out that an economic design can resist the commodification of nature.

SUPPORT FOR ARTISTS IN A COMMITMENT TO WORK/LIFE BALANCE

I never go to Oslo without taking the time to walk through the world's largest sculpture park made by a single artist—Gustav Vigeland. The park took decades to build. I've walked over the eighty acres in rain and shine, morning and sunset, and can never get enough of the 200-plus sculptures that display us humans in our vast range of expression.

The park came about because of a deal made in the 1920s between the city of Oslo and Vigeland, whose brilliance was recognized early. The city would give him a stipend and a building where he could work and live, and in exchange he would give the city all of his subsequent works.

Extending that tradition in their current economic design, Arts Council Norway (financed by the Ministry of Culture) provides guaranteed income for about 500 artists at a time. Additionally, it provides artistic grants for hundreds of artists.

Although any society might choose to support art for art's sake, I suspect that this is another place where synergy can be found: respecting artists as workers and not expecting them to starve in attics, combined with supporting their freedom, is likely to yield productivity that may unleash another Gustav Vigeland—and the cash-rich tourists who flock to Oslo to see the public park he built.

Even artists may get encouragement to maintain some balance in their work lives. To earn a little extra money in Norway, I once took a two-week job filling in for the pianist in a tourist hotel. The public employment agency that arranged the job (at no fee) said they would come by to check to see if I was doing okay.

About midway through my first evening a man came into the dining room and took a seat but ordered only coffee. After a couple of hours he signaled to me he'd like to talk. I met him and realized he was from the agency. He complimented me on my playing but suggested one change in my performance. I should, he said, take more breaks.

VOLUNTARISM

In my early periods in Norway I had the usual outsider's worry that strong economic participation by the state might reduce ordinary people's willingness to roll up their sleeves and do their share. The worry doubled when I learned about the low participation in organized religion, since in my country faith groups so often do the mobilizing to perform voluntary service. Still another reason that voluntarism in Norway might be undermined, I feared, is that a lot of the nonprofit organizations in civil society were funded largely by state grants rather than voluntary donations.

My assumptions took a beating when I rode the trolley to visit Berit's nephew Håvard and his partner Gerd. The pair and their young boys live in a part of Oslo high on the side of a mountain overlooking the Oslofjord.

Håvard works in a business and Gerd is a dancer active in Oslo's alternative-theater scene. We sat in their back yard with the customary coffee and chatted about our lives. Gerd mentioned that a big *dugnad* was coming up on the weekend when neighbors prepare their soccer field for the young people's fall season.

"Stop," I said. "What's this about the neighbors?"

"Maybe you haven't learned that word yet, George," Gerd said. "It's *dugnad*—barn-raising!"

Now I was confused, and said so. She laughed and described the strong Norwegian tradition of voluntary work when people work together to build a new boat landing, or assist a neighbor whose house partially burned, or even do a barn-raising.

Initially embarrassed not to have heard of this, I decided to forgive myself. The *dugnad* is under the radar, hard for foreigners to see. I later learned that the Danes have the same tradition, and use the same name for it. I found that that 40 percent of all Danes do voluntary work in cultural and sports associations, NGOs, social organizations, political groups, and so on.[114]

For Norwegians, the practice is so important that when Norway's national broadcasting service ran a contest among listeners to find the word that most expressed the national character, the winner was *dugnad*!

And, thanks to an economic model that fosters work/life balance, people have abundant time to volunteer in the community.

10

BREAKING BARRIERS TO EDUCATION AND LIFELONG LEARNING

There is no way that the ancient Vikings could have successfully braved the uncertain seas and explored unknown lands if they had not paid enormous attention to craft, to skill. They would also have been a one-generation wonder if they had not learned how to pass on their lore to the young. They did so for centuries. They clearly did what Brazilian educator Paolo Freire regards as the heart of learning: act, reflect, then act and reflect again.

It seems that the ancient Vikings, by paying attention to discovery, learning, and passing knowledge on, gave themselves extraordinary freedom at a time when many people would rather stay home.

Although today's Nordic education surely looks different from that of its forebears, the intention is still to give people an expanded opportunity to experience freedom. The first step is to invite individuals to educate themselves as far as formal institutions will take them, without personal expense getting in the way. The freedom for individuals builds on equality of access.

Free entrance to university education is now contested in many countries, including in Norway's former models, Germany and the UK. The Norwegians do not see the sense of adding tuition barriers to post-secondary education. Students can access loans and grants to handle living expenses while studying. Adding substantial debt to the shoulders of a young adult setting off on a career is a serious subtraction of freedom, and it also reduces the risk-taking that stimulates innovation and a dynamic economy. While free universities have disappeared from London and New York City, from Canada and California, the Nordics hold firm: they will not load tuition debt on the backs of their young people who want further education.

The seven Norwegian public universities are not the only institutions that are tuition-free. Free public post-secondary schooling is available for technical fields like seafaring, business, engineering, and agriculture; for arts fields like performance and visual arts; and for professions like medicine and law.

The goal is education for all—workers and farmers, as well as professionals. That is why Norwegians see education as a life-long, accessible resource. Adult education classes in a wide variety of subjects are so widely available that in any given year more than 750,000 adults take courses—about one-sixth of the population.

What is the economic result of the Vikings' priority on education? In 2009, the management consulting company McKinsey & Co. became curious about this very question. It ran the numbers and found that "if U.S. children did as well as students from nations such as Finland, our economy would be 9 percent to 16 percent larger." The study estimated that under-investing in education is costing the American economy $1.3 to $2.3 trillion every year.[115]

Educational under-investment actually undermines our historic claim to being a meritocracy in which talented working-class children are encouraged to shine. A new study by Sean Reardon of Stanford shows that the "gap in test scores between rich and poor American children is roughly 30 to 40 percent wider than it was twenty-five years ago."[116] Such a finding in the Nordic countries would prompt vigorous national discussion.

Quality education is smart economics, especially in a globalized economy. Setting a high standard of education and creating free access is a design that reflects, and further serves, equality and individual freedom.

TENSIONS AND CONTRADICTIONS

For my first ski vacation, Berit and I joined relatives in their hut in a remote valley. Once I learned enough to ski on my own—my proud teacher was ten-year-old Harald—I skied to the 1950s Norwegian equivalent of a rural "one-room schoolhouse." Because I was aiming for a teaching degree myself in Pennsylvania, I was curious about rural Norwegian education.

I arrived at recess time and found the children skiing on a steep slope behind the school. I was envious as I saw how easily they maneuvered. It obviously pays to be put on a pair of skis as soon as you can walk.

The teacher was happy to talk with me as we watched the children playing. I asked about teacher-student ratio in this school and wasn't surprised when he said that teachers had small classes. One of the most consistent findings of research in the United States is that class size hugely influences educational outcomes. The secondary school where I taught in Oslo had small classes.[117]

"Our school is slated to get an addition," he said. "A gym is to be built."

A wry smile spread across his face. "Country schools never used to have gyms because the children skied to school and were in excellent shape. Now, because of school buses, the department of education worries about the children's physical condition. So they are building gyms!"

I grinned back. There is no escaping contradictions.

A bigger conflict was posed by immigration. Some immigrant fathers who were eager to send their sons to school objected to sending their daughters.

On one side were Norwegians who insisted that respect for people with different cultural values requires that the fathers be accommodated. On the other side were feminists sticking up for equality.

The debate is settled. Now the fathers who want their daughters to stay in the kitchen must allow them to go to school. Fathers might complain that their freedom to continue their own tradition is not being respected, but in Norway freedom is not the only value that matters. Equality helps shape legislation.

What may have tipped the balance was the view that education is itself a core expectation in Norwegian society and only those who can accept education for all are welcome.

This chapter shares a few snapshots of Norwegian education from the point of view of the students moving through the system, paying particular attention to the design choices that enhance students' own freedom.

STARTING SCHOOL LATE, AND THEN CATCHING UP: HOW THE NORDICS ACCOMMODATE THE DIVERSITY OF YOUNG PEOPLE

Sweden, Denmark, Norway, and Iceland share roughly the same model of education. The children start school at age six or seven, late compared with some other countries.

In the first year, children play a lot of educational games and activities that help them to understand what intentional learning in a group is about. They learn the alphabet that year, and begin a bit of English. In Norway, the typical student goes through the seven years of elementary school in small classrooms without formal grades; feedback is given informally in light of individual differences, and students take tests home to show to their parents.

Grading starts at age thirteen or fourteen, when young people graduate into *ungdomskole* (the lower secondary school; literally translated, youth school). For the next three years they learn to take more individual responsibility for what, in the Nordic countries, is expected to be lifelong learning.

The children's slow start doesn't leave them out of the running internationally, judging from the OECD's Programme for International Student Assessment (PISA). Tested at about age fifteen, when they've had two years of *ungdomskole*, and compared with their peers in seventy-four countries, Norwegians ranked nineteenth in sciences, twenty-fourth in reading, and twenty-first in math. (The United States ranked respectively twenty-third, twenty-first, and thirty-first.)

Norwegians see no reason to be in a rush; most students will continue in the regular school system until they are nineteen.

In their second year of *ungdomskole* students get to choose an elective. These fourteen-year-olds' options usually include German, Spanish, and French, or additional Norwegian or English studies. (They have already been learning English since first grade.) Music is one of the core subjects.

UNICEF did a study of childhood well-being in which data were presented on career aspirations among fifteen-year-olds. Middle-class professionals generally assume that climbing the class ladder—"getting ahead"—should be the aspiration of all, since, for them, higher class position implies superiority.

As a sociologist, I find this assumption of superiority common among all groups that hold higher places in socially constructed vertical hierarchies. Examples are white people, men, heterosexuals, and members of a dominant religious affiliation. Lower-ranked personnel entering large organizations find it advantageous to conform to the expectations of their "betters," as when children of the working class, for example, mimic middle-class behavior to get preferred jobs.

Career aspirations of fifteen-year-olds, therefore, offer an interesting picture of just how classist any society is. Do the young people necessarily want what their teachers want for them? Wilkinson and Pickett took the cross-national UNICEF data and matched it with data on inequality in rich countries. They found that in the more equal countries more young people aspired to working-class jobs, while in countries with greater inequality more young people aspired to professional and even upper-class jobs.[118]

As we might expect, the "usual suspects" were on each end of that polarity, with more Nordic youngsters aspiring to working-class jobs while the highly unequal Portuguese and American youngsters were on the other. For a change, the UK was higher than the Nordics in percentage of fifteen-year-olds aspiring to low-skilled work, suggesting some retention of the robust British working-class culture of the early twentieth century.

As a Philadelphian, I am familiar with the youngster shooting hoops in a high-poverty neighborhood playground, who will be lucky to get any job at all, telling me that when he grows up he will be a star on a professional basketball team. I practice-taught in the third grade of such a neighborhood. One of our forty-four youngsters told me he planned to become a nuclear physicist.

One more cruelty visited upon young people in high-inequality countries is to induce star-struck dreams but to refuse to fund pathways to achieving satisfying outcomes, including high-wage working-class jobs.

THE SIXTEEN-YEAR-OLD GETS MULTIPLE OPTIONS

The sixteen-year-old graduates from *ungdomskolen* are finished with compulsory schooling. Those who are eager to get a job can take short vocational courses for free and look for a job. Another option is to become apprentices, a formal program in which they work for a wage and receive instruction at the same time.

As in Sweden, Denmark, and Iceland, most Norwegian sixteen-year-olds decide to go on to the three-year *videregående skole* (upper secondary school), which gives them many more options for a career. They choose between academic studies or vocational studies. Within each choice are multiple paths with choices of electives.

The youngsters often choose music as an elective even while taking their regular music class. When I lived in Norway I taught music in both lower and upper secondary school, so I taught the whole age range of thirteen to nineteen. On my first day with the nineteen-year-olds, several young men came up to me after class. They explained that they wouldn't be able to sing because they were tone-deaf.

Astonished, I laughed out loud. I couldn't hold back my spontaneous, although rude, reaction. In English, I asked, rhetorically, "Do you speak Norwegian?"

They waited to see what was next.

"You can't speak *Norwegian* if you're tone deaf!" I said with a grin. I said it again in Norwegian, exaggerating the melody in the sentence.

They laughed, and nodded sheepishly. They knew as well as I that the intonation in their language is so rich that it is almost like singing. The young men went on to enjoy our music classes. They didn't, however, join the school chorus I was starting.

Since my time there (1959–1960), Norwegians have expanded the role of music in schools. In elementary and lower secondary schools all students sing, dance, compose, and listen to music on a regular basis. They also have the chance to take instrumental or voice lessons at the local music or cultural arts school. (Every municipality must have, by law, a music or culture school.) Their lessons might be after school or during school hours as an elective.[119] One student in five takes advantage of this free opportunity.

Students in the upper secondary school—ages sixteen to nineteen—no longer have regular music classes, but they can still choose music as a major elective.

While visiting Norway in 2011, I encountered pop-up band

concerts in a variety of public spaces, including just outside the Oslo central railroad station. I talked with several of the band directors, each of whom told me the same thing: there has been a proliferation of bands in Norway—youth bands, community bands, and so on. They didn't find it remarkable. I guess it's not, considering the schools' intention to free as many Norwegians as possible to enjoy making music.

World Bank statistics show Norway, Sweden, and the United Kingdom in the mid–90 percent rates for secondary-school enrollment, with the United States coming in at 89.5 percent. Norway currently has the lowest high school dropout rate among OECD countries (4.6 percent).

Norway and Sweden have a low student-teacher ratio (about 1 to 10) while the UK and the United States come in higher, at about 1 to 14. It's another Nordic move that supports freedom: smaller classes give more space for students' diverse learning styles.

The vocational-studies track of upper secondary school has high standards; some courses have higher minimum entrance requirements than those for the academic-studies track. The main goal of the vocational track, called Vocational Educational Training (VET), is to prepare the nineteen-year-old graduate for a good job in one of nine fields, and also to prepare the graduate to go on to a Vocational Technical College for more advanced training if desired. It includes a very strong apprenticeship dimension, to build in learning-by-doing.

However, the school builds in a plan B, to enhance the freedom of the student. Educators designed the curriculum to enable graduates, if at that point they have become interested, to choose to enter university with only one year of additional preparation.

The other track in upper secondary school is academic, explicitly preparing the students to go on to a university or another post-secondary-school program like nursing or teaching. Graduates of this track, however, can still decide that thirteen years of schooling is enough and that they're ready to enter the labor market.

When the students near graduation, they call themselves "russ," and celebrate noisily around the town. As a teacher I was awakened one morning by a flatbed truck full of loud, excited nineteen-year-olds outside our apartment. It was early. The students wouldn't leave until I threw a coat over my pajamas and joined them on the truck, which transported them hooting and cheering to a breakfast in honor of us teachers.

CONTROVERSY IN SWEDEN OVER FOR-PROFIT CHARTERS

In 1992, the Swedish parliament, attracted to the idea of offering school choice, allowed for-profit secondary schools to be set up that would receive public money based on size of enrollment. One of the differences from charter schools in the United States is that, in Sweden, the teachers are members of the educators' union. Regional economic differences affect how much money a municipality can pay per student. By 2013, a quarter of Swedish students had enrolled and large corporations had set up chains of schools, finding them to be cash cows.

After two decades of experience, Swedes are turning against this model. Because the free-market model pits school against school, teachers feel pressured to give higher grades to attract more students. Some corporations were hiring underqualified teachers and stinting on library and other services in order to turn a larger profit. One of the chains, JB Education, owned by the Danish private equity firm Axcel, went bankrupt in 2013, leaving students stranded and about 1,000 people jobless.

The head of the largest teachers' union noted that the national education department had lost track of quality control. Another problem is that many of the best students flocked to the brandname private schools, which lowered the quality of the schools they left behind. Overall, secondary-school achievement has declined in Sweden, according to the OECD PISA scores. One interpretation of the experiment is that enhanced freedom for corporations resulted in diminished freedom for the students themselves as they prepare for life.

The Swedish Green Party, which originally voted for the school reform, issued a public apology in 2013: "Forgive us, our policy led our schools astray." A 2013 poll showed that 58 percent of Swedes are now opposed to introducing the profit motive into publicly funded education.[120]

OFFERING YOUNG PEOPLE THE FREEDOM TO REINVENT THEMSELVES

Adolescence being what it is—in Norway as elsewhere—there are young people who drift quite a bit before finding their motivation. If they quit school at sixteen, and discover after a couple of years that they do want to continue to *videregående skolen* (upper secondary school), it is their right to enter as late as age nineteen.

Alternatively, they can take advantage of the free follow-up career and training services provided to anyone of age fifteen to twenty-one who needs them and isn't working or in school already. One path (called "occupational rehabilitation") consists of up to three years of vocational training within the public educational system.

On graduation from *videregående skolen*, many nineteen-year-olds go to college, but an alternative is to attend a post-secondary vocational school, which offers a course of study from half a year to two years. Post-secondary vocational education gets high respect not only for its economic role but also for encouraging participation in society. In fact, the rates of civic and political participation for graduates of vocational post-secondary education are higher than for graduates of colleges.

Nordland Vocational College of Art and Film is an example of post-secondary vocational education. It's located in the traditional island fishing town of Lofoten in the far north of Norway. Its two-year courses offer a choice: film or visual art. The school says that many of its grads go on to institutions of higher education such as a university, while others go directly to work in film production or the arts. The school is public, owned by the county council, and free of tuition charge.[121]

To enter vocational colleges, students may not need to have graduated from upper secondary school, if they can show equivalent competence derived from work and informal learning experiences.

Still another dimension of freedom is the minimum of difficulty that Norwegians have in transferring from one kind of school to another: the universities (Norway has seven), the university colleges, and the specialized institutions at the university level (economics, music, sport sciences, veterinary science, architecture and design, and theology). Norway also has private higher-education institutions that charge tuition.

LIFELONG LEARNING OPPORTUNITIES

Norway gives its secondary public schools an additional mission: adult education and continuing education for lifelong learning. Nongovernmental organizations also get into the act, with substantial taxpayer support offering free adult education. To free more adults to study, these programs often come with gratis childcare.

The legacy of lifelong learning, however, long precedes today's secondary public schools. In 1864 a pair of teachers launched Norway's first folk high school, in the Eastern Norway town of Sagatun. They were inspired by the Danish visionary poet and writer N.F.S. Grundtvik, the bishop who inspired the Danes to renew themselves after Prussian chancellor Otto von Bismarck annexed a third of their country.

The folk high school movement pioneered popular education, creating boarding schools where both younger and older adults could learn informally, away from academic elitism, in an atmosphere of mutual respect and near-reverence for "the folk." In 2012, there were still seventy-seven folk high schools where students could take short courses up to a year, supported by public funding.

The education component dovetails with the larger economic model that enables Norway to adjust constantly to the changes of globalization, which includes so-called sunrise and sunset economic activities. Many Norwegians expect that during their working lives they will switch careers, learn new skill-sets, or both.

The economy as a whole benefits from an expectation of career flexibility: square pegs in round holes are not optimally productive. The universal health-care system, income support for people

who are laid off, and an abundance of free educational opportunities encourage people to reinvent themselves.[122]

Icelandic economist Thorvaldur Gylfason has warned about a
dynamic he observes in many countries that discover an extraordinary natural resource. Ironically, he finds such nations typically
"develop a false sense of security and become negligent about the
accumulation of human capital. Indeed, resource-rich nations can
live well from their natural resources over extended periods, even
with poor economic policies and a weak commitment to education." Applying his hypothesis to Norway, he observes that oil has
distorted part of its economy but has not weakened the Norwegian commitment to education. On the contrary, he notes: "The
proportion of each cohort attending colleges and universities in
Norway rose from 26 percent in 1980 to 62 percent in 1997."[123]

THE VIKING COUSINS

The Swedes experience the education ladder in a similar way to
the Norwegians, starting at age six, holding off on grades through
primary school, going on to lower secondary school and being allowed to leave at about age sixteen. Swedish fifteen-year-olds test
right in the median average of the OECD scores. If they continue
school, they, like Norwegians, get to choose between the academic
and the vocational tracks; also like the Norwegians and Danes,
about half of the Swedish students choose the vocational track.

Sweden also has a historic folk high school movement—about
150 schools—but the Swedish system offers more chance to prepare for college entrance than the Norwegian or Danish model
does.

Danish children have nine years of compulsory schooling, plus a tenth year if they want it to be sure to be ready for their next step—the labor market or more schooling. The distinction in Denmark between primary school and lower secondary school is not as sharp as in Norway, and the two units may be housed in the same building. In the historic birthplace of the folk high school movement, Denmark has more than seventy schools operating across the country.

Icelanders also start at age six; they have seven primary grades and three years in the lower secondary school. Their upper secondary school lasts four years, so the students typically finish at age twenty. Each of their four track options—academic, artistic, vocational, and general—each leads to the option of entrance to college. Gylfason told me that Icelandic music schools were made free of charge fifty years ago (when Iceland was a poor country), and enrollment jumped from 1,000 to 16,000!

The OECD in 2013 published numbers on countries' spending on formal education, calculated in various ways. As usual, over time, the Nordic countries play musical chairs at the top of the list of thirty-six countries. One OECD measure is the percentage of each country's GDP devoted to education. The 2010 list put Denmark in first place, Iceland second, Norway fourth, and Sweden thirteenth.

The United States was in sixth place.[124] The high rate of spending in the United States in the midst of widely deplored results by critics raises questions. Blaming American teachers is a popular indoor sport in my country, but there are other possible differences. One possibility is that education is like health care. The Nordics get "more bang for the buck" in health care by spending more wisely, relying mainly on single-payer systems rather than the United States' administratively top-heavy, wasteful market-based model.

Journalist Dana Goldstein's study of multiple educational systems offers what seems to me a more likely possibility. She concludes that broad educational outcomes cannot be isolated from other aspects of the economy that influence learning and achievement. She finds that teachers and public schools in other countries "are threads in a social fabric that includes affordable childcare, health coverage, and job training."[125]

U.S. schools are adding police to their budgets, by 2015 reaching 15,000 "school resource officers" in uniforms who sometimes carry weapons and are sometimes accused of targeting black students.[126] School police are another price education pays for the United States' failure to reduce poverty and racism.

If the holistic view makes sense, then once again the strength of Viking economics lies not only in individual institutions but in how they mutually reinforce one another to offer to individuals the freedom and equality that they want. A macro-design pays off.

"TOO MUCH SCHOOL"—A TENSION FOR NORWEGIANS

I was slow to catch a cultural nuance in Norwegians' enthusiasm for schooling. Compared with most other OECD countries, they prioritize spending for the schools for younger ages more than for colleges. Norwegians search for alternative pedagogical practices—they were early enthusiasts for Rudolf Steiner's Waldorf model—and they like informal learning.

I saw in their behavior a classic dilemma for egalitarians: how do you support excellence without becoming elitist? Sociologist Nils Christie, one of my teachers, said he worried about the tendency of schooling to simply replicate traditional Norway's class stratification. Christie voiced a deeply rooted populist theme.

Norwegians have a phrase: "*for mye skole*" ("too much school"). They love learning but, when structured by schools, they are wary of a possible top-down bias. Might schooling invalidate knowledge that comes from practical application? Might schooling diminish the wisdom and passion of an individual's inner, intuitive life? This is a people who cross-country ski and who watch a television program that simply features logs burning in a fireplace.

In 1959, when I began to study in Oslo, I was startled to be handed a several-page list of books and articles, and then to be told that my time was my own. The list of books was the *pensum*—the core content of sociology. I was invited to explore the field in a way that suited me while internalizing its basic set of concepts.

I was the only foreigner in our group, so I checked in with my new Norwegian classmates to see if they were as intimidated by this invitation as I was. They were not, because they expected it. "You are free to organize your time as you wish, George," they explained.

"I'll spend a lot of time this winter skiing," Anne-Lisa said with a grin, "but I'll take books along. When I'm prepared, I'll do what you'll do: tell them you're ready to take the exam."

"But what about the lectures and seminars?" I asked.

"Some are interesting and some are not," she said. "We can do what we want to about them. I mostly study on my own and with friends."

I found out about the examination process. When I believe I'm ready, I sign up to take two twelve-hour written exams, followed, if

I pass, by an oral exam. At the end I'll be notified whether I passed or failed.

Passing means completion of that chunk of my studies, the *grunnfag*, which took most students a year to a year and a half. The university degree itself usually took three years and was roughly the equivalent of an M.A. in the United States.

As it turned out, I found that I relished the freedom, the chance to fall in love with a particular writer and read everything he or she had written, or to spend a whole day obsessed with a provocative footnote I found. I usually studied in a large room with other sociology students, and when I got stuck I asked one of them to help me figure something out. Sometimes we had serial conversations about something really challenging or controversial, and sometimes I went to lectures.

I passed the exams for my *grunnfag* in sociology within a year; the structure worked for me. I did, though, meet "professional students" who were taking forever with their studies (along with beer halls and ski slopes).

The Norwegian university curriculum has become far more structured since my day, to conform to the Europe-wide "Bologna process." The change accompanies the larger trend of European integration, and aims to make schools and degrees more interchangeable from country to country. That, in turn, can increase freedom of opportunity.

Still, integrating into the more structured European university system spotlights the anti-elitist—and pro-intellectual—theme in Norwegian culture: how to keep alive for students their own free spirit of inquiry? Might "too much school" diminish reflective curiosity?

11

PAYING FOR WHAT YOU GET: THE VIKING APPROACH TO TAXES

The best-known aspect of the Nordic model may be the high taxes. I imagine that was true among people dominated by the ancient Vikings as well. If the marauding Norsemen didn't want to settle in your neighborhood, they were fond of setting up a tribute system, or what today we would call a protection racket: pay a yearly tax and you won't get hurt.

The Viking descendants are more efficient. They tax *themselves*: income, property, capital gains, and inheritance. Almost every time they buy something, they pay a sales tax. Taxes in Norway account for 42 percent of the gross national product. Taxes in Denmark, to take the most-taxed country, accounted for half the gross domestic product in 2014. The average in the OECD, the association of thirty-six of the world's richer states, was 34 percent.[127]

Because we in the United States are so familiar with the message that high taxes are a bad thing, I was astonished to read a comment by the former Norwegian prime minister, Jens Stoltenberg of the Labor Party, in *The New York Times*: "We won two elections promising not to lower taxes."

Surely this is not Viking practicality; at last we've found a piece of Viking insanity!

On the other hand, I remember an encounter I had with the U.S. Internal Revenue Service some years ago. The IRS and I had a difference that led me, appeal after appeal, to an officer I could really talk with. I didn't want him to misunderstand me, so I explained that I had no objection in principle to the graduated income tax approach. "In fact," I said, "when I lived in Norway I paid at a higher rate than I do here."

"Well," the IRS man replied, "in Norway you got what you paid for."

That's the basic attitude among Norwegians about their very high taxation rates. "To get a lot, we pay a lot."

Inc. Magazine sent senior writer Max Chaflin to Norway to interview entrepreneurs on their experience in a socialist-tinged environment. He interviewed Inger Ellen Nicolaisen, who founded and solely owns Nikita, the $60 million company that operates the largest chain of hair salons in Scandinavia. On Norwegian television she's famous for being the host of the nation's version of the Donald Trump show, *The Apprentice.*

Nicolaisen told Chaflin that she considers herself a political conservative. They talked about Norway's choice to add to the income tax, charging people like her a percentage on the amount of wealth they have.

"'Yeah, the wealth tax is a problem,' she says. 'But you have to make a choice. You can live in the Cayman Islands and pay no tax. But I don't want to live in the Cayman Islands. To live in Norway, you have to do what you have to. I think it's worth it.'"[128]

For their high taxes the Norwegians have gotten overall affluence, stability, opportunity, and a high level of services that make life easier and more secure. They got, for example, the *two hundred* tunnels they needed for one train line, between their two largest cities, Bergen and Oslo. And they expect to pay for what they get.

Nobel Prize–winning economist Joseph E. Stiglitz was chief economist for the World Bank and keeps close track of comparative economies. He recently countered the belief found in the United States that high taxes stifle economic growth: "Far from it. Over the period of 2000 to 2010, high-taxing Sweden, for example, grew far faster than the United States—the country's average growth rates have exceeded those of the United States—2.31 percent a year versus 1.85 percent."[129]

For his article, *Inc. Magazine*'s Chafkin asked other Norwegian entrepreneurs how they feel about their high taxes. He talked with Wiggo Dalmo, who started out as an apprentice to an industrial mechanic and got a job repairing mining equipment. Dalmo quit to be his own boss, hiring other mechanics, and soon his new company, Momek, was taking in $1 million a year. He built a machine shop and hired more people, and a decade later had a $44 million company with 150 employees.

Dalmo was a good person to ask. He pays nearly 50 percent of his income to the government, plus a substantial additional tax that amounts to about 1 percent of his total net worth. As a CEO he also pays payroll taxes, which are double those in the United States. When he goes to the store he pays sales tax, which at 25 percent is about triple the average in the United States. Chafkin wanted to know: what's Dalmo's attitude toward all that?

"The tax system is good—it's fair. What we're doing when we are paying taxes is buying a product. So the question isn't how much you pay for the product; it's the quality of the product."[130]

Something that builds public confidence about Norway's income tax system is that it is highly transparent, which guards against corruption and tax-cheating. Anyone can go online and read the returns of other Norwegians. If you know a corporate accountant who suddenly buys a Jaguar and builds a mansion, you can find out what she's declaring and blow the whistle.

The fairness embedded in the system, and the use of taxes to build an economic design that provides multiple benefits for everyone, apparently did not impress every person of wealth. John Fredricksen, a shipping tycoon with $7 to $8 billion in assets, renounced his Norwegian citizenship and went to live in Cyprus. According to Chafkin, Fredricksen is something of a folk hero to entrepreneurs back in Norway—but, significantly, most stay in Norway.

I asked Arne Isachsen, an economics professor at the Norwegian School of Business in Oslo, why more Norwegians with wealth don't send it abroad to be invested in global-south countries with higher rates of return. Capital flight has sometimes been a menace to countries seeking economic justice, after all. He said that to Norwegians the rate of return is only one value; a more important value to many people is stability. Norway's highly reliable economy, proven in the years following 2008, reassures investors who have grandchildren and great-grandchildren; they like security more than they like riding a financial roller-coaster.

EASING THE PAIN: TAXES FOR THE COMMON GOOD

Clearly, a basic principle in the Nordic model is taxing for the common good. The leftist parties that governed Iceland after the 2008 economic collapse had a tense confrontation with the IMF over exactly this issue. The Icelanders wanted to reduce the taxes on the working and middle classes and increase taxes on the rich. The IMF is famous for urging the opposite, as countries that continue to suffer from IMF-inspired austerity policies can tell us. In the case of Greece, 2015 found austerity hawks in the EU upping the ante on punishment to such an extreme that even the IMF could see it was self-defeating.

In 2009, Iceland won the argument with the austerity crowd and has made a stunning economic recovery. Every tax policy has, in the short run, winners and losers, and Icelanders wanted the winners to be workers and middle-class people, which in turn would end up benefiting everyone. It did.

Here we see in vivid colors how the outcome of a clash over tax policy—that is, over the value of equality—can build trust for a whole society. Two British medical epidemiologists have shown specific mechanisms through which the admittedly vague idea of "trust" is established. Richard Wilkinson and Kate Pickett called their 2009 international bestseller *The Spirit Level* after a humble carpenter's tool. When laid horizontally on a surface, the tool enables the carpenter to see by the position of the small bubble whether or not the surface is level.

In their book, the authors assemble peer-reviewed data from the world's richest countries. They find that inequality highly correlates with negative statistics in physical health, mental health, drug abuse, education, imprisonment, obesity, social mobility, violence, teenage pregnancy, and child well-being. They then argue that the correlations in fact represent causation, through a series of mechanisms. Their analysis of the international dataset also matched differences in equality among states within the United States.[131]

In addition to health indicators, Wilkinson and Pickett found data that enabled them to connect their equality hypothesis with trust. The European and World Values Survey asks random population samples from many countries whether or not they agree with the statement: "Most people can be trusted." Wilkinson and Pickett related the trust-survey data to the rich countries they had been tracking on the inequality variable. They found the same large differences they'd found with the health measures, following the same overall pattern. Sweden has the highest level of trust, with 66 percent of people feeling they can trust others. They are joined at the top by the other Nordics and Netherlands. The lowest level of trust is Portugal, with Greece (where people famously cheat on their taxes) in the same neighborhood.

Inside the United States, a similar range on the trust survey shows up: North Dakota at 67 percent along with Sweden on the high end and Mississippi at 17 percent along with Portugal on the low end. Overall, the states' trust indicators match their spots in relation to inequality.

The United States' overall place in the trust survey ranks halfway between the Nordics at the top and Portugal at the bottom. But public confidence in the economic elite is very low, outrun only by politicians in the race to the bottom. Macroeconomist Dean Baker helps us understand this. Federal income taxes are formally based on a system in which those who earn more pay a high percentage of their income in tax. The range is supposedly 15 percent for income between $18,000 and $75,000, 25 percent for income above $75,000 and under $150,000, and 39.6 percent for income above $465,000. The reality is that the country's 400 wealthiest families found ways to pay an average of just 17 percent of their income in taxes.

When trust is undermined by this kind of behavior, what is the result? Wilkinson and Pickett cite two U.S. political scientists, Harvard's Robert Putnam and Maryland's Eric Uslaner, each of whom has published studies of how trust levels influence society. Both scholars conclude that trust leads to cooperation. Uslaner writes, "People are more likely to donate time and money to helping others and to believe in a common culture where everyone should be treated with respect and tolerance. They are also supportive of the legal order."[132]

All this matters for follow-through on taxpaying. Equality also supports the social resilience that libertarians want us to depend on rather than government. Disasters provide illuminating moments when we can see social resilience operating, or not.[133] Climate change promises an increasing number of disasters, encouraging egalitarian tax policies that build community as well as governmental effectiveness for aid. The Nordic model, with its emphasis on equality and high taxes, has positive consequences for both community and government, and it maximizes capacity for the disasters certain to come in the future.

European countries have a history of taxing their corporations much more highly than we do in the United States. If we compare averages, corporate income tax revenue in the United States is about 25 percent below the average of the countries in the OECD. In 2013 during U.S. congressional hearings, the following question was raised: Why are so many large companies paying so little in taxes? According to Samuel Maruca, who served from 2011 to 2014 as IRS's first transfer pricing director, the issue "was pretty well in the shadows *for the past fifty years*."

Inside Europe, though, the differences have been substantial. In 2009, the United Kingdom got 2.8 percent of its taxes from corporations, while the Norwegians got 8.2 percent from that source.[134]

Personal income tax rates are not easy to compare, because some calculations include social security taxes and some don't. A further complication is that countries have been making adjustments since the 2008 economic crisis. Denmark and Sweden have a history of being leaders among those who tax their highest brackets the most; recent data had Denmark taxing at 59 percent and Sweden 57 percent. Norway was at 49 percent, about the same as the United Kingdom, but the UK's VAT tax is only 20 percent, compared with Norway's 25 percent. The United States within living memory had a robust economy while taxing its highest bracket at 70 percent, but now only taxes at about half that rate.[135] And economist Dean Baker reports the wealthiest actually paid only half of *that* number.

In Norwegian eyes, inheritance taxes also operate for the common good. Tax on inheritance from a parent is 6 percent for an estate worth $67,000 to $114,000, and 10 percent for estates over $114,000.[136]

As I've mentioned, the ordinary sales tax is about 25 percent. However, punitive taxes are levied on alcohol, tobacco, cosmetics, and other items that are viewed as luxurious or polluting.

The sales tax on cars can be higher than the actual price of the car itself. On the other hand, electric cars have little tax. Norway is not alone in using tax policy to tackle environmental issues. The OECD shows a number of countries raising significant revenue from environmentally related taxes, especially Denmark and Sweden (of course) but also the United Kingdom.

Despite Norway's being a leading oil exporter, it taxes gasoline at a very high rate to reduce consumption. A nationwide survey in 2010 showed a high level of support for taxes designed to protect the environment. Only a quarter of those polled wanted substantial reduction of fuel taxes. Thirty percent wanted a modest reduction, while 40 percent wanted the tax to remain the same or be notched a bit higher, and about 5 percent wanted the fuel tax doubled![137]

Although Americans are often stereotyped by our political class as anti-tax, the reality is often quite different. Pollsters have found that large majorities support a variety of taxes when they meet an important need and are for the common good.[138]

THE ECONOMIC COST OF VIOLENCE AND CRIMINALITY

A point of curiosity about the Nordics is the extraordinarily low rates of violence and criminality that they enjoy. Rarely do people consider the economic benefit that goes along with that. Mike Honda, the U.S. member of Congress who represents the Silicon Valley, has it very much in mind. Along with the U.S. Institute for Economics and Peace, he claims that that if the United States lowered its rates of violence and criminality to, say, Canadian levels, we could save hundreds of billions of dollars a year and add 2.7 million jobs.

To cross-check their findings, they compared the five states in the United States that have the lowest incidence of violence and criminality with the five states with the highest, and found very specific correlates for the most peaceful states in the United States: highest health coverage, high school graduation, educational opportunity, and greater income equality.[139] Tax policy influences each of those outcomes; abundant resources strategically used have their own value for each of these markers, plus lowering crime and violence. Safety-minded Americans might embrace the Nordic model for that reason alone.

ARE THE NORDICS IN DANGER OF KILLING THE GOOSE THAT LAYS THE GOLDEN EGGS?

Although Nordics value the vision, risk, and innovation contributed by entrepreneurs, they have a more complicated view of who lays the golden eggs. For one thing, they think the workers do a very large share of the egg-laying, which is why they invest so heavily in human capital and get higher productivity from their workers than in many countries. For another thing, their track record with cooperatives and with state-owned and municipal-owned enterprises gives them a positive perception of other sources of egg-laying. For the Nordics it would be simplistic to call entrepreneurs "*the* job-creators."

I already acknowledged one billionaire who left Norway for Cyprus, and the stubborn fact that the overwhelming majority of entrepreneurs remain in the country and pay enormous taxes. When *Inc. Magazine*'s Chafkin asked Nikita owner Inger Ellen Nicolaisen why she continued to grow her company, given the very large tax bite the government gets from the increased profit. Nicolaisen said, "I'm an entrepreneur. It's in my backbone."[140]

In reflecting, Chafkin reviewed his magazine's range of stories over the years about (mostly U.S.) entrepreneurs. He concluded that what drives creative entrepreneurship most of all is not the chance to spend money. It is the chance to make an impact.

In light of Chafkin's reflection, I thought of Norwegian Olav Thon. Everywhere I've gone in Norway I've seen one of his Thon Hotels in a premier location. Thon was once a farm boy who went to the city only to sell fox pelts. With 2013 assets estimated by *Forbes* magazine to be about $6 billion, he is the richest man in Norway.

Olav Thon continued to work well into his eighties, adding more hotels, retail stores, restaurants, and shopping malls to his empire, at home and abroad. When he turned ninety, he was asked for his plan for the future. He replied that he plans to give away his money through a trust when he dies.

HOW DO HIGH TAXES WORK OUT ON A MACRO LEVEL?

Among many of today's descendants of the Vikings it's a truism that paying high taxes results in getting high value. Their old-school shrewdness helped lead to the conversion of Jeffrey D. Sachs.

Sachs was one of the youngest economics professors in the history of Harvard University, and he made his initial reputation as a neoliberal advisor to Eastern European countries administering economic "shock therapy" to their populations. Now the Quetelet Professor of Sustainable Development at Columbia's School of International and Public Affairs, Sachs has changed his mind about the practicality of laissez-faire economics.

Reviewing the evidence, he wrote in *Scientific American* that the high-tax/high-spending Nordic countries have outperformed the low-tax/low-spending countries like the United Kingdom. "Most of the debate in the U.S.," he writes, "is clouded by vested interests and by ideology. Yet there is now a rich empirical record to judge these issues scientifically."

Sachs compares, on the one hand, Denmark, Finland, Norway, and Sweden, and on the other hand the low-tax, high-income countries that share a historical lineage with nineteenth-century Britain and its theories of laissez-faire: Australia, Canada, Ireland, New Zealand, the UK, and the United States. The contrast is stark: in the Nordic group the average portion of the budget given to social purposes is 27 percent of the gross domestic product, and in the Anglo-Saxon group it's just 17 percent.

He asks whether it's true, as claimed by followers of influential free-market economist Friedrich Von Hayek, that the high taxes needed to pay for high levels of social insurance reduce prosperity.

"On average, the Nordic countries outperform the Anglo-Saxon ones on most measures of economic performance . . . Von Hayek was wrong." In his conclusion, Sachs says that the Nordic model is not Von Hayek's "road to serfdom" but instead is the path to "fairness, economic equality and international competitiveness."[141]

Sachs's study gained further support from a Canadian think tank that researched the tax policies and economic outcomes of all OECD countries. The Canadian Centre for Policy Alternatives found that the high-tax countries generated overall superior performance to that of the United States and other low-tax members of the OECD.[142]

LITTLE NORWAY AND GREAT BRITAIN

Before learning about Sachs's conversion I was already puzzling about some of these issues. My father's ancestors came from Britain. In 1959 and 1960, I taught English in a Norwegian high school and it was the *British* version of the language, not the American version, that I was expected to teach. In 1969 and 1970, I lived in London, working and traveling widely in the UK.

Britain and Norway, both maritime nations, have historically been very close. Economically, Britain has been Norway's "big brother." Norway imported whole factories from Britain in their early days of industrialization. When Norwegian governmental leaders fled the country only one step ahead of Nazi German invaders, it was to London that they went. When Britain decided to stay out of the European Common Market, Norway did, too.

My biggest surprise in researching this book, therefore, has been gaining a picture of Britain and Norway that throws a startling light on Viking economics.

For starters, the size: Norway has a bigger land area than Britain. As I followed the geographical thread I realized that the two countries faced vastly different challenges in the practical tasks of building a modern economy.

Norway's population is dispersed widely, its small towns and villages separated by rugged mountains, fjords, and even glaciers. Because its latitude is high, the ice and massive snowfalls compound the difficulties. Building roads up sides of mountains and building bridges has been an enormous job, and maintaining them is not much easier.

The railroad age brought fresh obstacles; in Norway you can find the steepest-grade railroad in the world. I rode through two hundred tunnels on the train from Oslo to Bergen. Engineers additionally built sheds in a number of places to protect the tracks from snow.

Along with the era of airplanes came another challenge both

technical and financial. More than one hundred airports were built around Norway for a population that could fit in metropolitan Birmingham in England.

Population size raises another question: who is to pay for all this infrastructure? The population of Britain is roughly sixty million. During most of its development, Norway's population was less than four million—an almost pitiful tax base. Where was the wealth to come from for a massive investment in arduous-to-build infrastructure?

Moreover, Norway lacked the UK's abundant agricultural land; only 3 percent of Norway can be farmed. The UK had iron, copper, vast amounts of coal, and other resources to generate wealth; historical Norway had little besides water power, timber, and fish.

The UK, as a pioneer in industrialization, had a long lead-time to build its infrastructure; until 1905, Norway was linked to Sweden, a country focused on its own industries.

For hundreds of years, the UK was the center of a vast empire. At a time when Norway had a population of scattered farmers and a capital city of only tens of thousands, the UK was capturing wealth from Asia, Africa, and the Americas.

What began in my mind as geography, and the practical engineering challenge of infrastructure, became a fascinating economic question. By 2013, the government of the UK was claiming that the country was broke and had to raise tuition for higher education, cut maternity and childcare benefits and a half-million public-sector jobs, and take other measures that increase its already-high poverty levels.

The UK, an immensely wealthy country that has faced far less economic challenge than Norway and was far more blessed with resources, a large internal market, and a head start on industrialization—broke?

Because this is a book about the Nordics rather than the British, I leave it to citizens of the UK to ask themselves, in the midst of their government's austerity policy, just how their enormous wealth went missing. For the rest of us, putting the UK alongside countries that adopted the Nordic model helps us see more clearly the difference an economic design actually makes.

PART III

TODAY'S CHALLENGES, FOR THEM AND FOR US

12

ALLOWING RACIAL AND OTHER DIFFERENCES TO WORK FOR THE COMMON GOOD

Racism is a very personal issue for Berit and me because we twice adopted African American babies before being surprised by producing one by our (European-American, white) selves. Racism hurts white people as well, but through the lives of our black children, then grandchildren and great-grandchildren, we have lived in a special way with some of the dynamics of racial oppression.

The Nordics' history is very different from my country's large economic stake in both slavery and continuing racism today. Nevertheless, Nordic racism does exist, and I was eager to interview the director of Norway's Anti-Racism Center, Mari Linløkken. I started by acknowledging that my interest was personal as well as professional, then asked for her perspective on where racism comes from in Norway.

Mari somehow combined a no-nonsense manner with eyes full of warm attention.

"George, you might be forgetting that the African slave trade was a reality for Norway, too! We built slave ships, we benefited, we participated in the belief white people *everywhere* shared that slavery is legitimate because blacks are different from and inferior to us!

"An attitude that justifies monstrous evil doesn't just disappear. It hangs on, and that's why you find it here in Norway, too."

Her analysis resonated. I was brought up in a small town in rural Pennsylvania with no African Americans in my class in school, no black labor force to threaten the insecure Welsh and Cornish slate miners who settled there. The economic role of competition was given to immigrant Italians, and my town's economic elite—the mine owners—used the Italians' difference from the earlier settlers to divide and rule. My town's mostly Protestant Northern Europeans did indeed turn Italians into the "other." My miner grandfather, I remember, would not eat spaghetti; that was one way he expressed his prejudice.

But even though my town's Northern Europeans generated prejudice against the Italians, we had plenty of prejudice left over for African Americans. Indeed, wherever in the world I have encountered a settlement of white people, I've encountered racism. As Mari Linløkken said, why would the descendants of the Vikings be the exception?

Prejudice in today's Norway is expressed in many ways. *Bergenstidende* (*The Bergen Times*) reported that four out of ten Norwegians still perceive "immigration as a threat to the country's distinctive character." Over half believe that if a time of adversity comes, "employment should first be secured for Norwegians."[143]

Prejudice easily converts to discrimination, if you happen to have power. Mari told me that job applicants' chances of getting to the interview stage were 25 percent less if they had foreign names.

What many do not realize—in my country as well as in Norway—is that immigration is usually an economic plus. The fishing industry in northern Norway survives with the help of Tamils from Sri Lanka, along with Russians. In the task of maintaining the shipbuilding industry, Poles have played a major role.[144]

In Iceland, there is an interesting mismatch of perceptions of prejudice. A series of studies show that Icelanders report having a positive attitude toward immigrants, while the immigrants report that they experience prejudice and discrimination.[145]

On a fine summer day in Oslo, I saw at a corner newsstand a blaring headline with an article occupying most of the front page: "Born in Norway but Feel Like Foreigners: Less than half the teens in Oslo born of immigrants and brought up here feel themselves to be Norwegian. New study revealed in paper today."[146] I knew from my family's experience in the United States the alienating impact of being made "other" and being feared. I needed to understand better how fear was playing out in the Nordic countries and how their economic model was or was not a resource.

ISLAMOPHOBIA BECOMES DANGEROUS IN NORWAY: A PROPHETIC INTERVIEW

I'd been hearing about Thomas Hylland Eriksen, a social anthropologist who, although young, launched the interdisciplinary research program called Cultural Complexity in the New Norway. I caught up with him at the University of Oslo's Blindern campus in the western end of the city. Eriksen told me over coffee that even though only one-third of the newcomers to Norway are from Muslim countries, Islamophobes have succeeded in framing the public discussion about immigration.

Eriksen went on to describe what he called "mounting aggression against the 'elite' that let immigrants into the country." Ironically, what the Islamophobes call the "elite" is actually a succession of working-class-based Labor governments that have indeed been pro-immigration. With a tone of urgency, Eriksen said the situation was increasingly dangerous.

Eriksen's words proved all too prophetic. Two years after our conversation in 2009, Anders Behring Breivik set off a two-thousand-pound bomb that blasted the Labor Party headquarters and other government-related buildings. Breivik then went immediately to the small island of Utøya, where leaders of the youth wing of the Party were enjoying a conference at a summer camp. On the island, Breivik used automatic weapons to kill as many of the youths as he could. All told, 77 people lost their lives and 158 were wounded. July 22, 2011, was Norway's bloodiest day since World War II.

Operationally, it seems that Breivik acted alone. However, two years after his attack, Eriksen described a sinister background important to all of us who live in societies that suffer from racism. This is how he reported Norway's situation to the Washington, D.C.–based Migration Policy Institute:

> The most important view shared by all who associate with these loosely knit networks [of Islamophobia] is the belief that Muslims cannot become good Europeans, or good Norwegians, until they cease to be Muslims. This view has not only been voiced by members of Parliament (MPs) from the Progressive Party, but also by various commentators and intellectuals who do not identify with the right wing. Historian Nils Rune Langeland, in an interview

with influential left-of-center newspaper *Dagbladet* only days before the terrorist attacks, spoke of a coming *reconquista* (referring to the fall of Granada and the expulsion of the Moors in 1492), raised the possibility that the "Germanic peoples of the North may yet rise," and concluded by stating that Muslim girls may get good grades at university but "they will never crack the European code."

With the hindsight of the terrorist attack [by Breivik], Dr. Langeland's analysis reads almost like a recipe for armed revolt against creeping "Islamification by stealth" (a Progressive Party term) and the loss of honor and masculine strength among mainstream Norwegians. However, the interview was published without much initial controversy, which illustrates that this perception of Muslims has become so commonplace that Norwegians today hardly raise an eyebrow when they read statements like those made by Langeland. What is interesting, in other words, is the ordinariness of his generalizations and the trivialization of his contempt."[147]

CARTOONS IN DENMARK

The Danish newspaper *Jyllands-Posten* invited twelve different political cartoonists to submit caricatures of what the prophet Mohammed might have looked like. The paper published them on September 30, 2005. Many religious Muslims responded with outrage; they found the cartoons humiliating and sacrilegious. Muslims outside Denmark also responded strongly in many countries, even protesting at Danish embassies and consulates.

The newspaper defended itself by saying it was exercising its right to free speech. Despite its eagerness to assert journalistic freedom, I am not aware of the newspaper soliciting cartoons that demeaned Jesus or caricatured in an odious way the Danish king. Not only was the action an obvious act of aggression, but it was cowardly because it hid behind the superior power and privilege gained by centuries of dominance by the Western and Christian world.

The cluelessness of the Danish editor was then emulated in Norway by a Christian fundamentalist newspaper. We can doubt that the paper would find it acceptable if a Muslim newspaper turned Christ into a monstrous caricature.

Henrik Lunde, a leader of the Norwegian Anti-Racist Centre, wrote at the time about the Norwegian response to the Danish cartoons:

> The editors and all mainstream papers support the publishing of the drawings and proclaim this as an important battle for freedom of speech . . . The Islamic Council [of Norway] has done a terrific job and its spokesperson has made it perfectly clear that Muslims are angry and hurt, but will try to put this behind them and go forward because "we are all brothers in this country and must treat each other with respect."[148]

In 2015, the populist Danish People's Party gained so many votes that it became Denmark's second-largest party, after the Social Democrats. About the electoral campaign, *Politiken's* editor Bo Lidegaard wrote, "While steering clear of outright racism and Islamophobia, the [Danish People's Party] has set a strongly anti-immigrant tone in the public debate and drawn most other political parties into a competition to see who can be toughest on immigration."[149]

RIOTS IN SWEDEN, AND A NAZI GETS ELECTED

At least twice in recent years, immigrant youths have rioted in the Stockholm suburbs, in 2010 in Rinkeby, then in 2013 first in Husby and then spreading to Rinkeby and beyond. An estimated 85 percent of Husby residents were born outside Sweden. Police who were called to stop the youths from burning cars and buildings reportedly yelled racial epithets as they worked to bring the rioting under control.

The vigorous Swedish debate that followed in each case most often included veiled and open derogatory references to Muslims. The small anti-immigrant minority in Sweden has grown; in the 2010 election, a party named Sweden Democrats won 5.7 percent of the votes.

Nevertheless, the majority continued to give broad support for helping refugees. In 2012, 44,000 were given asylum from countries like Syria, Afghanistan, and Somalia, and Sweden is known as the world's most welcoming country for asylum-seekers. In 2015, Sweden stood out along with Germany for its hospitality to the flood of refugees fleeing Syria. By January 2016, however, the government called a temporary halt to the influx.

Given how open Sweden has been to immigration, I was puzzled by the young immigrants' rioting in relatively prosperous and egalitarian Sweden until I read of the study by a team of Norwegian peace researchers. They examined the relationship between local conflicts and a combination of micro- and macroeconomic measures. After studying a range of incidents of civil unrest in many countries, they found that violent conflict is more likely to erupt in areas with low absolute income, even if overall national GDP per capita is high. In particular, the researchers pointed to local areas with large deviations from national averages. Spatially distributed inequality increases the risk of conflict.[150]

The big picture in Sweden is that inequality grew more rapidly than in any other European country in the period between the mid-1980s to the late 2000s, according to the OECD.[151] Even though Sweden remains far more equal than most countries, something interesting is going on when we look at Husby and Rinkeby compared with Stockholm as a whole. In Husby unemployment is 10 percent, compared with 3.5 percent in Stockholm. Even those in Husby who are employed get 40 percent less income than the average earner in Stockholm.[152]

Although the study is compelling, we don't need to conclude that economics explains everything. As Swedish justice minister Beatrice Ask said after the 2013 riots, "Social exclusion is a very serious cause of many problems."[153] Camila Salazar, who works for Fryshuset, a Stockholm youth organization, told *The Guardian*: "For a lot of people who live in segregated areas, the only Swedes they meet are social workers or police officers. It's amazing how many have never had a Swedish friend."[154]

Still, it may be significant that Sweden cut back its public spending in the period before the riots, from 67 percent of GDP to 49 percent. Making those cutbacks while cutting taxes on the wealthy and corporations seems like asking for trouble. Twenty-three percent of young people in poor, largely immigrant communities do not achieve good enough grades to enter upper secondary education; Sweden had one of the highest ratios of youth to general unemployment in the OECD.[155]

Together, those trends *increase* the chance of social exclusion and resentment, followed by the blowback of racism from a majority population that is previously conditioned by its whiteness. In 2010, a self-identified Nazi was elected to a democratic assembly in Sweden for the first time since the 1940s. "The leader of the *Svenskarnas Parti* (Swedes' Party) won a seat on the Gråstorp municipal council in the south of the country, thereby making history."[156] The party subsequently declined and dissolved in May 2015.

Sweden Democrats is currently the only party taking a stand against immigration. It increased its percentage of the vote in parliamentary elections from 5.7 percent to 12.9 percent (in 2014). Sociologist Ulf Bjereld of the University of Gothenburg sees growing opposition within the working class to Sweden Democrats, despite that party's claim that it speaks for the workers more forthrightly than do the traditionally worker-based Social Democrats. Workers at a Volvo factory told Sweden Democrats' leader that he was not welcome to come to the factory to campaign for the 2014 election, as did the national organization of community centers, *Folkets Hus*.[157]

WHAT ARE THE STAKES FOR THE DESCENDANTS OF THE VIKINGS?

In researching this book, I have asked how people's life chances and choices are influenced by their economic model. The Nordics designed their economies to provide security and opportunity for economic advancement. Even though Mari Linløkken said we can expect residual white racism among the Nordics, why the intensity of the fear?

In conversation with pedagogy professor Hanna Ragnarsdottir of the University of Iceland in 2014, I made a breakthrough in my understanding of what the stakes are in these small countries. Since 1995, the number of immigrants in Iceland doubled, then doubled again.[158] To economist Thorvaldur Gylfason, this makes complete economic sense, and he argues for greater increases of immigration in the future. Hanna, on the other hand, described to me the Icelanders' sense of themselves as the only people in the world who speak Icelandic and love their culture. There are only 320,000 of them. They represent the strongest link to the ancient Vikings, who wrote a powerful literature and formed the first parliament.

I began to get it. If the Icelanders lost their culture, the world would lose something very precious. The legacy is theirs to protect. The newcomers to Iceland are not coming in order to celebrate, and join, the Icelandic culture. They are fleeing poverty and persecution. They are looking to earn a living. They want a fresh start and would prefer to keep their own cultures, wherever they are from. If the newcomers speak English, they can cope with daily life, since nearly all Icelanders speak English. What a relief it might be, from their point of view, not to have to engage with the tongue-twisting ordeal of learning how the Vikings talked.

The stakes are high, and this plays out, according to Hanna, in the schools. Should the newcomers learn Icelandic as a second language while also speaking their first language in school? But if they continue with their first language, how does anyone know whether they will *really* learn Icelandic?

The stakes are most compelling in Iceland, given the extremely small numbers of people there, but a similar sense of legacy exists for the Norwegians, of whom there are only 5 million in a world of billions. Norway accepts more immigrants per capita than the UK. Norway also has a higher percentage of its population that is foreign-born, at 14 percent, than the EU average.[159] Danes are 5.5 million, 10 percent of whom are immigrants. Of the 9.5 million Swedes, 14 percent are immigrants.

In the last fifteen years, the number of immigrants and their descendants has almost tripled in Norway. In a country of only 5 million, already one in seven isn't from Norway. "Who," they might well ask, "will speak my language and love my culture, when my children already tune in to American television and the English world of the Internet. Some Nordic pop singers compose and record their songs in English from the outset. As the years go by, will I continue to feel at home in my own country?"

On a recent visit to Oslo, I hung out in an outdoor museum filled with centuries-old houses, farm buildings, and an ancient stave church complete with carved wooden dragons. I enjoyed folk dance performances by laughing young people dressed in brightly colored handmade clothes of the old styles. I talked with their leader, who told me that there is a trend among young people of increased interest in the traditional dances and music.

"Do you have an idea where that trend comes from?" I asked him.

He took a moment to think, his eyes taking in the Hardanger fiddle in the hands of a nearby teen. "You know, these days young people mix in school with girls wearing the hajib, Somali boys listening to Afro-pop, a lot of cultural styles side by side. Maybe it encourages them to root themselves a bit more securely in their own ethnicity. Maybe that's it."

Maybe these young folk dancers are pointing the way, I muse. Instead of worrying about how others are different, *why not become more securely at home with one's own uniqueness?* Perhaps a world could be made safer for everyone.[160]

FIGHTING OPPRESSION: A TRACK RECORD BUILDS CONFIDENCE

The Nordics have an anti-oppression resource: their outstanding track record in important arenas of diversity. I've already described the rapid strides made in tackling sexism and the economic design's important role in that. The cabinet of the new Swedish government elected in 2014 has an equal number of women and men, a fact that goes largely unremarked within the Nordic countries, so usual has women's participation in leadership become. Americans who enjoy reading mysteries have no doubt noticed that many of the most prominent of the male Nordic novelists, such as Denmark's Peter Høeg, Iceland's Arnaldur Indridason, Norway's Jo Nesbø, and Sweden's Stieg Larssen and Henning Mankell, repeatedly explore feminist themes.

In 1971, during a time when a wave of young people on both sides of the Atlantic was inspired by a new vision of freedom, a group of squatters in Copenhagen founded *Fristaden Christiania*, the Free Town of Christiana. In 2014, I wandered through the stable community of more than 800 mostly long-term residents, in wonderment that a town of "anarchist hippies" could thrive for over forty years surrounded by a sea of Protestantism. Full of questions, I sat down with Kirsten Larsen Mhoja, a social anthropologist who has lived in Christiana for more than three decades.

Smiling as she recalled the struggle, Kirsten acknowledged that there had been multiple threats to the community. Survival, she said, required strategy, the cultivation of allies, and the development of strong norms of conflict resolution within the community itself.

The result? Christiana has proved itself so expert in sustainability, despite its marginal lifestyle within Denmark, that requests come from mainstream Danes for it to make itself a conscious laboratory for new approaches that support living on a changing planet.

Norway was the first country in the world to pass a law to protect homosexuals from discrimination, a major move for both equality and freedom. Since 1972, sexual activity between same-sex consenting partners has been legal. The age of consent was placed at age sixteen whether heterosexual or homosexual.

In 1979, Norwegian lesbians, gays, and bisexuals gained full rights and anti-discrimination protection in the armed forces. Two years later, the Storting prohibited hate speech directed at sexual minorities. In 1993, a civil partnership law took effect that gave many marriage rights to same-sex couples. (Denmark had already passed a similar law in 1989. Sweden followed in 1994.) In 2000, Norwegians gained the right to change their legal gender.

The Labor coalition government initiated a move for marriage equality in 2007, and the following year two opposition parties gave up their resistance to the initiative. The resulting parliamentary vote was 84–41, and the new law took effect on January 1, 2009. The law includes joint adoption by same-sex couples.

The city government of Oslo celebrated the law's passage by throwing a giant free party for gays and their allies on the roof of the new Opera House.

Sami (formerly known as Lapps) are the indigenous people of northern Norway, Sweden, Finland, and Russia. They speak a form of the Finno-Ugric language and have traditionally lived a nomadic life, moving with reindeer herds across the national boundaries of northern Scandinavia.

Ethnic Norwegians have a history of oppressing the Samis, including efforts to suppress their religion, language, and way of life. The Samis responded with a liberation struggle, found allies, and in Norway succeeded in amending the Constitution to require the Norwegian state "to create conditions enabling the Sami people to preserve and develop its language, culture and way of life."[161]

In Geneva, Switzerland, while teaching in a United Nations–sponsored seminar for indigenous leaders around the world, I met John Henricksen, permanent representative of the Sami Council to the Commission on Human Rights at the UN. He was a leader of the *Sameting* (Sami Parliament), which was established in 1989. He told me that the Sameting has considerable authority in the internal affairs of his people, including education, economic, and welfare issues, while the Norwegian state retains authority for international affairs and the overall economic direction of the country.

One point of tension is that the Sami people feel considerable solidarity *across* national lines—the drawing of boundaries called "Norway" and "Sweden" is a recent imposition with no real legitimacy for the indigenous people who were there when Norsemen were nowhere to be seen. The question still to be worked on is, how can the unitary peoplehood of the Sami be asserted, with these nation state boundaries getting in the way?

Nevertheless, more and more of the 40,000-plus Sami are *identifying* themselves as such in the Norwegian census. That may mean that the stigma is receding. Steps like the Sami people tak-

ing the global spotlight in the opening ceremony of the 1994 Lille-
hammer winter Olympics may be paying off.

RESPONSES TO THE ANTI-MUSLIM DRUMBEAT

Even while Denmark, Norway, and the other Nordics took diversity-
friendly steps, an anti-Muslim sentiment could be heard in the
background, occasionally erupting on the campaign trail largely
initiated by the anti-immigration politicians.

When I was visiting family in Skien in 2000, I browsed among
the vegetables and fruit on offer in the open market at the center of town. Political parties had booths, giving away their bro-
chures and urging people to vote for them. I was struck by the
assertiveness of the Labor Party brochure, showing on the front a
full-page photo of two young children playing together, one black
and the other white. I read with interest the accompanying text
that amounted to: Labor is the party you've trusted all these years
to build a strong economy that supports equality, democracy, and
freedom, and you can trust us also to handle the challenges of
building a strong multiracial society.

Other institutions resisted Islamophobia in 2000 as well. *Litera-
turans Huset*, an old and prestigious center of intellectual life in Norway, scheduled frequent forums and dialogues on diversity and issues
raised by immigration, and academics appeared frequently on the
radio and television dispensing light to go along with the rising heat.

As the Bishop of Oslo, Gunnar Staalsett, stood in the line of
a thousand years of history in the Church of Norway. This was
a church that stood against the Nazi oppression during World
War II. On December 28, 2000, he made history by being the first

bishop to visit a mosque. He chose Oslo's largest mosque and the important holiday of Id at the end of Ramadan.

In 2009, Siv Jensen, leader of the Progress Party, made an Islamophobic speech claiming that Norway was becoming a victim of "sneaking Islamization" (*snikislamisering*). Bishop Staalsett's successor, Bishop Ole Christian Kvarme, stepped up. Kvarme is regarded as centrist and moderate, but he urged politicians to create reconciliation, not confrontation, between faiths. He then followed up by publically visiting two Oslo mosques.

By that time Muslims had become the second-largest denomination in Norway, after the Church of Norway. In 2010, a year after Siv Jensen's speech, a group of Church of Norway bishops visited the Al-Aqsa Mosque in Jerusalem's Old City. Two years after that the Norwegian state finally ended its historic relationship with Christianity as the official religion. When I later met Halvor Nordhaug, the bishop of Bergen, he was visibly relieved. He was pleased that the mainstream Lutherans could now meet Muslims and other faith groups on a somewhat more equal playing field.

Inter-religious cooperation is growing. Imams are taking responsibility to end female mutilation, a custom used by Islamophobes to claim the moral high ground. Clergy actively oppose discrimination. Teachers in schools deliberately extend the range of what being "a Norwegian" is. The mass media write more stories about discrimination.

ANTI-RACISM ON THE EVERYDAY LEVEL

The Norwegian Center Against Racism (NCAR) is a nonprofit founded in 1978 that works with immigrants and supports dialogue between the newcomers and ethnic Norwegians. I smiled when Mari Linløkken told me about crusty old Norwegians with traditional skills like hunting and fishing who were eager to help the newcomers.

"We simply go to them and say, 'Ole, we've heard you are excellent at catching salmon and you can help us. We're in touch with people who have no salmon in their country and no idea how to catch them, but would like to learn. Would you be willing to teach them this marvelous Norwegian skill?"

I watched a video of another unusual program in which Center staffers ask Muslim immigrant families to invite ethnic Norwegian families to tea in their homes. Both families in the video are visibly awkward in the beginning. The stereotype about Norwegians being stiff and shy with strangers does, after all, have some basis in reality! The children in each family were the pacesetters, and a couple of hours later the adults allowed themselves to get curious about the deeper differences that enrich each of their lives.

By the time I caught up with the Anti-Racism Center (in 2009), Muslim families had already hosted 3,000 tea times in their homes. Early on, Princess Ingrid Alexandra famously participated in the program.

The rise in immigration to Norway coincided with the rise of the women's movement, which complicated how the newcomers were perceived by newly feminist Norwegians. By the 1980s and '90s, several experts told me, feminism had become absorbed into the narrative of what makes Norwegians an admirable people. Hip Norwegian young men gained points among their peers by their political correctness.

One reason to distrust and fear immigrants from notoriously patriarchal cultures, therefore, was stories of mistreatment of women and girls. The story of a father who wouldn't let his girls go to school would be widely, and righteously, discussed; forced marriage was gossiped about. Ethnic Norwegians could resist looking at their own racism by emphasizing their moral superiority to the sexism that was "invading" their feminist and egalitarian shores, and showing up in the apartment next door.

I asked Mari about how she began to untie this complicated knot. Her response reminded me of the Norwegians' historical approach to poverty, which was to develop a set of tools for handling a multi-layered problem. She emphasized the importance of assertively showing respect for cultural differences where there is no collision with one's own values. "Norwegians traditionally honor Christian holidays," she said. "Why not honor Muslim holidays? And what's the problem with providing important information in a variety of languages, to show respect for the language of others? Workplace cafeterias should of course offer Halal and vegetarian food."

I noted that the traditional practice of the Norwegian state is to provide maintenance grants to religious institutions, and the practice has been extended to mosques.

The second tool she sees is the calm and confident assertion that Norwegian law prevails. All girls as well as boys will go to school.

A third tool is relationship-building on the basis of equality. When a relationship is strong enough differences can be explored from a place of self-respect on both sides. "Tolerance" reflects fear rather than respect, Mari said. When Norwegians avoid one-on-one argument—or at least dialogue—about cultural differences, the avoidance implies a lack of respect. As Mari explained this I easily extrapolated to my own country, where whites often avoid building relationship with workmates and fellow students of color by skating on the surface rather than engaging about differences.

Mari told me that Norwegians should neither expect in advance to defer to the other's point of view, nor expect in advance that the other would defer to one's own. The intensity of honest dialogue about difference is to be welcomed, with some curiosity about the outcome, and openness to change.

I could see her point in daily interactions and in the larger picture. Cultures evolve, and they need to. Cultural defense implies rigidity; dialogue and debate implies openness to growth.

All that sounds good, so I pushed her. What if I'm an ethnic Norwegian living next door to a Muslim family where all the signs are pointing toward an upcoming forced marriage of the young daughter? What do I do?

Mari applied her set of tools. I should intervene, in the context of (a) having shown my interest in and respect for some of their cultural differences, and made the accommodations that a neighbor might, (b) having learned about the Norwegian law against forced marriage and the resources available for intervention from the law, (c) having had deeper discussions that included differences so that a measure of trust and mutual respect has been built.

The exact tactics for my intervention will be situational, and could include telling the youth about resources where she can get help. In an extreme case I would report the issue to the police to prevent the possibility of a murder, since such an extreme is not unknown when a daughter refuses to be married.

Mari said that difficult situations can come up for teachers as well as neighbors, and a creative resolution is more likely to come from discussion than from a procedural protocol.

As she talked I realized that once again *she was relying on the Norwegians' root value of equality.* In tough spots, I might be tempted to come from my place of higher rank (skin color, religion, citizenship) and try to power my way through the problem. Alternatively, I can stop pulling rank and turn to my inner strength, which includes willingness to be vulnerable. Mari's set of tools are an expression of equal relationship.

As when designing an economy, the creativity comes from choosing an alternative to the reigning paradigm.

VIKING ECONOMICS TAKES ON RACISM

For multicultural Americans encountering the descendants of the Vikings, what looks like the stain of nationalism can be an interest in cultural survival, not unlike the struggle of indigenous peoples in many parts of the world that are subject to extinction by larger populations prodded by globalization. On the defensive, many of today's Vikings may hesitate to embrace values and practices different from their own, even though an objective outsider can see the advantages of a pro-diversity stance.

The defensiveness is expressed by political polarization, and politicians gain votes by appealing to fear of immigration even though Norwegian visionaries tell me their country has comfortable physical space and resources for many more people than it presently contains. No one can know how the polarization will play out, among the Nordics or in my country. The question in this book remains, how is the Nordic economic model a resource in that situation?

We start with poverty. I've seen in my country how poverty supports the white narrative that black and brown people are inferior. In the United States, institutionalized scarcity pits people at the bottom against one another, within racial groups and across them, despite the fact that many roads to advancement depend on cooperation and collaboration. The overall class narrative brands people who are poor as "losers," which then erodes the confidence of all but the hardiest.

The Nordics offer the only economic model with a solid track record for minimizing absolute poverty. Full employment, with a living wage, is a deep commitment.

I've also seen in my country how racism and prejudice against immigrants are reinforced by putting obstacles before people who, if they've escaped poverty, want further economic opportunity. In Norway, Mari Linløkken told me, a larger percentage of immigrant girls take higher educational degrees than do ethnic Norwegians, when you control for the variable of parents' education. More young immigrants are speaking out, participating in debates, being role models. Some of them are taking the role of rebels, sparking more involvement from others—engagement is crucial, she said. Also more young adult immigrants are choosing to take careers in teaching and social work.

The Nordic model insists on wide-open doors to free education and training.

In my country, I've seen self-defeating behaviors among some immigrants and people of color reinforced by family histories, with insufficient outside resources to assist individuals to break out of family and neighborhood patterns. At present, a national campaign in my country seeks to defund schools and nonprofit centers that have in the past, even though inadequately, offered such resources. In Norway, Mari told me that dozens of Center staffers work behind the scenes advocating with government bureaucrats and coaching government workers on cross-cultural communication. They directly train immigrants as well, in job-interviewing skills, for example, and in how to relate to the education system. The Center had tutors representing more than a dozen countries with twenty-nine different languages.

The Nordic model generously funds agencies and programs that assist people who otherwise might lack opportunity. It seeks out barriers to advancement, such as the burdens of childcare and dependent elders, and tries to alleviate those to free everyone to move ahead. By universalizing such programs, as well as health care, vacations, access to public transportation, and other enhancements that otherwise can become racialized for disadvantaged populations, the model carefully avoids setting categories of people against each other.

Norwegian social scientists already find encouraging signs for their cumulatively increasing non-ethnic Norwegian population. Overall workforce participation among the immigrant population rose to 61.6 percent in 2010. That compares with 71.9 percent for the population as a whole.[162]

Length of time in the country matters. The longer that immigrants live in Norway, the more likely they are to get jobs.[163] The percentage of young people born to immigrant parents had jobs at a rate similar to their age-peers in families with Norwegian-born parents, 53 percent.[164]

Thomas Hylland Eriksen sums it up this way: "Over the past twenty years, successive governments have largely succeeded in creating a framework of equal opportunities for Norway's increasingly diverse population."[165]

To Mari Linløkken, that framework of equality means more room for diversity in Norwegian culture than there was in the 1970s, when she was young. She said that a recent attitude study showed *a majority of people are happy that diversity is growing in Norway.*

NORWAY'S ALTERNATIVE RESPONSE TO TERROR

When Anders Breivik launched his attack on July 22, 2011, he chose the right target, according to his views. The Labor Party and its allies had indeed given leadership for a diverse Norway. He parked the car loaded with a mixture of fertilizer and fuel oil in central Oslo, in front of the building housing Labor prime minister Jens Stoltenberg's office. The bomb severely damaged the headquarters of both the Labor and Liberal parties, the headquarters of the Trade Union Congress, and even the Supreme Court. Breivik's massacre of 69 young people at the Workers' Youth League summer camp on the island of Utøya, some as young as twelve, was intended to wipe out the next generation of Labor political leaders. He injured an additional 110 young people. Among the dead were personal friends of Stoltenberg.

At a press conference the morning after the attacks, Jens Stoltenberg vowed that the attack would not hurt Norwegian democracy, and the proper answer to the violence was "more democracy, more openness."[166]

Norwegians, joined by the royal family, packed the memorial service for the dead in Oslo Cathedral. According to *New York Times* reporter Steven Erlanger, "Long lines of people of all ages and colors waited patiently and quietly, some of them crying, to lay flowers or light candles at the spreading blanket of bouquets in front of the cathedral. Someone propped up a radio on a post so those waiting could listen to the service inside."[167]

At that memorial service, Stoltenberg quoted a girl in the Workers' Youth League who said, "If one man can show so much hate, think how much love we could show, standing together."[168]

The next day, July 25, at noon each of the Nordic countries held a minute of silence to honor the victims of the attacks.[169] Norway's minute of silence stretched to five minutes. Later in Oslo, a city of 600,000, an estimated 200,000 people participated in a "rose march." They gathered at Oslo's City Hall to mourn together.[170]

At his next news conference, Stoltenberg said, "It's absolutely possible to have an open, democratic, inclusive society, and at the same time have security measures and not be naïve . . . I think what we have seen is that there is going to be one Norway before and one Norway after July 22. But I hope and also believe that the Norway we see after will be more open, a more tolerant society, than what we had before."[171]

The New York Times interviewed young members of the Workers' Youth League including survivors of Breivik's attack, and found that they emphasized the importance of redoubling their efforts to keep Norway open to immigrants and fight climate change. Referring to Breivik, eighteen-year-old Helle Gannestad said, "He can take the lives from our friends but not their thoughts and wishes and beliefs, because that's going to go on with the rest of us."[172]

However, not all observers were sympathetic in the wake of the massacre. Fox News commentator Glenn Beck compared the Workers' Youth League with Hitler Youth.[173] When it became clear that Norway was not about to reinstate the death penalty that it proudly gave up in 1905, *The New York Times* published an op-ed by Thane Rosenbaum urging Norwegians to arouse their spirit of vengeance. He wrote derisively, "A country of such otherwise good fortune and peaceful intention is now unprepared—legally and morally—to deal with such a monstrous atrocity."[174]

Norway went ahead and implemented its own democratic and civil libertarian procedures for handling criminals. It gave Anders Behring Breivik a lawyer and his day in court, during which he acknowledged his disappointment that the state would not kill him and give him the martyrdom that he sought in his bid to inspire a Europe-wide movement against "*snikislamisering.*"

As it turned out, Norway's choice to live up to its highest values also was the pragmatically correct choice for minimizing the terrorist's impact. The sheer practicality of holding to the values of equality and freedom was ratified once again.

The Norwegians, not usually an emotional people, continued to grieve their losses. The year until the trial was hard for many; during my 2012 study trip I learned of a woman who'd been working in an affected government building whose trauma was so severe she still could not bear to return to her job. I walked slowly through the still-damaged government district, not letting my own tears distract me from noticing the lack of security guards and barriers. Even the *Storting* stood open as ever.

I asked everyone I met, "How has Norway changed since Breivik's attack?" and everywhere I received a reply that boiled down to this: "Well, it hasn't really changed. We are still ourselves."

Breivik was tried and convicted, sentenced to Norway's maximum imprisonment of twenty-one years with the condition that if he remains a danger to society he can be held longer. The Progress Party, whose rhetoric had been uncomfortably close to the fear that Breivik acted upon, did lose a considerable share of its vote in the next national election. From 2009 to 2013, it dropped from 22.9 percent to 16.3 percent. And even though as a coalition partner in the new government led by the Conservatives it presses to tighten immigration rules, the government coalition's 2014 policy statement acknowledges that immigration has contributed to Norway's economic growth. The statement goes on to say, "Immigration is a source of diversity, new ideas and cultural exchange. Variation contributes to new thinking, innovation, and creativity."[175]

For their part, the people at the grassroots found a new way to support each other during the prolonged pain of Breivik's trial. During the proceedings, the murderer claimed that a familiar song among Norwegians, "Children of the Rainbow," was Marxist brainwashing. The song was a translated version of "My Rainbow Race," composed by American folksinger Pete Seeger.

A couple of women in a small Norwegian town went to their central market and began to sing that song. Their action, a mix of sadness and determination, was picked up in other towns and spread rapidly across the nation. Soon there were tens of thousands of people in Oslo, gathered in the rain, standing by the trade union headquarters while holding umbrellas and roses, crying, and singing together the Norwegian version of Seeger's lyrics: "Together shall we live, every sister, brother, / Young children of the rainbow, a fertile land."

13

REACHING FOR HIGH GOALS ON CLIMATE CHANGE

In the spring of 2014, I flew from Iceland to Denmark. The weather was clear. As we approached the Copenhagen airport I looked out the window, alert for seagulls signaling our nearness to land. The objects I saw were white and graceful, but human-made: windmills, with blades slowly turning on tall masts rising from the sea.

On very windy days, Denmark meets all of its electricity needs from wind power and even produces a surplus to export to Germany, another country that is rushing into the twenty-first-century requirement of sustainable energy.[176] Germany is giving up nuclear and preparing to give up coal; to substitute, it's been making rapid strides with solar and still needs other sources, including wind power from Denmark.

Norway and Sweden trade renewables with their Danish cousins. The Nordic mountains across the *Skaggarak* have abundant hydropower, but when Norwegians and Swedes need more electricity, they import wind power from Denmark. When it needs to, Denmark imports hydroelectricity from Norway and Sweden.

Norway would like more wind power, so it is taking advantage of its oil-rig-building expertise to build the world's largest wind turbine, which will generate enough power for 2,000 homes.[177]

The Danes got a head start on wind, traceable to their people's movement that opposed nuclear power in the 1970s. With a history of shipbuilding leaving workers' skills and facilities in good supply, windmills provided an obvious alternative. To kick-start development, the government created an incentive for the grassroots to form local wind energy co-ops, which then proliferated alongside larger projects that were started on the regional and national level.

By 2014, the Danes had 4,737 onshore turbines in a country the size of Maryland, and 519 more offshore. They expect to generate 50 percent of their electricity from wind by 2020.[178] Additionally they invest in tidal, geothermal, biomass, and solar sources, along with practicing conservation.

In 2014, Copenhagen earned the title of world's most environmentally advanced capital city. Even though the city expects to add another 100,000 residents, it also expects to be carbon-neutral by 2025.

The stakes are high, according to a consensus of climate scientists, and Nordic leaders tend to believe scientists. In fact, one might argue that one reason for Nordic economic success over the years has been that social democrats believe in the value of evidence-based rationality, and therefore make a strong national investment in research, big-picture analysis, education, planning, and evaluation.

Nordics know they risk their credibility when they deny inconvenient truths. So when scientists predict that climate change will have enormous impact on economic opportunity and constraints, and carbon pollution can destroy much of what supports civilization as we know it, Nordic governments—sometimes pushed from below—set goals and design alternatives. Both Norway and Sweden fully intend to be carbon-neutral by 2050. By 2013, Sweden was already getting over half of its energy from renewables, while the EU average was 15 percent and the United States even less than that.[179]

UNCONVENTIONAL WISDOM

Conventional wisdom holds that the GDP and energy consumption have similar curves. When an economy grows, its energy use goes up; when it shrinks, energy use falls. A nation, therefore, cannot reduce energy use and at the same time be prosperous. Swedes and Danes are among those who disagree with conventional wisdom.

Sweden reduced its emissions by over 20 percent in the last twenty-five years. During that same period, the Swedish economy grew by more than 50 percent.[180] In the 1990s, Denmark also delinked GDP and energy consumption: the GDP continued to grow while energy consumption flattened. Danes believe that "energy efficiency" became the driver of *both* prosperity and sustainability.

Being practical people, the Danes used a number of tools to get their results. They put high taxes on gas for cars, even though they haven't needed to import oil because of their (modest) stake in the North Atlantic oil fields.

The high tax on gas makes bicycling attractive for many kinds of getting around. Bikes account for half of Copenhagen's commuting trips to school or work. While walking along Copenhagen streets beside an endless stream of whizzing bicycles, I noticed that the abundance means few riders bother to lock their bikes when they park them.

Forbes magazine points out that the Danes' biking actually contributes to the wealth of Copenhagen. "Researchers found that for every kilometer traveled by bike instead of by car, taxpayers saved 7.8 cents in avoided air pollution, accidents, noise and wear and tear on infrastructure. Cyclists in Copenhagen cover an estimated 1.2 million kilometers each day, saving the city more than $34 million each year."[181]

In transportation policy, I saw four goals in action: sustainability, efficiency, cost-saving, and better health through exercise.

Another tool the government used to promote energy efficiency was to hike the tax on electricity, to the point where Danes pay more for electricity than almost anyone in Europe. That in turn motivates businesses to eliminate energy waste and to innovate, and we know that innovation supports economic development.

At one of Copenhagen's numerous sidewalk cafes I interviewed Kristian Weise, the director of the economic think tank CEVEA. I was surprised to see such a young man heading the influential and prolific center, but he already had a range of national and international policy experience before he took the job. He told me that when Danes chose to make energy efficiency their new frontier, private enterprise lined up to participate and turn the initiative into profits. The result was a proliferation of businesses and jobs—more prosperity.

Weise noted that conventional economic thinking in Denmark used to be much like that in other countries, where people assume that a bold leap into reduced energy use would hurt the economy. Then Denmark proved the opposite—startling, and radical. He believes that it couldn't have happened without the visionary intervention of the state. When the state led, private enterprise followed.

I immediately remembered from my own country the almost overnight conversion of the giant U.S. auto industry from automaking to weapons manufacture at the beginning of World War II. The state led, private enterprise followed. *And*, with that massive stimulus economy-wide, the United States emerged from the Great Depression.

Weise told me about the tough negotiations among the nations in the European Union on reducing carbon emissions. Governments wanted an overall goal to reach by 2012. The negotiators finally agreed the overall goal would be reducing emissions to 8 percent below the level of 1990, then they went on to quarrel about how much each nation would contribute to that reduction. Caution ruled.

Weise smiled broadly as he told me that, when the negotiation became stalemated, Denmark issued a challenge. The other national representatives should add up the percentages that *they* could contribute to the overall goal and then, the Danish representative said, *his* country would do the rest![182]

WHERE DOES THIS NORDIC CONFIDENCE COME FROM?

The boldness that the Danish representative showed in European negotiations over global warming shows up again and again in these advanced democratic countries whose parties' job is to realize both freedom and equality.

In the 1990s, Denmark had 10 percent unemployment and the

economy was sluggish. The Social Democratic government stimulated the economy while at the same time putting more pressure on the unemployed to use their time off to prepare themselves for the new jobs being created. The government offered free education and training opportunities. The unemployment rate went down.

Weise told me that the Danish Central Bank president then reported to the Social Democratic prime minister that Denmark was doing as well as it could do. Structural unemployment, the official said, is 6 percent. The prime minister suggested lowering that to 5 percent, or even to 4 percent.

In fact, the rate went to 2 percent!

Politicians representing the working class find that it's a good thing to question neoliberal economic thinking, and overall that has paid off. This gives the politicians confidence, as when Iceland's leftist government defied the IMF's advice and made a remarkable recovery from one of the worst financial collapses in history—a stronger recovery than those in austerity-minded Ireland, Spain, Estonia, and the UK.

On energy, however, I found in Iceland serious division on the left regarding future energy development. About one-third of Iceland's international income comes from fish and another one-third from tourism. Energy presently provides the other third, for example through the hydroelectricity that refines aluminum.

Technological advance means the day may come when Icelandic-generated electricity could be directly exported to Europe. The country's central highlands are largely uninhabited, abundant with glaciers and untapped hydroelectric potential. But Iceland itself doesn't need much more electricity because of its small population and the abundance of geothermal energy for heating.

Icelanders who want to develop the water-power potential of the highlands argue that it could reduce European dependence on fossil fuels. In addition, selling the electricity would bring added income to Iceland, upgrading the level of public services it can provide.

On the other hand, internationally famous Icelandic singer Bjørk has joined other environmentalists in defending the central highland. They believe that using the water resources to generate electricity will inevitably harm the largest wilderness remaining in Europe.

As is true for the rest of us, the descendants of the Vikings face tough choices.

NORWAY AND ITS OIL DILEMMA

Norway is the one of the largest oil exporters on earth. In 2009, petroleum generated 22 percent of Norway's GDP and accounted for 47 percent of its exports. Norway already had widely distributed prosperity when the oil began to flow in the 1970s, and many Norwegians value the options that come with this new, shared wealth.

They are especially proud that they've used their oil money to create the world's largest sovereign pension fund, held in trust for future generations of Norwegians when the oil runs out. The pension fund by 2015 had grown to $900 billion and was widely invested around the world, with social responsibility and environmental criteria. However, if Norway stopped drilling and left the remaining oil in the ground, the growth of this pot of money would slow down.[183]

I caught up with Truls Gulowsen, the director of Norwegian

Greenpeace, in Oslo's Central Railroad station. A rugged-looking young man, Truls was wearing jeans and hiking boots and carrying a large backpack. He was about to start a vacation and was carrying the ticket for his train.

I knew that Greenpeace keeps a stern eye on Statoil, Norway's biggest player in oil and natural gas, which also buys stakes in oil fields in other countries. It has joined the global norm of multinational oil companies ceaselessly exploring and drilling wherever they can. One of those places is the Arctic, where melting ice has made exploitation more feasible.

I asked Truls what he thought about Norway's growth in this global game of oil production. He told me with a rueful smile that he found it alarming and wrongheaded. He went on to describe the Arctic situation, which is even more problematic than conditions in the North Sea. While it is *legal* for Norway to drill in the Arctic, the consequences would be terrible if an accident happened, given how fragile the ecology is and how tough it would be to clean up a spill.

Truls told me he was part of the crew on a Greenpeace ship that sailed close enough to a Norwegian drilling rig in the Arctic to hinder the drilling. He acknowledged that the Greenpeace crew was taking a risk, but said its mission is to create enough drama so people will take a fresh look at the situation. "We understand we may be arrested for that, but we need to take strong nonviolent action to make the point," he said.

Few would say that Norway's oil drilling has been irresponsible. The earlier finds of oil and natural gas were in the North Sea, which is extremely deep and also does not have a robust ecosystem. The Norwegian firm Statoil therefore invested in an additional fallback safety mechanism on its oil rigs which, had BP done the same on its rigs in the United States, might have prevented the disaster in the Gulf of Mexico.

In the hearings in the United States after that BP spill, the corporation revealed that it had decided against installing an additional fall-back safety mechanism in order to save money. Statoil, by contrast, is largely owned by a democratic and accountable government, so cutting corners on safety and environmental impact is not an acceptable option.

Still, Truls believes that the bottom line belongs to nature. Climate scientists have determined that the amount of oil and natural gas reserves that have *already* been identified by Norwegians and others will, if burned, take humankind over the brink.

Norway's most widely known literary writer, Karl Ove Knausgaard, helped to lead a resurgent effort in 2015 to end Arctic drilling. Knausgaard calls the drilling "shortsighted and stupid."[184] Anyone might ask why hardworking and productive Norwegians should still support further oil exploration if no one wants the climate outcome that will result?

EARLY WARNINGS LEAD TO COAL DIVESTMENT

Norwegians were among the first in the world to raise the alarm about climate change. Gro Brundtland, the doctor twice elected prime minister in the 1980s, whom Norwegians called "mother," pushed the United Nations to take climate change seriously. She led the UN's Brundtland Commission and laid the groundwork for the Kyoto conference.[185]

Through visionaries like her, Norwegian political culture became so sensitive to environmental issues that a government actually fell in 2000 over the question of whether additional energy should be generated by waterfalls or natural gas.

After Norwegians' head start, it's easy to see how environmentalists might now feel disappointed. I sought out a professor of environmental policy in her office at the University of Oslo. Karen O'Brien started studying climate change twenty-five years ago as a graduate student at the University of Wisconsin. She believes that Norway is not giving the exemplary leadership to the world that we might expect, given its legacy. "I see Swedes and Danes moving ahead of Norway in recycling, subsidizing public transport, promoting bicycling, and setting ambitious goals for reducing carbon emissions," she told me.

Thinking about the small population of Norway, living amidst mountains, I asked her how worried Norwegians really are about the impact of climate change at home. Professor O'Brien said that Norwegian leaders underestimate the impact within Norway itself, and therefore implement halfhearted policies and operate internationally in a "fix-it" mode that plays on their image as do-gooders and peacemakers.

An example of global "fixing" is Norway's $1.5 billion rainforest fund. Knowing that some countries in the developing world are financially pressured to destroy their forests for profit, Norway gives grants to governments to set aside vast tracts of forest as national parks.[186]

In 2011, the Ministry set goals to exceed its Kyoto commitment by 10 percent in the first period and to cut emissions in 2020 to only 30 percent of Norway's 1990-level emissions. Its carbon-neutrality goal is 2050. Norway is not currently on track to achieve that goal, but in 2013, carbon emissions dropped to their lowest level since 1995.

Norway's largest private pension fund, KLP, divested from coal in 2014. In the same year, its public Government Pension Fund Global (GPFG) divested from fifty-two coal companies, including the two primary U.S. mountaintop-removal companies in Appalachia, reducing its coal company holdings by one-third. Truls Gulowsen immediately criticized the GPFG for not dropping coal completely. Norway's largest environmental organization, Future in Our Hands, agreed. Arild Hermstad said, "The GPFG's coal investments are tiny in relationship to its total holdings, but the problems they cause around the world are huge."[187] In May 2015, the Storting decided to divest all the fund's holdings in coal, making it the largest fund ever to make a fossil fuel divestment.[188]

SWEDES PUSH ON GLOBAL, GRASSROOTS, AND CARBON TAX LEVELS

Considering the activist role that Sweden has played in the UN, it's not surprising that the Swedish pension fund AP4 catalyzed the portfolio decarbonization coalition through the UN's environmental program. By 2015, the coalition had gathered large institutional investors with over $600 billion of assets to commit to substantial divestment of their carbon assets. To set a strong example, the pension fund began to reduce its U.S. carbon assets by 50 to 80 percent in the short run, aiming toward 100 percent as soon as possible.[189]

Sweden has also been paying attention to grassroots-level cuts in carbon emissions. It has been choosing sites as laboratories; for example, the city of Kalmar, population 60,000, has its own carbonneutrality goal with national experts helping it out.[190]

A larger urban laboratory is in Sweden's capital city of Stockholm: the Hammarby Sjøstad waterfront district. The neighborhood uses biogas derived from wastewater to run kitchen stoves in 1,000 residences and has enough left over to help fuel public transportation. The district's full, integrated model is expected to be completed by 2016, but has already in 2007 won the World Clean Energy Award for innovative, practical projects that move renewable energy into the mainstream.

Swedish spokesperson Josefin Wangel commented about their work, "Most of the technical solutions aren't that hi-tech or sci-fi or special. What is special is the overall eco-model approach."[191]

Sweden, Denmark, and Norway were early adopters of carbon taxes in 1991; Iceland followed in 2009. Norway had some of the highest carbon taxes in the world, which raised the cost of energy production significantly. That made carbon capture economically feasible, at least in principle.

In May 2012, Norway inaugurated a facility that tests carbon capture and sequestration technologies. Skeptics claim such technology is impossible. Norway has invested more than $1 billion in the "impossible technology," however, and claims that it is on the verge of becoming viable. If the Norwegian plant proves successful, the technology could be used around the world, further benefiting Norway's economy.

In the meantime, its Environmental Ministry became dissatisfied with the results of its carbon tax, calculating that the years between 1991 and 1999 show a carbon-emissions drop of only 2.3 percent. Norwegians often call themselves stubborn, and their next step reinforced that image in my mind. In 2012, they decided to go for a critical impact, and doubled down on their carbon taxes.

CANADIAN TAR SANDS

One hot-button issue in Norway's oil extraction has been Statoil's decision to invest in the Canadian tar sands, which produce far more emissions in the extraction process than Norway's own North Sea oil. Environmental groups bitterly fought the decision. Despite the pressure, the government refused to dictate Statoil's investments. Greenpeace went to the Statoil shareholders' meeting and directly urged divesting from tar sands. In 2012, Statoil increased its production from tar sands by 60 percent.

More Norwegians joined the fight against tar-sands investment. In 2013, Norway's second largest insurance company, *Storebrand*, voted to exclude thirteen coal and six tar-sands companies from their investments. The reasons they gave were not just mitigation of environmental damage, but hard-headed financial priorities as well. Storebrand's head of sustainable investments explained, "If global ambitions to limit global warming to less than 2 degrees Celsius become a reality, many fossil fuel resources will become unburnable and their financial value will be dramatically reduced."

Finally, in 2014, Statoil pulled out.[192] Then in February 2015, the 800-pound gorilla spoke: the largest sovereign wealth fund in the world, Norway's pension fund (GPFG), announced that it had dropped its tar-sands investments because of both carbon emissions and destruction of water. The fund also divested palm oil and other climate change–related holdings, a total of 114 corporations. The practical Norwegians acknowledged in their statement that most fossil-fuel reserves must be left in the ground anyway, which from an investment point of view means stranded assets.[193]

GETTING AROUND EFFICIENTLY WHILE
SUPPORTING FREEDOM AND EQUALITY

Because the small population of Norway is widely scattered across an area the size of Great Britain, transportation poses a continuing difficulty in reducing emissions. One useful tool has been the policy of maintaining the highest car taxes in Europe—an SUV in Norway costs four times what it costs in the United States.

Another step is to encourage the use of electric and hybrid vehicles. Very high taxes on gas are helpful, and so is developing the infrastructure to support electric cars, trucks, and buses. Norwegians plan to put battery-charging stands around the country; electric cars will be charged in twenty minutes instead of seven hours.

More plug-ins require more electricity, but increasing the use of water power is opposed by Norwegians who defend their pristine mountains and waterways. That tension in turn puts more pressure on wind power to step into the gap.

People who own fully electric cars in Norway get free public parking and are allowed to use bus and taxi lanes. They don't need to pay tolls. They are exempt from sales tax, taxation as company cars, the annual road tax, and non-recurring vehicle fees.[194]

While reducing the carbon impact of cars, Norway continues its fundamental reliance on public transportation. The 1999 ban on sprawl, including large shopping malls outside city centers, helps.

Within the framework of that national law, most land-use decisions are made on the level of the municipal government, whether that government is in a city as large as Oslo or in a small

village. The decision-making is democratic rather than largely influenced by corporate interests, another power question that was
settled by the outcome of the class struggle in the 1920s and '30s.

Land use and public transportation are two more energy-
efficient ways that Norwegians express the values of both equality and freedom. Placing stores in centers of population density
means more people have a chance to shop near their homes. More
gain the freedom not to own a car. Norwegians also have many
places to hike, ski, and enjoy other aspects of nature. Their individual freedom is enhanced at the same time, as nature itself is
preserved through reduction of harmful pollutants.

Land-use and public-transportation policies support strong
communities and also, for individuals, better health by increasing
exercise and encouraging less time in cars eating fast food. Vital
communities and better health reduce health-care costs for Norway as a whole, an economic matter of some consequence, as in
any society.

Of course, equality and freedom are not the only values that
the Nordics hold dear. The descendants of the Vikings do care
about community, solidarity, and nature for their own sake. These
countries demonstrate is that, when democracy is securely in
place, it becomes possible to create an economic design that supports all five of those values while moving toward a sustainable
energy future.

In each of the countries, the debate continues: are we moving
toward sustainability fast enough?

14

HOW RELEVANT IS THE NORDIC MODEL TO THE UNITED STATES?

On returning home from research trips to the Nordic countries, I have given lectures to diverse groups, including hip urban young adults, suburban soccer moms, retirement communities, and even a small-town Rotary Club and a college faculty.

Listeners peppered me with questions and challenges about the Nordic model's relevance to the United States. Many emphasized ways that the Nordics are different from the United States, like small size, homogeneity, culture. Other listeners wondered whether Americans could mobilize enough power to make changes as significant as those that the Nordics achieved.

In this chapter, I'll share my responses to the most frequent questions.

Q. We have a substantially different culture from that of the Nordics. How can their model be expected to work here?

I agree that our country is unique, with its own history and mix of traditions. I also agree that no system offers a blueprint for others to copy. As we learn from the best practices of others, we still need to craft our version.

It is possible, however, to exaggerate cultural barriers to innovation. Consider some of the successes other countries have sometimes had in borrowing from us. Ken Burns described on PBS one of the standouts: national parks on a grand scale were invented in the United States and then picked up by *two hundred* other countries.[195] The United States pioneered voluntary service abroad, leading to its best-known example, the Peace Corps.[196] A number of other countries borrowed the idea.

In turn, the United States has adapted many practices first developed by others. The first modern urban public transportation system probably appeared in Nantes, France, in the early 1800s.[197] The foundation of the modern public library system was laid by the British Parliament in the 1850 Public Libraries Act.[198] Germany invented the modern social security system in 1883.[199]

Bullying has become a worrying issue in the United States, and some schools in Pennsylvania and New Jersey scanned the globe looking for best practices. They found the "Olweus Bullying Prevention Program" invented by Norwegians in the 1970s. The American schools tried it out and discovered that the low-cost program made a substantial difference.[200]

For fifteen years, I crisscrossed the globe as a trainer and consultant and met many international business and nongovernmental consultants who I began to see as honeybees. They were cross-pollinating. Sometimes a policy or best practice did not travel well, they said, but there were plenty of successes.

My conclusion is that because cultural difference does matter, we should let that fact influence the model we create for our country—but not stop exploring the potential of others' successes. One advantage of global diversity is that it produces a greater abundance of experiments to assess. As we consider adapting others' best practices, we would want to improve on them by using our own strengths.

The temptation we need to avoid, however, is diluting others' proven practices instead of improving them. The example of public health insurance clearly shows the downside of half-measures, and also reveals that the claims of culture can be exaggerated.

Many countries created governmental health insurance programs after World War II, for cultures as different as France and Germany. Within the United Kingdom, the system had to deal with *internal* diversity, since Scotland, Wales, and England were (and are still) very different from one another. No two national health programs were just alike, but they had in common the universal, single-payer approach of relying on their governments to simplify the accounting and meet individual needs in the whole society. According to the numbers gathered by OECD researchers, that approach to health care is much more extensive, and far less expensive, than the approach we are used to in the United States.

President Harry S. Truman proposed the universal governmental approach for the United States in the same period during which other nations were adopting it, after World War II. Special interests groups, including the medical profession, vetoed his proposal.

Two decades later, in 1966, the United States started Medicare, a limited borrowing of others' successful systems. Surveys tell us that the 50 million Medicare members rate their health insurance satisfaction higher than do people on private insurance plans. Studies by economists and the Congressional Budget Office find that Medicare is in fact a far more efficient way of providing health care for elders than the private market.[201]

It was not cultural difference that delayed governmental provision of health insurance for American elders. The satisfaction reported by elders could be matched for everyone if the United States had Medicare for all; it would mean care for everyone, enormous savings, and the United States at last joining the top tier of health practice in the world.[202] The reason the United States has failed to adopt universal health insurance is not because it violates our culture, but because special interests prevented the majority from getting what it was ready for.

The same could be said of many Nordic-like policies, which could fit just fine into American culture but were vetoed by special interests. Attacks on smart practices used by others routinely show up in this country for no valid cultural reason, like cutting budgets for building badly needed infrastructure. (Which American cultural value is threatened by modernizing our transportation, or electrical grid?) The educational program Head Start, validated by years of research, is threatened each year not because it is un-American to want the best for our children, nor because we Americans love the increased delinquency and crime when the children grow older without Head Start. Educating poor children simply does not line up with the intention to maximize profit.

In creating our own economic model that supports freedom and equality, I conclude that we can pay attention to culture without allowing "cultural difference" to become a smokescreen hiding the cold interplay of special interests.

Q. The Nordic countries are quite small compared with ours. Doesn't scale matter, and doesn't the internal homogeneity of their societies matter, too?

I made a startling discovery related to this question on an ordinary day in Oslo. On my way to a conference room to interview Jon M. Hippe and Tone Fløtten at the Fafø Research Foundation, I paused to look at framed photographs on the walls. One of them showed a Chinese delegation meeting with the researchers. Not only is China the most populous nation in the world, but it also contains substantial cultural diversity.

I immediately put the question of scale and homogeneity to my hosts. Fafø director Hippe told me they had raised those issues with their guests. The Chinese economists and policy experts said that sometimes scale matters, and sometimes it doesn't—it depends on the issue. They believe that they have much to learn from Norway.

I immediately thought of social security, which works in Norway and also in the United States even though our population is sixty-four times bigger. University of Oslo professor Lars Mjøset told me that Norwegians have relied on public banks and credit unions, and in the United States, 100 million people have joined credit unions, thereby saving $10 billion per year on fees and interest rates. According to the American Customer Satisfaction Index, credit unions get higher ratings than banks do from their users "on nearly every aspect of the customer experience."[203]

Another example where scale is not a major issue is clean air. The United States used to have famously dirty air, then made huge strides in cleanup through a national program called the Fresh Air Act, enforced by the Environmental Protection Agency. In fact, our country is well-known for very large-scale government projects that are the envy of many countries, such as the Interstate Highway System started under President Dwight Eisenhower.

Now our infrastructure is falling apart; the McKinsey Global Institute estimates that we need to spend an additional $150 billion a year on infrastructure to meet our needs. The American Society of Civil Engineers gave a grade of D-plus to our infrastructure in 2013, and since then there have been more budget cutbacks, such as the Congressional move to cut back on Amtrak immediately after a fatal, and preventable, crash in Pennsylvania in 2015 for lack of an infrastructure improvement. Europeans typically spend about 5 percent of their gross domestic product on infrastructure, while the United States spends half that![204]

A big and wealthy country like ours can take on many projects that are beyond the reach of smaller countries, which makes all the more remarkable the sight of our transportation infrastructure falling behind. The *Los Angeles Times* reports that in 2015 the Central Japan Railway tested magnetic levitation trains that exceeded 350 miles per hour. [205] There are many ways in which the United States could use its advantages of scale to *exceed* the achievements of the Nordics; for example, we can end carbon pollution by using our vast access to solar energy.

What I've just said also responds to the question about the assumed advantage that homogeneity gives economies that promote equality and freedom. For example, how does making higher education free depend on homogeneity? For years in the United States, free higher education was offered in the most culturally diverse place in the nation: New York City. The top-ranked college where I taught, Swarthmore, deliberately *increased* the racial and class diversity of its student body because the college knew that diversity promotes a higher-quality education for all, including for rich white students who otherwise miss an abundance of perspectives. The choice to include class diversity required Swarthmore to offer free education to low-income students—simply good educational policy.

Free education can be offered on a national scale, as was done in the Nordic countries *when they had far less wealth available than we do.* The United States, which once offered free quality higher education in many state institutions, is currently going in the opposite direction, defunding higher education.

HOMOGENEITY AND EQUALITY.

Wilkinson and Pickett suggest another way of thinking about the role of homogeneity: compare Portugal and Spain.[206] The two countries have many similarities: they share the Iberian peninsula, the Roman Catholic religion, and similar ancient ancestral ethnicities. They are racially seen as the same, have been traders who built empires, and each had a political dictatorship until recently. Compare their societies on equality, however, and it turns out that they are very different: Portugal is one of the most unequal nations in the world, while Spain is average.

The two nations differ in other important respects, but again in ways that contradict the notion that homogeneity and small size pay off in building an egalitarian society. Spain has over four times Portugal's population size, contains sub-nations that still speak their own language and struggle for autonomy, includes more native-born citizens from its former colonies including racially different Africans and Latin Americans, and has a higher percentage of recent immigrants. Spain is larger and far more diverse than is Portugal, *yet has been more successful in developing an egalitarian society.*

DIVERSITY AND ECONOMIC DEVELOPMENT

I pointed out earlier that homogeneity is actually a liability when it comes to economic development; innovation flourishes in the presence of multiple perspectives. And as we saw in the chapter on entrepreneurs, start-ups flourish in Norway not because of historical homogeneity but because of present-day support from an economic system that begets equality and freedom.

The greater cultural diversity in the United States in fact gives us an economic edge over the Nordic countries, if we choose to use it. Those who worry that the U.S. rate of innovation is in trouble might ask about cutbacks in American research and development budgets.

California's lieutenant governor, Gavin Newsome, tells the story of how proud he was of upgrading governmental computer capacity during his two terms as San Francisco's mayor. Toward the end of his period as mayor, he crossed paths with Estonia's premier. Newsome bragged to his guest, describing specifically the breakthrough systems he was installing. The Estonian remarked casually that his government had installed the same capacity years before.

I heard the humbled Newsome tell this story on public radio as his way of inviting fellow Americans out of our nationalistic bubble.

In short, like the Chinese delegation that came to Oslo, we can be open to learn from others as we improve our country. We also can take account of differences of scale and degree of cultural diversity as we design a new economy that supports freedom and equality. Robert Kennedy put it this way: "There are those who look at things the way they are and ask why . . . I dream of things that never were and ask why not?"[207]

Medical epidemiologists Wilkinson and Pickett offer a tantalizing picture for the United States if we were to adopt policies that resulted in reducing our income inequality to the level of the Nordics and produced similar correlations: prison populations reduced by 75 percent, rates of mental illness and obesity cut by almost two-thirds, a 75 percent increase in the number of people who feel they can trust others, and an average increase in longevity while working the equivalent of two months less per year![208]

Q. In recent decades, haven't most Americans moved away from wanting what the Nordics have?

The major political parties have in recent decades backed away from anything close to the Nordic model. The Democratic and Republican policies are reflected in both the economists' numbers and the daily lives of the American majority.

The trend is clear. Joseph E. Stiglitz has been chief economist of the World Bank and the chair of President Bill Clinton's Council of Economic Advisers. He observes that "the United States not only has the highest level of inequality among the advanced industrial countries, but the level of its inequality is increasing in absolute terms relative to that in other countries."[209]

To find out what most Americans actually want, we need to bypass the politicians and ask the people themselves.

Stiglitz reviewed the opinion research and found that the American majority believes there is too much inequality. These views "were held broadly across very different demographic groups, men and women, Democrats and Republicans, and those at the top and those with lower incomes." In one of the studies, participants were shown two different income distributions, in the form of pie charts. Without saying so, one chart reflected the distribution in Sweden and the second chart that of the United States. 92 percent said they preferred the first.[210]

How important is it to the public to change policies regarding inequality? A *New York Times*–CBS News poll reported that 65 percent of Americans believe the gap between rich and poor is a problem that needs immediate attention. In the same poll, 74 percent said corporations have too much influence in American life and politics; only 3 percent disagreed.[211]

For the past couple of decades, elected officials have been cutting taxes for the wealthy, but a *Washington Post* poll in 2014 showed a majority of people in favor of tax *increases*.[212] A study of Asian Americans who earn over $250,000 per year found that 62 percent supported raising taxes on their category to provide more government services.[213] A 2014 Gallup poll showed that even among Republicans, 45 percent believe that upper-income people paid too little in taxes.[214]

For decades the airwaves have been full of anti-government rhetoric insisting that only private business can be "job creators." However, almost half those polled in 2014 wanted the government to provide a job to any citizen who cannot find work in the private sector. Such a policy would actually be more radical than that of the Nordics![215]

In 1994, conservative Republicans took control of Congress.

When polltakers asked a random sample of the American people whether it is the responsibility of government to care for those who can't take care of themselves, 57 percent thought so. Then change happened, in two directions. In the following decade, both parties shifted toward greater conservatism. The people, in contrast, *shifted during that time toward the Nordic model*: by 2007, the number believing that government should take responsibility for the poor rose to 69 percent. Over two-thirds of the public said government should guarantee every citizen enough to eat and a place to sleep.[216]

Some politicians claim that a majority of citizens fear big government and want to shrink it. However, two-thirds said in 2007 that they want the government to guarantee health insurance for all citizens. Citizens are urged to beware of governmental regulation, yet three-quarters *even of self-identified Republican small-business owners* said they favored raising the minimum wage by more than $2. In 2014, voters in four Republican states did raise the minimum wage: Alaska, Arkansas, Nebraska, and South Dakota.[217]

The Nordics are famous for high taxes, and U.S. politicians claim that our people would not tolerate that, but some polls show otherwise. In Pennsylvania, a staggering 83 percent said they wanted to maintain support for public schools even in bad times, and are willing to raise state taxes to do so.[218]

The degree to which the leadership of both national parties are out of touch with the majority is remarkable. In 2014, national polls revealed that a majority of Americans want to address global warming. A year later the Senate appointed its leading climate-change denier to be head of the Senate's committee on the environment.

Polls in 2014 revealed a strong class difference among Republicans, with many of the blue-collar males who become Republicans in recent decades refusing to sign on to the 1 percent's agenda. In addition, 45 percent of Republicans believe that the rich should pay more in taxes. More Republicans favor increased spending on Social Security, Medicare, education, and infrastructure than favor cutting those programs. *The New Yorker*'s George Packer sums up the evidence this way: "Although government activism is anathema to conservative donors and Grover Norquist, it's fine with a lot of Republicans making less than fifty thousand dollars a year."[219]

The mainstream media continue to report the discourse of the political class as if it accurately reflects what Americans think. I find that many people in my audiences who think that Nordic-style policies are sensible have no idea that they are in fact members of the American majority. They assume that their views are shared only by a small minority. It was therefore a large surprise that Presidential candidate Senator Bernie Sanders, a democratic socialist, attracted the largest crowds of any candidate in the Democratic race in the summer of 2015 despite the reluctance of the mass media to cover him.

If Americans were allowed to hear the Nordic story, even larger majorities would want to adapt that model for this country. North Dakota, the state with the largest population of Norwegian Americans, offers evidence for that. When North Dakota struck it rich in oil it knew from Norway's experience that it is possible to gain public revenue from the oil and at the same time avoid dependency on that source. It therefore created what it calls a Legacy Fund for use in the longer run. Boom-and-bust has little allure when a population knows enough about the Nordic model to know that a much better alternative exists.[220]

In short, multiple sources suggest that the major political parties are lost in their bubble of manipulation and money. A majority of Americans do want the greater equality of opportunity and freedom that the Nordics have.

Q. But don't Americans distrust government too much to want it to play a larger role?

The Nordic model's dependence on the state can easily be overblown. I've described earlier the enormous vitality of the cooperative sector as well as the under-the-radar activity of civil society. In these ways, Norway, for example, is similar to the United States, whose sector of cooperatives is once again growing. Political economist Gar Alperovitz' important book *What Then Must We Do?* describes an American abundance of thriving co-ops and innovative public-private partnerships that are breathing new life even into deindustrialized areas that corporations abandoned decades ago.[221] As in the Nordic countries, cooperatives show they can scale up as well as down, and provide the flexibility that corporations at their best provide, and more staying power than most corporations are interested in.

On the other hand, the widespread American distrust of government is real. A century ago, most Norwegians also distrusted their government, as did their Viking cousins. They had every reason to distrust government when they realized that the government consistently served the economic elite instead of the people as a whole. The government failed to hold up its end of the implicit social contract between citizen and state.

Norwegians are now happy to pay high taxes because they

trust the new political class they have installed. They gave the Labor Party a chance to come through and it did, abundantly, forcing the other parts of the political landscape to shift significantly to the left in order not to remain completely isolated on the margin. During my interview with the head of the leading Conservative think tank Citiva, I was struck by Kristin Clemet's observation. She is a prominent conservative politician and said that, in Norway, President Obama would be considered right-wing. She said she would be happy to have him as a member of her party.

The Swedish political spectrum is similar. And in Denmark the joke I heard making the rounds is that the multi-party Danish system is composed entirely of social democratic parties!

As I mentioned previously, Norwegians see themselves as "a nation of complainers." They don't expect their state to be anywhere close to perfect, and have abundant built-in mechanisms to force transparency and accountability. This realism—built on a foundation of peoples who empowered themselves through creating mass movements that forced nonviolent change—makes Norway, Sweden, and Denmark democratic and minimizes corruption. The result is government people can trust.

My conclusion is that the question of trust in government is incorrectly framed. According to a poll reported by *Harper's Magazine* in 1966, two-thirds of Americans said they trusted the government most of the time. Only one-fifth say that now.[222] This dramatic decline is explained by other polls showing majorities, even of Republicans, believing that the government has been prioritizing the interests of the economic elite.[223]

Economic democracy produces governments people can trust. Recent elections in the Nordic countries attract up to twice the percentage of voters as our elections in the United States. The Nordic example shows that people can make a U-turn on the trust issue after a power shift delivers democratic governance.

Q. Isn't the growth of inequality just the result of market forces like globalization and technology? Why blame the government for that?

Nobel Prize–winning economist Paul Krugman challenges the conventional wisdom that exploding inequality in the United States and the UK in the 1980s and '90s was driven by two things: a rising demand for highly skilled labor—an aspect of spreading information technology—and imported goods like textiles replacing the need for less-skilled labor. By contrast, he points out that Canada, France, Japan, the Netherlands, Spain, and Switzerland lived with the same market forces and did not experience steep inequality growth. The same is true in the Nordic countries.

The UK's experience is relevant to this question. After the harrowing experience of World War II, during which the British experienced enormous solidarity and the British Communist Party grew substantially, the UK turned to its social democratic Labour Party and aimed for an economic system much like that of the Nordics.

The Brits didn't get there, but they made sufficient strides so that the UK shows up in most international ratings in a better light than the United States. In his article refuting globalization and technology as causes of our ills, Krugman writes that the UK and the United States experienced a similar source for their declines in equality: attacks on trade unions, abandoning productivity sharing agreements with labor, and the offensive by the political right with resulting changes in taxes and benefits.[224]

We don't usually think of liberal Krugman and centrist Harvard economist Lawrence Summers in the same camp, but Summers's comment on taxes as a wealth-equalizer on national public radio bears repeating. Summers was Secretary of the Treasury under President Bill Clinton. When asked about French economist Thomas Piketty's proposal to reduce the wealth gap by creating a "wealth tax" for rich people, Summers said it was a good idea. He also said it was not politically possible in the United States.[225]

Q. The Nordics used the power of the vote to create their model. How can we do that with big money corrupting our system?

This question makes two assumptions, one correct and one not. Getting this right opens the door to good old-fashioned American optimism, by pointing to the real source of hope.

The correct assumption made by the questioner is that big money corrupts our system. This is not new. With its *Citizens United* decision the Supreme Court opened the floodgates for billions of dollars to enter the electoral system. But the evidence shows that the problem goes much deeper than that.

In 2014, two U.S. political scientists released a broad empirical study that reveals who actually has the say in public policy. Martin Gilens of Princeton and Benjamin I. Page of Northwestern examined the 1,779 specific policy issues that came to a head for national decision over the two decades between 1981 and 2002, long before the current money rush. On each issue they determined from opinion polls and other evidence what the majority of the public wanted and what the economic elite wanted. When those two views differed, the scholars wanted to know whose view prevailed. They took into account the fact that ordinary citizens often combine to form mass-based interest groups like the American Association of Retired Persons (AARP).

What they found was that, when there was a difference, the economic elite—and not the majority—almost always got their way.

Even the mass-based interest groups had little or no independent influence. In the scholars' words, "In the United States, our findings indicate, the majority does *not* rule—at least in the causal sense of actually determining policy outcomes."[226]

The BBC account of the study used the word "oligarchy" to describe the findings of the research, although Gilens and Page did not reach a conclusion on whether it is the top 1 percent or the top one-tenth of 1 percent who are the most influential within the category "economic elite."

The new study flatly contradicts what high school and college teachers taught in my day, and probably in yours: that the United States is a pluralist democracy in which decisions are made legislatively as a result of shifting coalitions of interest groups including the majority of Americans. The Princeton study's more accurate picture of reality is sobering, but it is also freeing. The study invites us to let go of frustration and the discouragement felt by many Americans who keep returning to the electoral well in hopes of change, only to find that the well is dry. It is not our fault. The U.S. electoral system truly is rigged against progressive change.

The incorrect assumption from my questioner is that the Nordics used the power of the vote to change their economies and societies. Like us, a century ago the Norwegians, Danes, Swedes, and Icelanders all had electoral systems that pretended to be responsive to the people, but were not. They all came to realize that their "liberal democracies" were in fact oligarchies, incapable of birthing what is now called the Nordic model.

In each country, the people took to the streets to force an opening for the will of the majority. The Norwegians, Danes, and Swedes went the farthest, displacing their economic elite as the hegemonic force directing society. Once they did that, they had the political space to create a new economic model.[227]

Iceland showed its people-power more recently when, after their 2008 crash, they took to the streets and refused to accept austerity, high unemployment, and a stagnant economy. If Americans had done the same after our own crash of 2008, we could have narrowed the wealth gap as the Icelanders did theirs, kept families in their homes, retained high wage-earners in high-paying jobs, avoided skyrocketing college debt, broken up banks and imposed rigorous regulation on them, and reduced levels of mental and physical illness. But Americans had failed to learn from our own historical legacy of nonviolent direct action that forced change when the electoral channel was clogged.

At any time we choose, Americans could decide to learn from our own abundant experience of people-power triumphing despite harsh opposition. In the 1960s, the civil rights movement faced down the largest terrorist movement in U.S. history, the Ku Klux Klan, as well as lawless police. Brave African Americans with white allies won gains and took casualties, while a largely indifferent federal government looked on. Finally the federal government was forced to act—by that same civil rights movement.[228]

Frances Fox Piven, the former head of the American Sociological Association, has shown that many gains that we Americans take for granted were the results of the turbulent 1960s and '70s, as well as the flourishing mass movements of the 1930s.[229] A short list would include social security, Medicare, limits on the length of the work week, rights for people with different abilities, rights for black people and others of color, rights for women and elders and children. All those gains resulted from movements using the leverage of nonviolent action. Two of the most distinguished scholarly books on inequality conclude that only social movements can overcome the economic elite's power and privilege.[230]

Some gains made by Americans in the 1960s and '70s—gains that depended on direct action and that were in the majority-supported direction of the Nordic model—were lost in the decades since the 1970s. During the 1980s, "Reagan revolution," several important movements went on the defensive in an effort to keep previously won gains. As the wily old strategist Mohandas Gandhi pointed out long ago, justice-seekers cannot win by going on the defensive.

Billionaire Warren E. Buffett described the post-seventies era in his 2006 wide-ranging interview with Ben Stein of *The New York Times*. Stein noted that, when unfair tax rates are discussed, some people accuse others of being engaged in class warfare. Buffett replied, "There's class warfare, all right, but it's my class, the rich class, that's making war, and we're winning."[231]

That was 2006, and Mr. Buffett's class has multiplied its wins since then. In the "recovery" after the financial sector's crash in 2008, the wealth gap grew even more. In contrast, Iceland became more equal as it picked up the pieces after its crash and returned to prosperity.

In the United States after 2008, most progressives fell back on lobbying and the electoral arena, clearly the wrong venue. Further, they failed to learn from either Gandhi or our own history: they tried to protect previous gains, instead of going on the offensive as Americans did after the crash of 1929. After 2008 freedom and equality continued to lose ground in our country.[232]

The good news is that not all American movements forgot the American legacy of what works when the ballot box does not. The lesbian, gay, bisexual, and transgender (LGBT) movement staged its first national demonstration at Independence Hall on July 4, 1965. While the movement did selectively use electoral means later on, the activists' remarkable progress rested mainly on their unstinting use of nonviolent action. This very American movement arguably ranks with the best of the Nordic movements in its use of people-power, and helps us to answer the listener's question about leverage.

The tactics included sit-ins and street demonstrations. Countless individuals, including me in 1973, undermined the oppression by "coming out of the closet." The nature of homosexual and gender injustice depends heavily on maintaining a cultural narrative that renders otherness invisible. Coming out, therefore, is an act of noncooperation in the classical Gandhian sense (refusing to participate in an oppressive system), and yet is accessible in everyday settings. Decade after decade since the 1960s, LGBT people have been coming out of the closet despite a near-toxic homophobic atmosphere, courageously performing this action millions of times in one of the longest-running confrontations in history.[233] When Republican elected officials desert their party's stand against gay rights, they routinely acknowledge the power of friends and family coming out of the closet.

As with the civil rights and labor movements in their day of strong nonviolent campaigns, LGBT people experienced imprisonment, injury, and death in their struggle. As Dr. King used to say, "Freedom is not free." LGBT people challenged oppression thousands of years old by steadily going on the offensive with multiple nonviolent tactics. They continue to reap stunningly rapid change by taking the offensive. In 2015, both Indiana and Arkansas passed legislation that arguably permitted discrimination against LGBT people; the counterattack by gays and allies was fierce and both states backed off. Some movements at that point might rest on its laurels, but a headline in the *Philadelphia Inquirer* tells a different story: "Gay-rights *push follows* successes." (Italics mine.)

Gandhi would be proud of the LGBT movement's strategic smarts. The example is a challenge to other movements: find your own creative nonviolent tactics and take the offensive![234]

Q. In the United States, the movements of the 1930s and '60s did not gain the significant power shift achieved by the Nordics. Why would another round of turbulence give us a better chance for genuine democracy?

Conditions are very different now than they were in those days, and some of the changes favor an outcome that leads to greater freedom and equality. Here are five ways that today's circumstances are quite different from those of the 1960s.

Then, the prevailing order still had enormous legitimacy. The overall context of the 1960s contained remarkable prosperity and expansion of opportunity. Nearly everyone saw the United States as the best of all possible worlds: "There's nowhere to go but up."

This legitimacy was reinforced on the ideological front by "American exceptionalism." Princeton historian Kevin Cruse has described the religious dimension in detailing "how corporate America created Christian America."[235]

Early in his career, Dr. King in his speeches accepted the American Dream and demanded access for African Americans. Only later did he question the economic structure and urge us to rethink our attachment to free-market capitalism. After all, in the 1950s and '60s, wages were rising, higher education was cheap (and sometimes free), bipartisan problem-solving reigned in Washington. The 1960s ferment was a "revolution of rising expectations."

In that context, many older and calmer minds believed that the United States had the correct political economic model and that impatient young people just needed some maturity to realize that some piecemeal reforms like a "war on poverty" would take care of our major problems.

In contrast, today's older people see widespread evidence of stuckness, even general deterioration. Many of their children have dimmer life prospects than they themselves had as young people. It is obvious that the United States is falling in international ratings of equality and freedom and that the policies of both parties are dominated by the economic elite.

Everyone complains about the "gridlock" in Washington and notes that cadidates who promise to "reach across the aisle" fail to do so when they arrive at the House and Senate. Dysfunction increases on a state level as well. A trio of researchers investigated the question: Might increasing political polarization be related to another powerful U.S. trend?

Political scientists Nolan McCarty, Keith T. Poole, and Howard Rosenthal posed that polarization is closely related to economic inequality. For decades after World War II, white male inequality in the United States was relatively low and governance largely bipartisan in spirit. As their research shows, our politics began to polarize at the same time that economic inequality widened.

As the two increased together, growing dysfunctionality plagued both economy and governance. The researchers' book, *Polarized America*, was published two years before the Great Recession of 2008. Since then, polarization has accelerated along with income inequality. No structures are yet in place to change this trend, but grassroots movements are growing.[236]

Just as in the Nordic countries in the 1920s and '30s, the legitimacy of the U.S. political economy is shredding. Already in 2006 billionaire Warren Buffett acknowledged to *The New York Times* that what he called "the class war" had escalated in recent decades. Buffett's statement reminds me of the boy who said the emperor wears no clothes. Now, because legitimacy has eroded, we can go well beyond the piecemeal reforms yielded in the '60s that kept the power structure in place.

Then, the economic elite offered plans for amelioration. President Lyndon Johnson declared a war on poverty. President Richard Nixon promised to clean up the environment. Now the economic elite denies the problem or its magnitude (climate change, lack of opportunity), or avoids mentioning the problem (growing insecurity and poverty). The alienation felt widely in working-class African American neighborhoods is spreading well beyond them, as pressing problems disrupting the lives of nearly all Americans remain unaddressed by the country's leadership. Each climate-change-induced disaster is, like Hurricane Katrina, California wildfires, and Superstorm Sandy, another event exposing the rot at the top.

Then, there was little economic grassroots organizing for empowerment. The 1960s remnant of largely bureaucratized cooperatives from the 1930s was nothing like the recent vitality and empowerment described by Gar Alperovitz. Today, support for equality and freedom has a growing grassroots base, far outstripping the tentative storefront co-ops of the 1970s, with increased skills and confidence to match the track record of success.

We should not count out trade unions in this scenario. Organized labor *is* growing where grassroots approaches are tried and coalitions are built between unions and community groups. Even after all the battering and slanted mass-media coverage of recent decades, a significant part of the public still believes in labor. According to Gallup polls, a majority of people say they generally side with labor in disputes and only 34 percent side with management. Fifty-three percent believe that unions help the economy and only 36 percent believe that they hurt.[237]

Now our country has a headstart in grassroots activism and organization.

Then, there was little knowledge or understanding of people-power. Since the 1960s, social scientists have researched the technique of change called "civil resistance," "people-power," or "nonviolent struggle." This technique includes boycotts, demonstrations, occupations, and strikes familiar in both Nordic and American history, plus a hundred other tactics that effect change. A web-based searchable database now comprises more than 1,000 cases of nonviolent action in 200 countries, complete with narratives for each case.[238] The campaigns range from local issues to national struggles that brought down military dictatorships, all by nonviolent struggle used when the ballot box did not work.

Along with investigation of tactics have come striking new insights about strategy. The newly burgeoning knowledge changes the playing field for those who want to work for change. A recent award-winning study by political scientists Erica Chenoweth and Maria Stephens, for example, found by comparing mass struggles since 1900 that the movements choosing nonviolent action rather than armed struggle doubled their chances for success.[239] The 1960s activists in the United States who argued for (and even experimented with) armed struggle had no access to this modern knowledge bank. Those activists' often brave and always misplaced emphasis on violence scared allies away and reduced the potential impact of their campaigns.[240]

Scientific support for the existence of a technique for change *more powerful than either electoral campaigns or armed struggle* encourages grassroots movements who want to go beyond piecemeal reforms to bring about real democracy in the United States. As the growing experience of empowerment at the grassroots links to a macro-strategy for change through nonviolent struggle, the movements of the future will be stronger and more confident, less factionalized and romantic than most were in the 1960s and '70s.

Now, when people give up on electoral contests that usually result in unaccountable elected officials who follow the direction of the economic elite, they can turn to a wealth of knowledge to create strategically sound, pragmatic, nonviolent campaigns that will create more powerful mass movements for change.

Then, alternative economic designs were either speculative or scary. Visionary thinking in the 1960s was clouded by the specter of a Soviet Union that pretended to be democratic and socialist and was neither. Piecemeal improvement projects within the design of liberal capitalism then seemed the only sensible option.

Now the Nordic alternative is drawing increasing attention. It is a design with a long track record of delivering freedom and equality well beyond the Anglo-American model. When the alternative is regarded not as a blueprint but as an invitation to create our own design inspired by what works there and in our own experience, a majority of Americans might find it simply pragmatic rather than scary.

A growing movement pressing for economic democracy will no doubt meet resistance from those who label it "socialistic." Fortunately, "socialism" is losing its scariness in U.S. political discourse, despite the best efforts of Fox News. While the neoliberal *Economist* magazine has tried to claim the Nordics as "capitalist," *Inc. Magazine* entitled its laudatory article, "In Norway, Start-ups Say Ja to Socialism."[241]

The Pew Research Center surveyed Americans in 2010 on identification with socialism, two years after the 2008 economic crisis spurred a massive barrage of propaganda against socialism from the media and many politicians. In the Pew poll, only 52 percent reacted favorably to the word "capitalism" while 29 percent reacted favorably to the word "socialism. Among eighteen- to thirty-year-olds, support of socialism and capitalism was evenly divided at 43 percent each. Support for socialism is dramatically higher among women, people of color, and people who make less than $30,000 per year. The poll found that interest in socialism has grown despite the propaganda campaign against it.[242]

The Gallup poll taken in the same year found that a majority of Democrats said they felt positive about socialism, and a third of the entire population was favorable.[243]

The Pew Center resurveyed this question in 2011 and found that "among voters under the age of thirty, forty-nine percent had a positive view of socialism. (Only forty-six percent had a positive view of capitalism.)"[244]

In a May 2015 poll, Yougov found Democrats evenly divided in their favorable views of socialism and capitalism: 43–43. Five months later, the same source found 49 percent of Democrats viewed socialism favorably, while capitalism fell to 37 percent.[245]

Mass media pundits routinely called Senator Bernie Sanders's candidacy for the 2016 Democratic presidential nomination the entry of a socialist in the race, with no noticeable shudders in the mainstream.

Now the door has opened in the United States for consideration of alternatives.

Q. What's next for building movements for a power shift supporting freedom and equality?

In the 1920s and '30s, we Americans were similar to the Nordic peoples in that we honored the process of envisioning a new society. The Nordics continued to cherish their visionaries, although I did interview some who believe that the visionary muscle has lately been losing its strength. Americans, however, let go of that thread decades ago, and by the 1990s, a U.S. president got away with referring dismissively to "the vision thing."

In the Bible, we find the observation that "without a vision, the people perish."

The next step for readers of this book might be to support the progressive social movements emerging around us and to embrace the value of design, to project the contours of what a political economy could look like that would support their cause.

Change requires hard work: social movements need many skills, many talents. Movements need organizers, communicators, advocates, funders, nurturers, researchers, trainers, musicians and artists, nonviolent warriors, and "foot soldiers," as well as visionary designers. All those were present in the Nordic movements that challenged a thousand years of poverty and oppression, took the offensive, and built democracy.

I'm an American. I know that at our best moments we have changed our society significantly for the better. I believe that, given the new circumstances and forces at work, plus applying the new knowledge about making change, we can go much farther than we have before. We can take up the struggle on a larger scale, this time decisively changing our country's direction toward freedom and equality.

Acknowledgments

I have been greatly helped by interviews with:

Eirikur Bergmann, Director of the Centre for European Studies at Bifrost University in Iceland.

Kristin Clemet, businesswoman, board chair of investment firm Norfund, formerly Conservative Party minister of education.

Jon Ivar Elstad, sociologist, Senior Researcher at Norwegian Social Research.

Thomas Hylland Eriksen, anthropology professor at University of Oslo.

Thorvaldur Gylfason, economics professor at University of Iceland.

Håken Haugli, Norwegian LGBT leader and deputy representative from city of Oslo to Parliament.

Knut Heidar, political science professor at University of Oslo.

Arne Jon Isachsen, economics professor at BI Norwegian Business School.

Jørgen Jørgensen, peace studies author and lecturer in Sweden, Denmark, and Norway.

Knut Kjeldstadli, history professor at University of Oslo, author of eight books on Norwegian history and specialist in the Labor Party.

Theo Koritzinsky, professor of education and international studies, Oslo Teachers College.

Mari Linløkken, former director of Norway's Anti-Racism Center.

Kirsten Larsen Mhoja, social anthropologist, longtime resident in Christiana, Denmark.

Lars Mjøset, professor of sociology and human geography at University of Oslo.

Hanna Ragnarsdottir, education professor, University of Iceland.

Dag Seierstad, a college lecturer and a leader in the Socialist Left Party.

Timothy Szlachetko, political scientist, Directorate of Minorities and Inclusion in the Norwegian government.

Hørdur Torfason, actor, leader of the Icelandic "Pots and Pans revolution."

Asbjørn Wahl, elected officer of the International Transport Workers' Federation and advisor to the Norwegian Union of Municipal and General Employees.

Kristian Weise, director, Cevea, an independent center-left think tank, Denmark.

Bo Wirmark, author, active in the Swedish Peace Council and World Council of Churches.

The book couldn't have happened without a strong support team: Berit M. Lakey and Liv Ingrid Lakey. Swarthmore College, particularly Director Joy Charlton and other colleagues at the Eugene M. Lang Center for Civic and Social Responsibility, research assistants M. Schlotterbeck and Elowyn Corby, and Professor Lee Smithey; Nathan Schneider and my agent, Krista Ingebretson; and friends, Johnny Lapham, Viki Laura List, Antje Mattheus, and Daniel Hunter.

Notes

Chapter 1: Vikings as Iconic Adventurers, Then and Now

1. Global Age Watch Index rates Norway as the best place to grow old, after studying quality of later life in ninety-six countries. Sweden is close behind at number two. www.bbc.com/news/world-29426 (accessed October 16, 2014). Published on the UN International Day of Older Persons. Measures four areas: income security, healthy, personal capability, and whether the person lives in an "enabling environment" (quote from BBC story). See also, "How Sweden cares for its elderly population," August 5, 2014, *BBC Health News*, www.bbc.com/news/health-28654739 (accessed October 16, 2014).

2. worldhappiness.report (accessed August 25, 2015). The index, compiled by the UN Sustainable Development Solutions Network, is based on measures like healthy life expectancy, freedom to make life choices, and social support. The rank of the United States is 15, and the UK, 21. The rankings in 2015 are very similar to those published in 2013.

3. The OECD's Better Life Index rated the United Kingdom eighteenth and the United States fourteenth. www.oecdbet-

terlifeindex.org/topics/life-satisfaction/. Switzerland, whose methodology is explained on its website, came in first for this index.

Chapter 2: Making Their Way in a Globalized World

4. The U.S. census data in 2015 reports a home-ownership rate in the United States of 63 percent, erasing nearly all the increase from the previous two decades. The drop happened in the eight years since the Great Recession began. Alan J. Heavens, "Fewer Own Homes; It's a Most Telling Sign." *Philadelphia Inquirer*, July 19, 2015, p. J8. According to *Bloomberg News*, home-ownership has fallen to the lowest reading since 1967. *Philadelphia Inquirer*, July 29, 2015, p. A12.

5. The 2014 summary of Norway's asylum resettlement program can be found in the online report from the International Organization for Migration, which states that refugees will come chiefly from Syria, Afghanistan, and Congo. www.iom.int/cms/en/sites/iom/home/where-we-work/europa/european-economic-area/norway.html (accessed August 8, 2014).

6. The 2015 Commitment to Development Index (CDI), created by the Center for Global Development. www.cgdev.org/cdi-2015/country/NOR (accessed January 6, 2015).

7. The Commitment to Development Index (CDI) ranks twenty-seven of the world's richest countries based on their dedication to policies that benefit poor nations: aid, trade, finance, migration, environment, security, and technology. The United Kingdom rated sixth, and the United States, twenty-first. The index is created by the Center for Global Development. www.cgdev.org/cdi-2015 (accessed January 6, 2015).

8. Asbjørn Wahl, *The Rise and Fall of the Welfare State* (London: Pluto Press, 2011), chapters 6 and 7.

Chapter 3: Vikings Get Lost, Bankers Go Wild

9. Richard Orange, "Tough on Finance, Tough on Migrants: How Stefan Løfven Brought Sweden's Left In from the Cold." *The Observer*, July 13, 2013.

10. Claire Ellicott and David Wilkes, "Thatcher's Plan to Use Army in Miners' Strike: Previously Secret Files Reveal How Former PM Planned to Mobilize Troops." *Mail Online*, January 2, 2014. www.dailymail.co.uk/news/article-2532995/Thatchers-plan-use-army-miners-strike-previously-secret-files-reveal-former-PM-planned-mobilise-troops.html.

11. www.encyclopedia.com/topic/Denmark.aspx.

12. "Workers Protest as Danish Government Tries to Settle Labor Conflict." *Associated Press*, March 29, 1985.

13. www.apnewsarchive.com/1985/Workers-Protest-as-Danish-Government-Tries-to-Settle-Labor-Conflict/id-037882bce-5569de93d252d1b35848fbf (accessed July 29, 2014). Another source, although not directly referring to the 1985–86 Danish struggle, acknowledges that the minority center-right government was not able to implement a number of the changes that it wanted to make. See Johannes Kananen, *The Nordic Welfare State in Three Eras: From Emancipation to Discipline* (Farnham, England: Ashgate Publishing Limited, 2014), p. 119.

14. As late as 2015, the claims for a U.S. recovery were padded by misleading statistics. In February 2015, for example, the U.S. Labor Department claimed an unemployment rate of 5.5 percent. That claim did not take into account the 6.6 million people working part-time who wanted full-time work, nor the part-timers who

needed more hours (short of full time) to be able to pay their bills. The statistic also leaves out people who have become so discouraged that they have given up seeking work. An authentic report would also acknowledge how many jobs replacing the jobs lost in the Great Recession are now low-waged. Jane M. Von Bergen, "Unemployment Rate Falls to Seven-Year Low" (*Philadelphia Inquirer*, March 7, 2015). Iceland's economy crashed in the same year that the United States faced its financial crisis, but Iceland experienced one of the worst collapses in history. Rejecting the neoliberal austerity approach taken by much of Europe and by the United States, Iceland rebounded quickly. By early 2015, its unemployment rate, measured in the same way as that of the United States, declined to 4.6 percent. The next chapter tells the Icelandic story. www.tradingeconomics.com/iceland/unemployment-rate (accessed August 24, 2015).

Chapter 4: Iceland Creates the Biggest Crash, then Rebounds

15. Thorvaldur Torfason wrote an amusing article comparing Icelandic bankers to the American Savings and Loan scandal and the Mel Brooks play *The Producers.* economistsview.typepad.com/economistsview/2010/08/mel-brooks-and-the-bankers.html.

16. H. H. Gissurarson, "Miracle on Iceland," *Wall Street Journal*, January 29, 2004. Cited by Stuckler, David and Basu, Sanjay, *The Body Economic: Why Austerity Kills* (New York: Basic Books, 2013), p. 172.

17. In an article in the Reykjavik newspaper *Morgunbladid*, November 17, 2007, cited by Stuckler, David and Basu, Sanjay, *The Body Economic*, p. 60.

18. Bergmann, Eirkur, *Iceland and the International Financial Cri-sis: Boom, Bust and Recovery* (New York: Palgrave Macmillan, 2014), p. 52.

19. Bergmann, *Iceland and the International Financial Crisis*.

20. *Inside Job*, 2010, directed by Charles Ferguson, written by Charles Ferguson and Chad Beck.

21. Bergmann, *Iceland and the International Financial Crisis*, p. 8.

22. Iceland previously had broken ground when it came to gen-der, thanks to a mass women's movement in the 1970s. In 1980, Iceland's Vigdis Finnbogadøttir was the first woman demo-cratically elected president in the world, and she remained in office for sixteen years. At one point, three of Iceland's top four office-holders were women: Supreme Court Chief Justice, Pres-ident of the Althing, and President of the country. At that time, the prime minister (the most powerful of the four) was a man, so the 2009 election of a woman to prime minister was still a breakthrough.

23. Stuckler, David and Basu, Sanjay, *The Body Economic*, pp. 64–65.

24. Stuckler, op. cit., p. 63.

25. Bergmann, op. cit., describes a number of specific policies that protected people, including handling the mortgage problem, to prevent poverty, pp. 159–62. An additional policy was to avoid laying off people by reducing hours for individuals while re-taining them. transform-network.net/blog/archive-2013/news/detail/Blog/the-other-way-of-iceland-analysing-a-case-of-no-bail-out.html (accessed April 15, 2014).

26. www.tradingeconomics.com/iceland/unemployment-rate (ac-cessed August 24, 2015).

27. Omar R. Valdimarsson, "Let Banks Fail Is Iceland Mantra as 2 percent Joblessness in Sight," *Bloomberg News*, January 27,

2014.   www.bloomberg.com/news/2014-01-27/let-banks-fail-becomes-iceland-mantra-as-2-joblessness-in-sight.html   (accessed July 21, 2014).

28. This is described by Eirikur Bergmann in the last chapter of his book. Thorvaldur Gylfason was elected one of the writers of the new draft constitution, and describes his experiences on the online magazine Opendemocracy.net.

Chapter 5: How Norwegians Empowered Themselves to Adopt the Nordic Model

29. I chose to write the story of the Norwegians' (and, to a smaller extent, the Swedes') struggle without footnotes, since scholarly accounts exist elsewhere. In gratitude, however, I want to acknowledge the following sources: Gøsta Esping-Andersen, *The Three Worlds of Welfare Capitalism* (Princeton, NJ: Princeton University Press, 1990); Penny Gill Martin, "Strategic Opportunities and Limitations: The Norwegian Labor Party and the Trade Unions," *Industrial and Labor Relations Review*, Vol. 28, No. 1, October 1974; Jan Fagerbert, Ådne Cappelen, Lars Mjøset, and Rune Skarstein, "The Decline of Social-Democratic State Capitalism in Norway," *New Left Review* 181, May/June 1990; Asbjørn Wahl, "Labour and Development: What Can Be Learned from the Nordic Model?" *Labour, Capital and Society* 40: 1 and 2, 2007; Sten Sparre Nilson, "Labor Insurgency in Norway: The Crisis of 1917–1920," *Social Science History*, Vol. 5, No. 4, Autumn 1981; Lars Mjøset, Ådne Cappelen, Jan Fagerberg, Bent Sofus Tranøy, "Norway: Changing the Model," Perry Anderson and Patrick Camiller (eds.), *Mapping the West European Left* (London: Verso, 1994). University of Oslo history professor Knut Kjeldstadli, the author of eight books on Norwegian history, kindly gave me two long interviews. My

interpretations and the resulting narrative remain, of course, my own.

30. *An American Dilemma.* Myrdal wrote the 1,500-page book with the assistance of Ralph Bunche, a leading African American intellectual who went on to become Deputy Secretary-General of the United Nations. Myrdal was chosen for the study by The Carnegie Foundation for the Advancement of Teaching because as a Swede he might be more objective than an American (New York: Harper & Brothers, 1944).

Chapter 6: More Start-ups than the United States: Support for Entrepreneurs, Workers, and the Equality of Women

31. Global Entrepreneurship Monitor, cited by Max Chafkin, "In Norway, Start-ups Say Ja to Socialism," *Inc. Magazine*, January 20, 2011. www.inc.com/magazine/20110201/in-norway-start-ups-say-ja-to-socialism.html/7 (accessed August 2, 2013).

32. "In Norway, Start-ups Say Ja to Socialism," *Inc. Magazine*, January 20, 2011. www.inc.com/magazine/20110201/in-norway-start-ups-say-ja-to-socialism.html/7 (accessed August 2, 2013).

33. Mark Zandi, "Economy still doesn't feel right," *Philadelphia Inquirer*, April 27, 2014, p. C3.

34. The Norwegian Center for Multicultural Value Creation organizes the program.

35. Jonathan Jopkin, Vitor Lapuente, and Lovisa Moller, "Lower Levels of Inequality Are Linked with Greater Innovation in Economies." blogs.lse.ac.uk/politicsandpolicy/archives/39215 (accessed June 8, 2014).

36. www.nytimes.com/interactive/2012/01/04/us/comparing-economic-mobility.html?_r=0 (accessed August 1, 2013).

37. Markus Jantti and colleagues, "American Exceptionalism in a

New Light: A Comparison of Intergenerational Earnings Mo-
bility in the Nordic Countries, the United Kingdom and the
United States," January 2006. IZA DEP No. 1938, Discussion
Paper Series, Institute for the Study of Labor, Bonn, Germany.

38. Iceland's recovery from one of the worst economic collapses
in history makes an interesting comparison with that of the
United States. Iceland's recovery was guided by the Nordic
model: the country bounced back quickly from the 2008 disaster and decreased inequality at the same time. The United
States recovery has been slow and halting while simultaneously
increasing its population's inequality.

39. *Viking Age: Everyday Life During the Extraordinary Era of the
Norsemen* (New York: Sterling, 2013).

40. www.guardian.co.uk/commentisfree/2011/jul/18/diversi-
ty-boardroom-corporate-decisions (accessed August 5, 2011).
The author of the article claims she has done research showing
that meetings with 40 percent women are reported by participants to be more professional: "Greater female representation
seems to make meetings a little more pleasant, the preparation
material is tidier and more comprehensive, and the processes
more formal. Our respondents call it professionalisation." As
of 2011, 95 percent of board members of Fortune 500 companies were white men. Charles A. Gallagher, "'Minority'
Nation?" *Philadelphia Inquirer*, November 28, 2015, p. C1. In
2015, in the United States, 104 women held 19 percent of the
House and Senate seats in Congress. That gender proportion
is lower than that of the parliaments of a number of countries,
including Afghanistan, Rwanda, and Ecuador, according to the
World Bank. Justine McDaniel and Caitlin McCabe, "Struggle
for Political Equity Persists," *Philadelphia Inquirer*, November 29, 2015, p. A14. Statistics on gender comparing Denmark

with the United States can be found here: www.bbc.com/news/
world-europe-34528366.

41. www.savethechildren.net (accessed August 30, 2015).

42. www.norway.org/aboutnorway/society/welfare/benefits/ (accessed July 31, 2013).

43. Strocel.com.

44. John Weeks, *Inequality Trends in Some Developed OECD Countries.* Working Paper No. 6. (New York: United Nations Department of Economic and Social Affairs, 2005.) www.un-.org/esa/desa/papers/2005/wp6_2005.pdf (accessed August 28, 2015). Cited by Wilkinson and Pickett, pp. 244–45.

45. David Dayen, *The Fiscal Times*, Quoted in *The Week*, September 18, 2015, p. 34. The U.S. Conference of Mayors commissioned a study of post-2008 wage trends, which revealed in 2015 that "the nation lost 8.7 million jobs in 2008 and 2009 that paid average wages of $61,637. The jobs that have replaced them, at least through the middle of last year, have a corresponding average wage of only $47,171." The study was conducted by the consulting firm IHS Global Insight. Joel Naroff, "Widening Pay Gap," *Philadelphia Inquirer*, November 1, 2015, p. E9.

46. Joseph E. Stiglitz, *The Price of Inequality* (New York: W. W. Norton, 2012), p. 81.

47. For information on the relationship of party and unions in Norway, see Penny Gill Martin, "Strategic Opportunities and Limitations: The Norwegian Labor Party and the Trade Unions," *Industrial and Labor Relations Review*, Vol. 28, No. 1. (October, 1974), pp. 75–88.

48. In the UK, 25.8 percent of workers were unionized and in the United States, 11.1 percent. Among the descendants of the Vikings: Norway, 54.7 percent, Sweden, 67.5 percent, Denmark, 68.5 percent (in 2010), and Iceland, 79.3 percent (in 2008).

49. Wahl, Asbjørn. 2011. *The Rise and Fall of the Welfare State.* London: Pluto Press, p. 55. Wahl reports that Germany has lost 48 percent of its union membership since the high of 1991 and the European Union as a whole has sunk to 23 percent union density (p. 69). Figures like this help us to understand how so many governments in the EU were able to force austerity on the working and middle classes following the financial sector's failure in 2008. Middle-class Americans have also been experiencing the harsh outcomes of lowered union density in the working class.

50. Wahl, p. 74. Wahl claims that governments in Sweden and Denmark have moved on several fronts to weaken the Nordic model, more so than in Norway.

51. Brooks, Neil and Thaddeus Hwong. (2006). *The Social Benefits and Economic Costs of Taxation.* Ottawa: Canadian Centre for Policy Alternatives, p. 28. www.policyalternatives.ca/sites/default/files/uploads/publications/National_Office_Pubs/2006/Benefits_and_Costs_of_Taxation.pdf (accessed August 30, 2015).

52. Galbraith, *The Predator State*, p. 190.

53. In Norway, Start-ups Say Ja to Socialism," *Inc. Magazine,* January 20, 2011. www.inc.com/magazine/20110201/in-norway-start-ups-say-ja-to-socialism.html/7 (accessed August 2, 2013).

54. Brian Miller and Mike Lapham, *The Self-Made Myth and the Truth about How Government Helps Individuals and Businesses Succeed* (San Francisco: Berrett-Koehler Publishers, 2012).

55. www.commondreams.org/views/2014/10/20/top-heavy-planet-nordic-nations-show-path-healthier-wealth-equity.

56. 2015 report. www.keepeek.com/Digital-Asset-Management/oecd/social-issues-migration-health/income-inequality_9789264246010-en#page25 (accessed January 9, 2016).

Chapter 7: Family Farmers and Cooperatives:
Key Players in the Nordic Model

57. International Cooperative Alliance, "Cooperatives create sustainable growth and quality employment." ica.coop/en/co-operatives-create-sustainable-growth-and-quality-employment (accessed May 3, 2016).

58. International Labour Organization, 2010. "Cooperatives and the crisis: 'Our customers are also our owners.'" www.ilo.org/global/publications/magazines-and-journals/world-of-work-magazine/article (accessed July 19, 2014).

59. Birchall, John. and Hammond Ketilson, L. 2009. *Resilience of the cooperative business model in times of crisis.* Geneva, ILO.

60. www.greatplacetowork.net/best-companies/europe/europe/50-best-large-workplaces-in-europe (accessed August 2, 2013).

61. www.thenews.coop/49090/news/general/view-top-300-co-operatives-around-world/#.U5UKVy-aluk (accessed June 8, 2014).

62. Sources for comparative business resilience and reducing turnover include Steven Dawson and Sherman Kreiner, *Cooperative Home Care Associates: History and Lessons* (New York: Home Care Associates Training Institute, 1993); Andrew Robinson and Hao Zhang, "Employee Share Ownership: Safeguarding Investments in Human Capital," *British Journal of Industrial Relations*, vol. 43, no. 3, pp. 469–88.

63. "Cooperative Housing in Sweden." ICA [International Cooperative Association] Housing. 2014. www.chfcanada.coop/icahousing/pages/membersearch.asp?op=country&id=14 (accessed July 19, 2014).

64. Pestoff, Victor. "Co-Production as a new perspective for the Swedish welfare state?" 2013. Governance International Blog. He cites Johan Vamstad (2012), "Co-Production and Service

Quality: A New Perspective for the Swedish Welfare State," in *New Public Governance, the Third Sector and Co-Production* (edited by Victor Pestoff, Taco Brandsen and Bram Verschuere), pp. 297–316. www.govint.org/news/blog/tags/parent percent2ocooperatives/?no_cache=1&cHash=8a52a8d-85077754cfe7bf824116e1964 (accessed July 19, 2014).

65. Wizelius, Tore. 2014. *Windpower Ownership in Sweden: Business models and motives* (London: Taylor & Francis), p. 47.

66. Lange, Even, Espen E. and Merok, E, "A successful latecomer: Growth and transformation of the Norwegian consumer co-operatives 1920–2000." Paper to be presented at the XIV International Economic History Congress, Helsinki, August 21–15, 2006. www.helsinki.fi/iehc2006/papers2/Lange.pdf (accessed July 19, 2014).

67. Sejersted, Francis. 2011. *The Age of Social Democracy: Norway and Sweden in the Twentieth Century* (Princeton, NJ: Princeton University Press), p. 263.

68. www.jarlsberg.com/us/about.

69. epp.eurostat.ec.europa.eu/statistics_explained/index.php/Farm_structure_in_Norway (accessed July 31, 2013).

70. blog.norway.com/2011/04/12/farmers-demanding-higher-income/ (accessed August 1, 2013).

71. www.norwaypost.no/index.php/news/latest-news/28249-norwegian-farmers-incomes-up-5-per-cent.

72. Numbers from the International Cooperative Alliance. hereandnow.wbur.org/2011/03/23/entrepreneurs-norway. www.britannica.com/EBchecked/topic/420178/Norway/214109/Demographic-trends. Helpful on demographic and big picture of economic production. (Accessed August 1, 2013.)

73. "The Cooperative Movement in Sweden." Fact sheet on Sweden published by the Swedish Institute, October 1983. digital.

lib.usu.edu/cdm/ref/collection/coops/id/5571 (accessed July 18, 2014).

74. www.danishdairyboard.dk/History.aspx (accessed August 30, 2015).

Chapter 8: Preventing Poverty: Nordics Learn How an Advanced Economy Can Abolish Poverty

75. Numbers were not available for Iceland. The calculation for the United States is 22.4 percent, placing it the twenty-second-lowest. Child poverty increased 12 percent in the United States between 1996 and 2013, as reported in Harper's Index for September 2013.

76. UNICEF, *A League Table of Child Poverty in Rich Nations*, Innocenti Report Card, Issue No. 1, June 2000, p. 6. www.unicef. is/efni/report_card/UNICEF_report_card_1.pdf   (accessed July 28, 2014).

77. www.thelocal.se/20120316/39720.

78. U.S. Department of Health and Human Services. aspe.hhs. gov/frequently-asked-questions-related-poverty-guide-lines-and-poverty (accessed August 30, 2015).

79. UNICEF, *A League Table of Child Poverty in Rich Nations*, Innocenti Report Card, Issue No. 1, June 2000, p. 11. www.unicef. is/efni/report_card/UNICEF_report_card_1.pdf   (accessed July 28, 2014).

80. Nina Berglund, "Concerns Rise over Poverty in Norway," *News in English*, August 31, 2011. www.newsinenglish.no/2011/08/31/ concerns-rise-over-poverty-in-norway (accessed May 4, 2016).

81. Op. cit., p. 11.

82. Although the United States has a law on the books (the Humphrey-Hawkins Act) stating that full employment is its goal, in practice it has no such policy. The Congress rejected Pres-

ident Obama's effort to pass a second stimulus plan after the U.S. financial sector caused the Great Recession of 2008. As late as 2015 the true unemployment rate, including people who wanted full-time work but could only get part-time jobs, and the people so discouraged about their job prospects that they had not looked for work lately, was 11 percent. Jane M. Von Bergen, "Unemployment rate falls to seven-year low," *Philadelphia Inquirer*, March 7, 2015, p. A1. Based on latest release of U.S. Department of Labor statistics.

83. www.worldfinance.com/home/top-5/top-5-countries-with-the-lowest-unemployment (accessed January 12, 2016).

84. See Asbjørn Wahl, *The Rise and Fall of the Welfare State* (London: Pluto Press, 2011), Chapters 6 and 7.

85. Op. cit., p. 14.

86. I put "war on poverty" in quotes because, even in the original conception, it was far from a serious effort. Bayard Rustin, a major advisor to Dr. Martin Luther King, Jr., was at that time an ally of President Johnson's. When LBJ's plan was publically announced, I happened to be in a large meeting with Rustin. "This is the first time," Bayard said in a tone of exasperation, "that America has gone to war with a BB gun!"

87. See, for example, the platform on the Danish People's Party website: www.danskfolkeparti.dk/The_Party_Program_of_the_Danish_Peoples_Party (accessed August 29, 2015).

88. In the United States, the trend has been ominous. "Poverty among the elderly is growing. And deep or extreme poverty—defined by the government as a single person earning $5,700 a year or less—has taken a jump that even experts find astonishing. For men over age sixty-five nationwide, the rate of deep poverty increased 23 percent between 2011 and 2012, according to analysis by the National Women's Law Center, a

nonprofit advocacy group. For women, it went up 18 percent. Overall, that means a total of 442,000 elderly men and 733,000 elderly women were living in deep poverty in America in 2012, the center's figures show." Alfred Lubrano, "Extreme poverty rising for elderly," *Philadelphia Inquirer*, October 20, 2013, p. A3.

89. The study was done in 2007 and published in the *Health Policy Journal*. www.commonwealthfund.org/~/media/images/publications/in-the-literature/2011/sep/preventable-death-l.gif (accessed January 12, 2015). Health expenditures as a percentage of the GDP use the latest available numbers (2013), and are found in the OECD health data website: www.oecd.org/els/health-systems/health-data.htm (accessed January 13, 2016).

90. Again drawn from the latest available data, 2013, in the OECD's data website: www.oecd.org/els/health-systems/health-data.htm (accessed January 13, 2016).

91. "Why Pharma's Patents are a Drug on the Market," *The Guardian*, May 31, 2011. www.theguardian.com/commentisfree/cifamerica/2011/may/31/healthcare-pharmaceuticals-industry (accessed January 26, 2016).

92. "Britain tops the fuel poverty league table," by Simon Read. *The Independent*, March 29, 2013. www.independent.co.uk/money/spend-save/britain-tops-the-fuel-poverty-league-table-8554723.html (accessed July 29, 2014).

93. Association for the Conservation of Energy. "Energy efficiency and excess winter deaths: Comparing the UK and Sweden," November 2013. www.energybillrevolution.org/wp-content/uploads/2013/12/ACE-Research-Comparing-the-UK-and-Sweden-3.12.13.pdf (accessed July 29, 2014).

94. By comparison, the rate in the UK is 154 prisoners per 100,000 and the United States, the highest in the world, has 730.

95. UN, Survey on Crime Trends and the Operations of Criminal Justice Systems, cited by Wilkinson and Pickett, p. 148.

96. "Why Violent Crime Is So Rare in Iceland." BBC News. www.bbc.com/news/magazine-25201471.

97. Public Radio International, December 3, 2013. www.pri.org/stories/2013–12-03/iceland-grieves-after-police-kill-man-first-time-its-history. The chief of police said in his statement: "The police are deeply saddened by this tragic event and would like to extend their condolences to the family of the individual in question." Grief counseling was offered immediately to the police officers involved. www.theguardian.com/world/2013/dec/02/iceland-armed-police-shoot-man-dead-first-time.

98. Landon Thomas, Jr., "Thriving Norway Provides an Economics Lesson," *The New York Times*, May 14, 2009. www.nytimes.com/2009/05/14/business/global/14frugal.html (accessed May 4, 2016).

Chapter 9: Creating Work/Life Balance

99. Hiscott, Rebecca. "Sweden to Experiment with Six-Hour Workday." *The Huffington Post*, June 5, 2014 (accessed July 21, 2014).

100. OECD Labor Productivity: stats.oecd.org/Index.aspx?DataSetCode=LEVEL.

101. Hiscott, Rebecca, op. cit. Not all workplaces find people becoming more productive, or happier, with a shorter day. Evidence from various countries suggests that the outcome may relate to the kind of job, and also to expectations about the degree of informal communication in the workplace itself. One firm found that within its own worksite, people in some jobs had positive outcomes from shorter days (in both productivity

and morale) and people in other kinds of jobs had less. Michelle Goodman, "Do shorter workdays really make us more productive?" BBC.com, July 30, 2014. www.bbc.com/capital/story/20140729-do-shorter-workdays-really-work   (accessed August 2, 2014).

102. Schulte's book is *Overwhelmed: Work, Love, and Play When No One Has the Time*, published by Farrar, Straus and Giroux/Sarah Crichton Books, 2014. The *Fresh Air* interview is from March 14, 2014.

103. www.britannica.com/EBchecked/topic/420178/Norway/214109/Demographic-trends (accessed November 10, 2011).

104. Bowles and Y. Park, "Emulation, inequality, and work hours: was Thorsten Veblen right?" *Economic Journal* (2005) 115: F398–F412. Cited in Parkinson and Pickett, *The Spirit Level* (New York: Bloomsbury Press, 2009), p. 228. Wilkinson and Pickett found a parallel variability on advertising. In more unequal countries more of the GDP is spent on advertising, with the United States and New Zealand spending twice as much as Denmark and Norway. Presumably, advertising is the carrot held in front of the donkey to keep it working.

105. Better Life Index, 2013. www.oecdbetterlifeindex.org (accessed May 13, 2014).

106. www.norway.org/aboutnorway/society/welfare/benefits/ (accessed July 31, 2013).

107. www.huffingtonpost.com/2013/10/22/denmark-happiest-country_n_4070761.html (accessed July 21, 2014).

108. According to a 2011 study by Ronald Rindfuss, David Guilkey, Philip Morgan, and Oystein Kravdal titled "Child-Care Availability and Fertility in Norway." www.ncbi.nlm.nih.gov/pmc/articles/PMC3099220/#R21. In 2004, 72 percent of women with

children under the age of three were employed. www.norway. org/aboutnorway/society/Equal-Opportunities/gender/work-force/ (accessed April 3, 2011).

109. *Statistics Norway 2007*, cited in Øystein Kravdal's article, "Why Is Fertility in Norway so High?"

110. James Surowiecki, "The Cult of Overwork," *The New Yorker*, January 27, 2011, p. 23.

111. www.huffingtonpost.com/2013/10/22/denmark-happiest-coun-try_n_4070761.html (accessed July 21, 2014).

112. Wilkinson and Pickett draw their data from the World Bank, the World Health Organization, the UN, and the OECD. See pp. 22–23 and 174–75.

113. www.loe.org/shows/segments.html?program-ID=99-P13–00003&segmentID=2 (accessed November 20, 2011). "The Land Tenure System in Norway, and Local Democ-racy in Relation to Land Issues," www.caledonia.org.uk/land/tenure.htm. Anders Anderssen, Advisor to the County Gover-nor, Sogn og Fjordane (accessed November 20, 2011).

114. www.huffingtonpost.com/2013/10/22/denmark-happiest-coun-try_n_4070761.html (accessed July 21, 2014).

Chapter 10: Breaking Barriers to Education and Lifelong Learning

115. Laura Vanderkam, "The permanent recession: It's no secret that the educational system in the USA doesn't stack up well against the rest of the world. What's less-known is the severe economic consequences." *USA Today Weekly International Edition*, June 19–21, 2009, p. 7W. It is true that the United States does invest considerable sums in education, but that is often in defiance of the results of educational studies pointing to what is in fact effective. Research for many years has shown overwhelmingly

that learning goes up when the number of students in a class goes down. The new, top-down educational "reform movement" ignores these studies and instead insists on frequent, widespread (and expensive) testing. This not only results in larger classrooms but also, significantly, more taxpayer money diverted into the private sector via testing companies.

116. Sean F. Reardon, "The Widening Academic Achievement Gap between the Rich and the Poor: New Evidence and Possible Explanations," in R. Murnane and G. Duncan, eds., *Whither Opportunity? Rising Inequality and the Uncertain Life Chances of Low-Income Children* (New York: Russell Sage Foundation, 2011), pp. 91–116.

117. As I write this, the national campaign by the United States' 1 percent to defund public schools has resulted for Philadelphia in the likely prospect of classrooms with 40 students. The campaign uses the classic strategy, which is first to run down the quality of a public service, then to amplify the public's dissatisfaction and channel it into blaming the teachers and administrators themselves, thus provoking a popular readiness to "try something else"—that is, educational taxes being placed in private hands.

118. UNICEF Innocenti Research Centre. *Child Poverty in Perspective: An overview of child well-being in rich countries* (Florence: Innocenti Report Card, 2007). Wilkinson and Pickett, p. 116.

119. Studies in the United States show that enhancing music programs for working-class children in Harlem, West Philadelphia, and Chester, PA, pays off in increased academic achievement as well. These programs are funded by privately raised money, since the running-down of public schools includes abandoning music and arts programs.)

120. Niklas Pollard, "Insight: Sweden rethinks pioneering school

reforms, private equity under fire," Reuters, December 10, 2013 (accessed August 29, 2015).

121. www.kunstfilm.no/english/ (accessed July 23, 2014).

122. A useful overview of the Norwegian tertiary education system, including an explanation of the loans and grants available to students as income support while they go to school, is: gse.buffalo.edu/org/inthigheredfinance/files/Country_Profiles/Europe/Norway.pdf (accessed July 23, 2014).

123. Thorvaldur Gylfason, "Natural resources, education, and economic development." *European Economic Review* 45 (2001): 847–59.

124. *Education at a Glance, 2013: OECD Indicators.* www.oecd.org/edu/eag2013 percent20(eng)—FINAL percent2020 percent-20June percent202013.pdf (accessed July 24, 2014). This source also presents information on the comparative rates of student attainment in the various countries, including graduation rates and success in gaining jobs.

125. Goldstein, Dana, *The Teacher Wars: A History of America's Most Embattled Profession* (New York: Doubleday, 2014), p. 274.

126. *The Week*, November 6, 2015, p. 7.

Chapter 11: Paying for What You Get:
The Viking Approach to Taxes

127. These OECD statistics can be found here: stats.oecd.org/Index.aspx?DataSetCode=REV.

128. Chaflin, Max. "In Norway, Start-ups Say Ja to Socialism," *Inc. Magazine*, January 20, 2011. www.inc.com/magazine/20110201/in-norway-start-ups-say-ja-to-socialism.html/7 (accessed August 2, 2013).

129. Joseph E. Stiglitz, *The Price of Inequality* (New York: W. W. Norton, 2012), p. 28.

130. Chaflin, op. cit.

131. The authors respond to frequently asked questions and update their data on the website of a nonprofit, www.equalitytrust.org. uk/spirit-level. *The Spirit Level: Why Greater Equality Makes Societies Stronger* (New York: Bloomsbury Press, 2009).

132. Wilkinson and Pickett, pp. 55–56. In Putnam's book *Bowling Alone*, he defines "social capital" as the sum total of people's involvement in community life. "Social capital and economic equality moved in tandem through most of the twentieth century [in the United States]. In terms of the distribution of wealth and income, America in the 1950s and 1960s was more egalitarian than it had been in more than a century . . . those same decades were also the high point of social connectedness and civic engagement." R.D. Putnam, *Bowling Alone: The collapse and revival of American community.* (New York: Simon & Schuster, 2000). Eric Uslaner's book is *The Moral Foundations of Trust.* (Cambridge: Cambridge University Press, 2002.)

133. Wilkinson and Pickett analyze the grounds for the international condemnation of the U.S. response to Hurricane Katrina: "Countries around the world offered aid and assistance, while their news coverage was filled with criticism." The authors note that Louisiana is a high-inequality state within the United States and demonstrated the expected lack of social trust and resiliency; pp. 49–50.

134. AmericanProgress.org, June 2011 (accessed June 8, 2014).

135. In the United States, President Reagan's administration began a march downward in personal taxes for the wealthy (as high as 70 percent). Joseph Stiglitz tells us that, considering that municipal bonds, a favorite haven for the rich, are not even

taxed at all, the 400 top income earners in the United States
paid an average tax rate of just 19.9 percent in 2009. The top 1
percent in general pay between 20–24 percent, which is lower
than Americans with moderate incomes. Joseph E. Stiglitz, *The
Price of Inequality*, New York: W. W. Norton, p. xxxi. Warren
Buffett, the second-richest person in the United States, stated
that his taxable income was taxed only at 17.4 percent, a frac-
tion of what others pay who earn much less. In 2007, he said,
"Dynastic wealth, the enemy of a meritocracy, is on the rise.
Equality of opportunity has been on the decline." For that rea-
son, he backs estate taxes. Brian Miller and Mike Lapham, *The
Self-Made Myth* (San Francisco: Berrett-Koehler, 2012), p. 76.

136. www.norjus.no/visartikkel.asp?art=254.

137. Kallbekken and Saelen, 2010.

138. Noting a consistent drumbeat from politicians of both parties
decrying increased taxes, a series of polls were taken in Pennsylvania in 2011 to check that out. Fifty-seven percent were
willing to pay higher fees for driver's licenses and registration
if the money went toward road and bridge repairs. Seventy-one
percent want to tax Marcellus Shale gas drilling. (The governor refused.) Seventy-two percent want smokeless tobacco and
cigars to be taxed. Eighty-three percent want to maintain support for public schools even in bad times, and are willing to
raise state taxes to do so. (The governor then lowered taxes—on
corporations in the state—and substantially reduced funding
of public education.) Timothy Potts, "Major parties vs. the majority," *Philadelphia Inquirer*, December 28, 2011, p. A22.

139. In 2015, the IRS pursued more than one thousand "transfer
pricing" cases: corporations accused of transferring income
away from higher-tax U.S. operating units to tax-protected
affiliates, hoping to collect up to $194 billion in unpaid taxes.

These include Apple ($16.3 billion), Vanguard Group ($34.6 billion), and Amazon ($1.5 billion). The numbers are estimates. Joseph N. Distefano, "The IRS's Intensifying Fight Over Income Taxes," *Philadelphia Inquirer*, November 1, 2015, p. E1.

140. Chafkin, op. cit.

141. Jeffrey D. Sachs, "The Social Welfare State, beyond Ideology." *Scientific American*, November 1, 2006. Norwegian writer Asbjørn Wahl cites another study, of OECD countries, that comes to the same conclusion in comparing national tax policies and economic and social outcomes. The Canadian Centre for Policy Alternatives compared high-tax and low-tax countries on the basis of social and economic indicators. Among other things, the study found productivity (GNP per hour worked) was higher in the high-tax states. Brooks, N. and Hwong, T. (2006). *The Social Benefits and Economic Costs of Taxation*. Ottawa: Canadian Centre for Policy Alternatives. www.policy-alternatives.ca/documents/National_Office_Pubs/2006/Benefits_and-Costs_of_Taxation.pdf. Wahl, Asbjørn (2011). *The Rise and Fall of the Welfare State*. London: Pluto Press, p. 6.

142. Brooks, N., and Hwong, T. (2006). *The Social Benefits and Economic Costs of Taxation*. Ottawa: Canadian Centre for Policy Alternatives. <www.policyalternatives.ca/documents/National_Office_Pubs/2006/Benefits_and-Costs_of_Taxation.pdf> . Quoted extensively by Wahl, Asbjørn, 2011. *The Rise and Fall of the Welfare State*. London: Pluto Press. The productivity citation is on p. 7.

Chapter 12: Allowing Racial and Other Differences to Work for the Common Good

143. August 28, 2011. Cited by Felice Blake in her article "Black in Norway," Al Jazeera.com, August 20, 2011. www.aljazeera.

com/indepth/opinion/2011/08/201182984256236502.html (accessed August 8, 2014).

144. Eriksen, Thomas Hylland. 2013. *Immigration and National Identity in Norway.* Washington, D.C.: Migration Policy Institute, p. 12.

145. "Manifestation of hidden discrimination and everyday prejudice toward immigrants in Iceland," 2013, Guðrún Pétursdóttir . *InterCultural Ísland* . www.ici.is/assets/Everyday_discrimination_in_Iceland.pdf (accessed February 4, 2014).

146. *Aftenposten*, the major national newspaper of Norway. July 10, 2012.

147. Eriksen, Thomas Hylland. 2013. *Immigration and National Identity in Norway.* Washington, D.C.: Migration Policy Institute, p. 12. See also his book *Paradoxes of Cultural Recognition*, coedited with Sharam Alghasi and Halleh Ghorashi, Ashgate Publishers (now Routledge/Taylor & Francis), 2009.

148. The letter, dated February 3, 2006, was published on the UK blog of the Institute for Race Relations. www.irr.org.uk/news/we-are-very-close-to-violence/ (accessed August 8, 2014).

149. Bo Lidegaard, "Denmark's Far-Right Kingmakers," *The New York Times*, June 21, 2015.

150. Halvard Buhaug, Kristian Skrede Gleditsch, Helge Holtermann, Gudrun Østby, Andreas Forø Tollefsen, "It's the Local Economy, Stupid! Geographic Wealth Dispersion and Conflict Outbreak Location." *The Journal of Conflict Resolution*, October 2011, vol. 55, no. 5. jcr.sagepub.com/content/55/5/814.abstract (accessed August 9, 2014).

151. OECD, "Divided We Stand: Why Inequality Keeps Rising." 2011. www.oecd.org/els/soc/49499779.pdf (accessed August 9, 2014). Sweden still remains far more equal than most countries.

152. Richard Orange, "Swedish riots spark surprise and anger: As

inequality and segregation start to rise, the spread of youth disorder has shaken ethnic Swedes and older immigrants alike." *The Observer*, May 25, 2013. www.theguardian.com/world/2013/may/25/sweden-europe-news (accessed August 9, 2014).

153. en.wikipedia.org/wiki/2013_Stockholm_riots (accessed August 9, 2014).

154. May 25, 2013. www.theguardian.com/world/2013/may/25/sweden-europe-news (accessed August 9, 2014).

155. Liam McLaughlin, "The Swedish riots: What really happened? Inequality, not immigration, was what sparked the unrest." New Statesman, 14 June 2013. www.newstatesman.com/economics/2013/06/swedish-riots-what-really-happened (accessed August 9, 2014).

156. www.mynewsdesk.com/uk/expo/pressreleases/tag/expo-foundation (accessed August 8, 2014). The website contains Expo Foundation's white supremacy reports; the quote is from its press release dated May 13, 2011. The famous author Stieg Larsson was editor of the foundation's magazine, *Expo*.

157. Ylva Nilsson, "Immigration not a topic for Swedish mainstream parties," online periodical *EU Observer*, May 6, 2014. euobserver.com/eu-elections/124013 (accessed August 29, 2015).

158. blogs.helsinki.fi/ije4d-journal/files/2012/11/IJE4D-Vol.-1-article-21.pdf.

159. Mats Persson, "If EU Migration Is the Problem, Switzerland and Norway Are Not the Answer." *The Telegraph*, September 12, 2015. www.telegraph.co.uk/news/uknews/immigration/11190269/If-EU-migration-is-the-problem-Switzerland-and-Norway-are-not-the-answer.html (accessed January 13, 2016).

160. As I noted in the chapter on education, generous public support in the Nordic model to all things cultural supports the respect for ethnic Norwegian cultural identity, along with other identities, that is reflected through dance and music. The disestablishment of the state Lutheran Church while taxes continue to maintain church buildings—and mosques—again creates a universal solution consistent with the model's principles.

161. www.minorityrights.org/1499/norway/sami.html. On website of World Directory of Minorities and Indigenous Peoples (accessed August 11, 2014).

162. Anders Ekeland (2011).

163. Eriksen, Thomas Hylland. 2013. *Immigration and National Identity in Norway.* Washington, D.C.: Migration Policy Institute, p. 5.

164. Anders Ekeland (2011). "Stabil yrkesdeltakelse og ledighet" [Stable workforce participation and unemployment rates] (in Norwegian). "Tabell:05111: Personer i alderen 15–74 år, etter kjønn, arbeidsstyrkestatus og alder" [Persons aged 15–74, by gender, workforce status and age] (in Norwegian). Statistics Norway (accessed August 11, 2014).

165. Eriksen, Thomas Hylland. 2013. *Immigration and National Identity in Norway.* Washington, D.C.: Migration Policy Institute, p. 1.

166. "Vi er alle rystet av ordskapen," Aftenposten. Quoted in Wikipedia article, "2011 Norway attacks." en.wikipedia.org/wiki/2011_Norway_attacks (accessed August 14, 2014).

167. "Amid Tears, Flickering Candles and Flowers, a Shaken Norway Mourns." July 24, 2011. www.nytimes.com/2011/07/25/world/europe/25oslo.html (accessed August 11, 2014).

168. Batty, David; Godfrey, Hannah, "Norway attacks: Sunday 24 July rolling coverage: 1.13pm," *The Guardian.* Quoted in Wiki-

pedia, "2011 Norway Attacks." "Vi er alle rystet av ordskapen," en.wikipedia.org/wiki/2011_Norway_attacks (accessed August 14, 2014).

169. Svensson, Olof and Josefin Karlsson. "Hela Norden hedrade offren med tyst minut." *Aftonbladet* (Sweden), July 25, 2011. Quoted in Wikipedia article, "2011 Norway attacks." en.wikipedia.org/wiki/2011_Norway_attacks (accessed August 14, 2014).

170. "More than 200,000 mourn in downtown Oslo." *Verdens Gang* (Norway). July 25, 2011. Quoted in Wikipedia article, "2011 Norway attacks." en.wikipedia.org/wiki/2011_Norway_attacks (accessed August 14, 2014).

171. "Norway's Premier Vows to Keep an Open Society," by Michael Schwirtz, *The New York Times*, July 27, 2011. www.nytimes.com/2011/07/28/world/europe/28norway.html (accessed August 11, 2014).

172. "Young Survivors Find Their Faith in Norway's System Is Even Stronger," by Matthew Saltmarsh, July 27, 2011. www.nytimes.com/2011/07/28/world/europe/28iht-youth28.html (accessed August 11, 2014).

173. "Glenn Beck sammenligner AUF med Hitlerjugend," *Bergens Tidende*, 26 July 2011.

174. "Letters: Norway and the Vengeance Factor." August 2, 2011. Quoted in Wikipedia article, "2011 Norway attacks." en.wikipedia.org/wiki/2011_Norway_attacks (accessed August 14, 2014). www.nytimes.com/2011/08/03/opinion/norway-and-the-vengeance-factor.html (accessed August 11, 2014).

175. *The Foreigner*, August 9, 2014. theforeigner.no/pages/news/norways-new-immigration-and-asylum-policies/ (accessed August 9, 2014).

Chapter 13: Reaching for High Goals
on Climate Change

176. www.sierraclub.org/sierra/2015-1-january-february/feature/ leading-edge (accessed August 25, 2015).

177. inhabitat.com/norway-to-build-the-worlds-largest-wind-turbine/. Once it's in place, they want to make more of them offshore. "Norwegian oil and gas champion StatoilHydro (NYSE:STO) has teamed up with German infrastructure giant Siemens (NYSE:SI) to build the first floating wind turbines for deep-water use. With centers of gravity deep below the surface and moorings tied to the seabed, these rigs would go farther offshore than any pylon-based wind turbine could. The first application for such a far-flung power generation system would actually be to help power oil and gas rigs that sit atop the North Sea's dwindling petroleum reserves"—www.greenchipstocks.com/articles/ norway-wind-power-law/440. Already wind power plays a role in Norway: "The Smøla wind park was built in two steps that opened in September 2002 and September 2005, respectively. It has 68 wind turbines producing 450 GWh of electricity per year. It is the largest land-based wind generating facility in Europe"— Liana Müler in "Wind Power in Norway: Innovation Strategy" www.iet.ntnu.no/~ralf/muller/pubs/wind.pdf. This wind-farm provides power for nearly 25,000 households.

178. www.sierraclub.org/sierra/2015-1-january-february/feature/ leading-edge.

179. Mike Corder, "Court orders Dutch to do more on climate," *Philadelphia Inquirer*, June 25, 2015, A8.

180. Elizabeth Kolbert, "The Weight of the World," *The New Yorker*, August 24, 2015, p. 28.

181. www.huffingtonpost.com/2013/10/22/denmark-happiest-country_n_4070761.html.

182. Denmark's lead representative in the negotiations was the late Svend Auken, known as "the father of Danish climate energy policy." Auken was one of the few Danish politicians ever to be honored in the U.S. House of Representatives. A leading Social Democrat, he was a member of *Folketinget* (Parliament) for thirty-eight years and minister for environment and energy from 1994 to 2001.

183. Norway's government in 2013 estimated the remaining reserves of the Norwegian Continental Shelf (NCS) equivalent to 84 billion barrels of oil.

184. www.theguardian.com/environment/2015/may/19/karl-ove-knausgaard-condemns-norways-arctic-oil-drill-plans (accessed September 28, 2015).

185. Before Brundtland came Arne Naess, who attracted an international following with his teaching of deep ecology. Naess was a philosophy professor at the University of Oslo known for his mountain climbing and pacifism. When a student in Oslo I met him and read his study of Gandhi; years later, I would hear that he'd been arrested for protesting the development of a hydroelectric dam in his beloved mountains.

186. Critics say that saving rain forests elsewhere takes Norway off the hook for reducing its own emissions, but the Ministry of the Environment responds by saying that "efforts to reduce these emissions must be additional to and not a replacement for efforts by developed economies to reduce their emissions."

187. www.theguardian.com/environment/2015/mar/16/norways-sovereign-wealth-fund-drops-over-50-coal-companies.

188. 350.org, in a broadcast e-mail May 28, 2015.

189. unepfi.org/pdc/ (accessed January 15, 2016).

190. www.worldwatch.org/node/6039.

191. "Swedish City Recognized for Efforts to Support Sustainable

Communities," WorldWatch Institute online newsletter (accessed July 23, 2014).

192. www.pri.org/stories/2014-10-21/big-companies-are-pulling-plug-their-projects-albertas-tar-sands (accessed August 8, 2015).

193. news.mongabay.com/2015/02/norway-sovereign-fund-drops-coal-tar-sands-gold-mining-companies/ (accessed August 8, 2015).

194. www.treehugger.com/cars/cheapest-new-cars-in-norway-are-electric.html.

Chapter 14: How Relevant Is the Nordic Model to the United States?

195. "All Things Considered," National Public Radio, September 25, 2009.

196. Peace Corps members are paid a small stipend but many other programs are not. Another pioneer was Service Civile Internationale, founded by Pierre Ceresole in Switzerland.

197. en.wikipedia.org/wiki/Public_transport#History.

198. en.wikipedia.org/wiki/Public_library#Modern_public_libraries.

199. Wikipedia entry.

200. Dan Hardy, "Rising up to stop bullying," *Philadelphia Inquirer*, November 14, 2010, p. B1.

201. Joseph E. Stiglitz, *The Price of Inequality* (New York: W. W. Norton, 2012), p. 461, n58.

202. The *Los Angeles Times* reported one of the many studies showing the United States lagging behind on health care. The Commonwealth Fund found that the United States ranked last among eleven industrial nations on health-care quality and access, despite having by far the costliest care. (The United States

spent $8,508 per person compared, for example, with the top-ranked Britain which spent only $3,406 per person.) Chad Terhune, "U.S. last on health care list," reprinted by *Philadelphia Inquirer*, June 17, 2014, p. A9.

203. Jim Nussle, "Don't punish credit unions for big banks' sins," *Philadelphia Inquirer*, May 11, 2015, p. A14. Credit unions protect their members' accounts from loss in their own version of the Federal Deposit Insurance Corporation, in the rare case of a local credit union failure. Because the structure of credit unions is decentralized, they are never "too big to fail" and do not ask for taxpayer bailouts.

204. See the *Philadelphia Inquirer*'s front-page story on the Amtrak crash and Congress, May 17, 2015. In the same newspaper are reported the other facts by Robert Puentes, "With many infrastructure needs, time to get moving," May 17, 2015, p. C-1.

205. The *Los Angeles Times* reported that Central Japan Railway is running magnetic levitation trains exceeding 350 mph on a test track. *Philadelphia Inquirer*, April 19, 2015, p. A6.

206. Wilkinson and Pickett, pp. 185–86.

207. www.brainyquote.com/quotes/quotes/r/robertkenn121273.html.

208. Wilkinson and Pickett, p. 268.

209. *The Price of Inequality* (New York: W. W. Norton, 2012), p. 27. Stiglitz judges that the U.S. economy has "not been performing well" for over a third of a century, and notes how misleading GDP growth is as a measure. "Although it has managed to increase GDP per capita, from 1980 to 2010 by three-fourths, most fulltime male workers have, as we've noted, seen their incomes go down." The income growth, he notes, occurs among the top 1 percent, and inequalities in wealth are even greater than of income.

210. Michael I. Norton and Dan Ariely, "Building a Better America—One Wealth Quintile at a Time," *Perspectives on Psychological Science* 6, no. 1 (2011): pp. 9–12. Cited by Joseph E. Stiglitz, *The Price of Inequality* (New York: W. W. Norton, 2012), p. 160. Wilkinson and Pickett report that in Britain for the past couple of decades polls have shown that 75–80 percent of the people believe income differences are too big. *The Spirit Level*, p. 249.

211. *Washington Post* columnist Dana Milbank, "Endless source of controversy," reprinted in the *Philadelphia Inquirer*, June 10, 2015, p. A18.

212. Zachary Goldfarb reviewed recent polls for *The Washington Post* and was cited by Eric Alterman in *The Nation*, December 1–8, 2014, p. 6.

213. Karthick Ramakrishnan, director of the National Asian American Survey (www.naasurvey.com) and associate professor at the University of California at Riverside, reported by Michael Smerconish in the *Philadelphia Inquirer*, November 18, 2012, p. C6.

214. Cited in *The Nation*, "The Invisible Primary," May 11, 2015, p. 3.

215. Harper's Index, *Harper's Magazine*, April 2014.

216. The Pew Research Center for the People and the Press reviewed opinion polls between 1987 and 2007. The study, "Trends in Political Values and Core Attitudes: 1987–2007," is reported by Rick Perlstein in *The Nation*, "Will the Progressive Majority Emerge?" July 9, 2007, p. 11. The last finding was dated 2007.

217. More on minimum wage, in this connection: voters in four Republican states voted in the November 2014 election on the question of minimum wage. Nebraskans approved a ballot measure to raise minim wage to $8 per hour next year and $9 per hour in 2016; South Dakotans voted to raise it to $8.50 next

year; Arkansas voters approved gradual increase to $8.50 by 2017; Alaskans agreed to raise it to $9.75 by 2016. Charles Lane, "Grand bargain on minimum wage would take politics out of wages," *Philadelphia Inquirer*, November 10, 2014, p. A10.

218. Timothy Potts, "Major parties vs. the majority," *Philadelphia Inquirer*, December 28, 2011, p. A22.

219. "The Republican Class War," *The New Yorker*, November 9, 2015, p. 28.

220. Barry G. Rabe, public policy professor writing in the *Philadelphia Inquirer*, "How Pa. can get severance tax right," August 2, 2015, p. C1.

221. Alperovitz, Gar. *What Then Must We Do? Straight Talk about the Next American Revolution*. White River Junction, Vermont: Chelsea Green Publishing, 2013.

222. *Harper's Index*, April 2016.

223. "In a recent ABC/Washington Post poll, 68 percent agreed that we live in a country whose economic system favors the rich rather than the rest of us. (About half of Republicans agreed with this too.)" Eric Alterman, "Inequality in Campaign Mode," *The Nation*, September 28–October 5, 2015. "A June 2015 New York Times/CBS News poll found that more than 80 percent of Americans believe money plays too great a role in campaigns, while two-thirds say that the wealthy have a greater chance of influencing the electoral process than other Americans." Senator Sheldon Whitehouse, "Super-PAC Tsunami." *The Nation*, October 12, 2015. "Seventy Percent (70%) of Likely U.S. Voters Think Government and Big Business Often Work Together in Ways That Hurt Consumers and Investors." www.rasmussenreports.com/public_content/politics/general_politics/september_2013/70_think_government_big_business_often_work_together_against_consumers_investors (accessed

December 14, 2015). "The view that government and big business work together against the interests of others is shared across partisan, demographic and ideological lines. Seventy percent (70%) of liberals hold that view, along with 69% of conservatives. Seventy-one percent (71%) Republicans think it's true, and so do 64% of Democrats." February 7, 2011, Rasmussen Reports. www.rasmussenreports.com/public_content/politics/general_politics/february_2011/68_believe_government_and_big_business_work_together_against_the_rest_of_us (accessed December 14, 2015).

224. Paul Krugman, *The Conscience of a Liberal: Reclaiming America from the Right* (New York: W. W. Norton, 2007). Cited by Wilkinson and Pickett, pp. 242–43.

225. "Here and Now," interviewed by Jeremy Hobson, National Public Radio, January 27, 2016. www.npr.org/podcasts/510051/here-x26-now (accessed January 28, 2016).

226. Martin Gilens and Benjamin I. Page, 2014. "Testing Theories of American Politics: Elites, Interest Groups, and Average Citizens." scholar.princeton.edu/sites/default/files/mgilens/files/gilens_and_page_2014_-testing_theories_of_american_politics.doc.pdf. p. 576.

227. The result of the Icelanders' mass insurgency is still unclear as of this writing. One goal was a new constitution that would strengthen democracy. In 2016, Icelanders again showed their ability to force accountability through mass nonviolent action by forcing the resignation of their prime minister for sending money to an offshore account after having urged the people to keep their money in Icelandic banks (www.theguardian.com/world/2016/apr/05/iceland-prime-minister-resigns-over-panama-papers-revelations). If the U.S. public were to take to the streets in outrage over a governmental action in the same pro-

portion as Icelanders had in 2016, the total number of Americans would be 10 million. wagingnonviolence.org/feature/what-if-americans-protested-like-icelanders/.

228. An excellent place to start absorbing the lessons of the civil rights movement is the book about the 1963 campaign in Birmingham, Alabama, by Martin Luther King, Jr.: *Why We Can't Wait*. Taylor Branch won the Pulitzer Prize for his history of the Civil Rights Movement; *Pillar of Fire* (1963–65) is a good place to start (Simon & Schuster, 1998). I analyze briefly one of the movement's strongest strategies here: wagingnonviolence.org/feature/how-to-create-a-multi-level-movement-for-climate-justice/. The largest assembly of civil rights campaigns can be found on the searchable Global Nonviolent Action Database: nvdatabase.swarthmore.edu.

229. Frances Fox Piven, *Challenging Authority: How Ordinary People Change America* (Lanham, MD: Rowman and Littlefield, 2006).

230. Joseph E. Stiglitz, *The Price of Inequality*, preface to the paperback edition (New York: W. W. Norton, 2013), p. xxxiv; Richard Wilkinson and Kate Pickett, *The Spirit Level: Why Greater Equality Makes Societies Stronger.* (New York: Bloomsbury Press, 2009). Multiple examples of successful direct-action campaigns in the United States (and almost 200 other countries) are offered on the searchable website Global Nonviolent Action Database: www.nvdatabase.swarthmore.edu.

231. Ben Stein, "In Class Warfare, Guess Which Class Is Winning," *The New York Times*, November 26, 2006.

232. Wisconsin gave our country a clear example of this, first bravely and nonviolently defying Governor Scott Walker's attack on the labor movement and setting the stage for a win by going on the offensive, then instead turning to the ballot box. Labor lost

once again. The Koch brothers, satisfied with the governor they sponsored, are among his backers for U.S. President.

233. The documentary film *How to Survive a Plague* reveals the dynamics of one of the most confrontational campaigns, that of ACT-UP opposing the health industry's neglect of the AIDS epidemic. See also my brief article highlighting strategic principles used in the LGBT movement: wagingnonviolence.org/feature/lessons-from-the-lgbt-equality-movement/.

234. "Gay-rights push follows successes." Headline in *Philadelphia Inquirer,* April 5, 2015. Article by Tom Davies and Andrew Demillo of *The Associated Press* that describes the response by LGBT advocates to their victory in Indiana and Arkansas where legislatures changed their recently passed religious-objections laws to make sure that they did not allow discrimination. This is typical of the campaigning style of LGBT people that has, since 1965 in the United States, taken the offensive against a form of oppression that has lasted a millennium.

235. Kevin M. Kruse, *One Nation Under God: How Corporate America Invented Christian America* (New York: Basic Books, 2015).

236. Nolan McCarty, Keith T. Poole, and Howard Rosenthal, *Polarized America* (Cambridge, MA: MIT Press, 2006).

237. Reported by Rick Perlstein in *The Nation,* "Will the Progressive Majority Emerge?," July 9, 2007, p. 11.

238. "A Recent Gallup Poll on Americans' Confidence in US Institutions Put 'Big Business' Second to Last—Above Only Congress." *The Economist* cites the poll, quoted by *This Week,* October 16, 2015, p. 38. Even Republicans are showing up in polls as increasingly critical. "[In 2014, a Gallup poll found that 45 percent of Republicans think that the rich should pay more in taxes. Another Poll, by the Pew Research Center, showed that more Republicans favor increased spending on Social Security,

Medicare, education, and infrastructure than favor cutting those programs." George Packer, "The Republican Class War," *The New Yorker*, November 9, 2015. The Rasmussen Survey Organization reported that 71 percent of Republicans believe that the government and big business work together against the interests of others. www.rasmussenreports.com/public_content/ politics/general_politics/february_2011/68_believe_government_and_big_business_work_together_against_the_rest_ of_us (accessed December 14, 2015).

239. Erica Chenoweth and Maria J. Stephan, *Why Civil Resistance Works: The Strategic Logic of Nonviolent Conflict* (New York: Columbia University Press, 2011).

240. Chenoweth and Stephan addressed this question in their book; they found that movements double their chances of success by focusing on nonviolent tactics. I have written frequently on this subject on waging nonviolence, for example wagingnonviolence. org/feature/a-diversity-of-tactics-a-paucity-of-participants/, wagingnonviolence.org/feature/the-black-panthers-militarist-error/, and wagingnonviolence.org/feature/unlikely-allies/.

241. *Inc. Magazine*, January 20, 2011. www.inc.com/magazine/20110201/in-norway-start-ups-say-ja-to-socialism.html/7.

242. people-press.org/2010/05/04/socialism-not-so-negative-capitalism-not-so-positive/.

243. www.gallup.com/poll/125645/socialism-viewed-positively-americans.aspx.

244. Margaret Talbot, "The Populist Prophet," *The New Yorker*, October 12, 2015, p. 64.

245. John Nichols, "Progressive Honor Roll 2015," *The Nation*, January 4, 2016, p. 18.

About the Author

GEORGE LAKEY was the Eugene M. Lang Visiting Professor for Issues in Social Change at Swarthmore College, and is a Quaker. He has led 1,500 workshops on five continents, as well as activist projects on local, national, and international levels. He is the author of many books and articles and has written for *Waging Nonviolence* and *Common Dreams*, among other publications.